Adobe® Premiere® 6.0

Classroom in a Book®

Adobe

www.adobe.com/adobepress

Written and designed at Adobe Systems Incorporated, 345 Park Avenue, San Jose, California 95110, U.S.A.

Printed in the U.S.A.

ISBN: 0-201-71018-8

10-9-8-7-6-5-4-3-2

Contents

Adding Audio

Lesson 5

Additional Editing
Techniques

Lesson 6

**Advanced Editing
Techniques**

Lesson 7

Creating a Title

Lesson 8

Applying Video and
Audio Effects

Duplicate Clips and
Virtual Clips

Getting Started

DV in, Web out. That vision is now a reality for Macintosh® and Windows® users alike. With Adobe Premiere® 6.0 software, you can effortlessly capture Digital Video (DV), employ best-of-breed tools to craft your video productions, and then output to the leading Web streaming formats or to any type of medium. Whether you are a video professional or an aspiring producer, you'll enjoy the versatility, ease of use, and power of Adobe Premiere software.

About *Classroom in a Book*

Adobe Premiere 6.0 Classroom in a Book® is part of the official training series for Adobe graphics and publishing software developed by experts at Adobe Systems. The lessons are designed to let you learn at your own pace. If you're new to Adobe Premiere, you'll learn the fundamental concepts and features you'll need to master the program. If you've been using Adobe Premiere for awhile, you'll find that *Adobe Premiere 6.0 Classroom in a Book* teaches many advanced features, including tips and techniques for using the latest version of Adobe Premiere.

Although each lesson provides step-by-step instructions for creating a specific project, there's room for exploration and experimentation. You can follow the book from start to finish or do only the lessons that correspond to your interests and needs.

Prerequisites

Before beginning to use *Adobe Premiere 6.0 Classroom in a Book*, you should have a working knowledge of your computer and its operating system. Make sure that you know how to use the mouse and standard menus and commands and that you know how to open, save, and close files. If you need to review these techniques, see the printed or online documentation included with your Windows® or Macintosh® operating system. It is also helpful, but not necessary, to have experience with Adobe Premiere, Adobe Illustrator®, Adobe Photoshop®, and Adobe After Effects®.

Installing the Adobe Premiere program

Before you begin using *Adobe Premiere 6.0 Classroom in a Book*, make sure that your system is set up correctly and that you've installed the required software and hardware. You must purchase the Adobe Premiere 6.0 software separately. For system requirements and complete instructions on installing the software, see the *InstallReadMe* file on the Adobe Premiere 6.0 Application CD.

You must install the application from the Adobe Premiere 6.0 Application CD onto your hard disk; you cannot run the program directly from the CD-ROM. Follow the on-screen instructions. Make sure the serial number for your Premiere software is accessible before installing the application; you can find the serial number on the registration card, on the CD sleeve, or on the back of the CD case.

Important Note: After installing the Adobe Premiere 6.0 software from the Application CD, you must download and install the most recent updates from the Adobe Web site. Please visit www.adobe.com/support/downloads/main.html and check the Premiere section to find and install the appropriate updates for your operating system.

Installing QuickTime

QuickTime® 4.0 is required for playing the QuickTime movies you create in Adobe Premiere on both Windows and Mac OS systems. In addition, to play sound:

• On a Windows system, a sound card and speakers must be installed.

• On a Mac OS system, sound playback hardware is built in, although the quality varies by model. For best quality when previewing audio, you may want to connect external speakers to your system.

If QuickTime 4.0 is not already installed on your system, you can install it from the Adobe Premiere application CD-ROM. See the *Adobe Premiere 6.0 User Guide* for installation instructions.

Starting Adobe Premiere

You start Premiere just as you would any software application.

1 Launch the program as follows, depending on your operating system:

• In Windows, choose Start > Programs > Adobe > Premiere 6.0 > Adobe Premiere 6.0.

• In Mac OS, open the Adobe Premiere folder, and double-click the Adobe Premiere program icon. (If you installed the program in a folder other than Adobe Premiere, open that folder.)

In Premiere, if you are starting the program for the first time or if you have deleted the preferences (as you will be instructed to do in the lessons in this book), the Initial Workspace selection box appears. Lessons in the *Adobe Premiere 6.0 Classroom in a Book* are taught in the Single-Track Editing mode. Click the Single-Track Editing Mode button to select this mode. In the lessons that follow, you will learn about this and the other editing workspaces available in Adobe Premiere 6.0.

2 In the Load Project Settings dialog box, choose Multimedia or Multimedia Quicktime (depending on your operating system), and click OK.

Note: For the lessons in this book, you will work with a QuickTime preset or the lesson will specify a different setting, based on the source material you will be using for that lesson. For your own work, you will typically use the preset included with your capture card software or the appropriate preset included with Premiere.

♡ *Adobe Premiere 6.0 is very easy to customize. When working on your own projects, if you don't see a preset that matches your video, select the preset that most closely matches your editing environment, and then click Custom, specify your project settings, and then click Save. In the Save Project Settings dialog box, type a name and description if desired) and click OK. The new settings are saved as a preset file that appears in the list of available presets in the Load Project Settings dialog box. For more information, see "Specifying Settings", in Chapter 1 of the* Adobe Premiere 6.0 User Guide.

3 After you click OK, the Adobe Premiere application window appears. You will see the Single-Track Editing mode workspace and its three main windows (the Project window, the Monitor window, and the Timeline window) and the default palettes. If necessary, you can rearrange windows and palettes so they don't overlap, by choosing Window > Workspace > Single-Track Editing. The workspace components automatically adjust.

4 Choose Edit > Preferences > General and Still Image and select Open Movies in Clip Window if it is not selected.

Installing the *Classroom in a Book* fonts

To ensure that the lesson files appear on your system with the correct fonts, you may need to install the *Classroom in a Book* font files. The fonts for the lessons are located in the Fonts folder on the *Adobe Premiere Classroom in a Book* CD. If you already have these on your system, you do not need to install them now. If you have ATM* (Adobe Type Manager*), its documentation describes installation of fonts. If you do not have ATM, you can install it from the *Classroom in a Book* CD; in this case, ATM will automatically install the necessary fonts.

You can also install the Adobe Premiere 6.0 Classroom in a Book *fonts by copying all of the files in the Fonts folder on the* Classroom in a Book *CD into Program Files/Common Files/Adobe/Fonts (in Windows) or into System Folder/Application Support/Adobe/Fonts (in Mac OS). If you install a Type I, TrueType, OpenType, or CID font into these local Fonts folders, the font appears in Adobe applications only.*

Copying the *Classroom in a Book* files

The *Adobe Premiere Classroom in a Book* CD includes folders containing all the electronic files for the lessons. Each lesson has its own folder, and you must copy the folders to your hard drive to do the lessons. To save room on your drive, you can install only the folder for each lesson as you need it, and remove it when you're done.

To install the *Classroom in a Book* files:

1 Insert the *Adobe Premiere Classroom in a Book* CD into your CD-ROM drive.

2 Create a folder named Pr60_CIB on your hard drive.

3 Copy the lessons you want to the hard drive:

• To copy all of the lessons, drag the Lessons folder from the CD into the Pr60_CIB folder.

• To copy a single lesson, drag the individual lesson folder from the CD into the Pr60_CIB folder.

Note: *If you are installing the files in Windows, you need to unlock them before using them. You don't need to unlock the files if you are installing them in Mac OS.*

4 In Windows, unlock the files you copied:

• If you copied all the lessons to your hard drive, double-click the unlock.bat file in the Pr60_CIB/Lessons folder.

• If you copied a single lesson, drag the unlock.bat file from the Lessons folder on the CD into the Pr60_CIB folder. Then double-click the unlock.bat file in the Pr60_CIB folder.

Note: As you work through each lesson, you will overwrite the Start files. To restore the original files, recopy the corresponding Lesson folder from the Classroom in a Book *CD to the Pr60_CIB folder on your hard drive.*

Restoring default preferences

Adobe Premiere 6.0 provides *default*, or factory preset, settings. Like many software programs, Premiere 6.0 also maintains a *preferences file* that stores the settings you most recently used in the program. Each lesson in this *Classroom in a Book* indicates whether you need to set preferences or delete preferences to return the Premiere options to their *default*, or factory preset, settings. You may also find instances in your own projects when restoring the default preferences will be useful.

Note: Deleting the preferences file also resets the window and palette positions.

To quickly locate and delete the Premiere preferences file:

1 Do one of the following:

• In Windows, choose Start > Find > Files or Folders and search for prem60.prf. Choose Options > Save Results and then File > Save Search.

• In Mac OS, create an alias for the Preferences folder. Locate and select the Preferences folder, found within the System folder. From the title bar, choose File > Make Alias, or hold down the Command key and type the letter "m." A file called Preferences alias will appear within the System folder. Move this file to your desktop, or to another convenient location (such as the Apple Menu Items folder within your System folder to make it accessible as a menu item under the Apple icon in the title bar). Double-clicking the alias (or selecting it under the Apple icon) will open the Preferences folder to give you quick access to the Adobe Premiere 6.0 Preferences file.

2 Double-click the saved search file (Windows) or alias (Mac OS) any time you want to open the Preferences folder.

To restore default preferences for Premiere:

1 If Premiere is running, exit Premiere.

2 Do one of the following:

• In Windows, delete the Prem60.prf file from the folder containing the Premiere 6.0 software program.

• In Mac OS, delete the Adobe Premiere 6.0 Prefs file found in the Preferences folder in the System folder.

To save your current Premiere preferences:

1 Exit Adobe Premiere.

2 Do one of the following:

• In Windows, select the Prem60.prf file from the folder containing the Premiere 6.0 software program.

• In Mac OS, select the Adobe Premiere 6.0 Prefs file found in the Preferences folder in the System folder.

Note: The default location of the Adobe Premiere 6.0 Settings folder varies by operating system; use your operating system's Find command to locate this folder.

3 Drag the preferences file to your desktop or to another folder that you can locate quickly while you are working.

To restore your saved settings after completing the lessons:

1 Exit Premiere.

2 Drag the preferences file from the desktop back into the Adobe Premiere 6.0 Settings folder.

3 In the Warning dialog box that appears, confirm that you want to replace the existing version of the file indicated.

Additional resources

Adobe Premiere 6.0 Classroom in a Book is not intended to replace documentation that comes with the Premiere 6.0 program. Only the commands and options used in the lessons are explained in this book. For comprehensive information about program features, refer to these resources:

• The *Adobe Premiere 6.0 User Guide*, which is included with Adobe Premiere 6.0 software, contains a complete description of all features in the software.

• Online Help, an online version of the *User Guide*, is accessible by choosing Help > Contents (Windows) or Help > Help Contents (Mac OS) from the Premiere title bar.

• The Adobe Web site (www.adobe.com), can be viewed by choosing Help > Adobe Online if you have a connection to the World Wide Web.

• Adobe Premiere Technical Guides can also be found in the support area of the Adobe Web site (www.adobe.com/support/techdocs/topissuespre.htm). You may find them useful for additional information as you develop your skills.

Adobe Certification

The Adobe Training and Certification Programs are designed to help Adobe customers improve and promote their product proficiency skills. The Adobe Certified Expert (ACE) program is designed to recognize the high-level skills of expert users. Adobe Certified Training Providers (ACTP) use only Adobe Certified Experts to teach Adobe software classes. Available in either ACTP classrooms or on-site, the ACE program is the best way to master the use of Adobe products. For Adobe Certified Training Programs information, visit the Partnering with Adobe Web site at http://partners.adobe.com.

A Tour of Adobe Premiere

This Tour helps you understand and work with basic concepts and features of the Adobe Premiere program. You'll run through a typical series of steps for creating a video piece, including basic editing techniques, adding transitions, motion, and transparency. Completing this Tour should take approximately one hour.

Over the course of this Tour, you'll create a promotional television spot for a fictional bicycle company using video and audio clips provided on the CD-ROM included with this *Adobe Premiere 6.0 Classroom in a Book*. You'll be working with clips that have already been digitized as QuickTime files. If you were actually producing this project from the start, you would likely capture clips from the original video tapes and digitize them yourself, using Premiere.

Starting the Tour

To begin, you need to launch Adobe Premiere 6.0, set up your workspace, create a new project, and then import the video clips.

1 Make sure you know the location of the files used in this lesson. Insert the *Adobe Premiere Classroom in a Book* CD-ROM disk. Copy the Tour folder to your hard drive. For help, see "Copying the Classroom in a Book files" on page 14.

2 To ensure that the Premiere preferences are set to the default values, exit Premiere, and then delete the preferences file as explained in "Restoring default preferences" on page 15.

3 Start the Premiere 6.0 program.

When you start Premiere for the first time, or after deleting the preferences, the Select Initial Workspace dialog box appears so you can select an initial workspace.

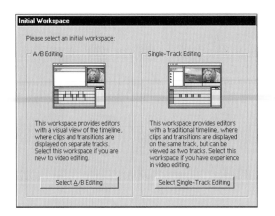

4 For this Tour, click Select Single-Track Editing to select that workspace.

5 Now, the Load Project Settings dialog box, appears. Click Cancel. For this first step in this Tour, no settings are required. You'll return to the Load Project Settings dialog box after watching a finished version of the movie you will be creating in this Tour.

Load Project Settings

Available Presets

	Description
▷ 📁 DV – NTSC	Compressor: Cinepak
▷ 📁 DV – PAL	Frame Size: 320x240
📄 **Multimedia QuickTime**	Frame Rate: 15fps
📄 Multimedia Video for Windows	Audio: 22050, 16-bit, Mono
📄 NTSC 640x480 QuickTime	
📄 NTSC 640x480 Video for Windows	**Video Settings**
📄 NTSC 720x480 QuickTime	Compressor: Cinepak
📄 NTSC 720x480 Video for Windows	Frame Size: 320 x 240
📄 PAL QuickTime	Frame Rate: 15.00
📄 PAL Video for Windows	Depth: Millions, Quality: 100%

Buttons: OK, Cancel, Custom..., Delete, Open..., Help

Audio Settings
Rate: 22050, Format: 16 – Mono
Compressor: Uncompressed

Rendering Options
Field setting: No Fields

Note: If you are unsure about which preset to select, choose the one that best corresponds to your capture device.

6 Choose File > Open and double-click the zfinal.mov file in the Tour folder you copied from the *Adobe Premiere Classroom in a Book* CD-ROM to your hard drive. Now, the Zfinal.mov file appears in its own Clip window.

7 Click the Play button (▶) and the video program will begin playing as shown below.

8 Choose File > Close when the finished movie stops running.

Starting the Tour as a new project

Now, you're ready to start creating the movie you just watched.

1 Choose File > New Project.

2 The Load Project Settings dialog box appears again. This time, you will choose a setting for the Tour project. Select Multimedia or Multimedia QuickTime (depending on your operating system), and click OK to proceed with the project.

3 After you click OK, you will see the Single-Track editing mode Workspace and its associated windows and its default palettes.

4 Choose Edit > Preferences > General and Still Image and deselect Open Movies in Clip Window if it is selected. Click OK.

Now, you're ready to import the clips you'll be using for your video program. A clip can be digitized film, video, audio, a still image, or a sequence of still images.

There are several ways to bring clips into a project. In this Tour, you'll import clips directly into the Project window. This is the place that Premiere lists all source clips you import into a project, though you don't have to use every clip you import.

A Project window includes a *Bin area*, which shows the bins that have been added to the project. The Bin area appears on the left side of the Project window, and can be resized or hidden. When the bins in the Bin area contain other bins, the hierarchical structure appears, much like the graphical view of folders and subfolders in your operating system.

5 To import the movie clips you need to create the Tour movie, choose File > Import > File, and then open the Tour folder that you copied to your hard drive from the *Adobe Premiere 6.0 Classroom in a Book* CD-ROM. Hold down the Control key (Windows) or the Shift key (Mac OS) and select these four files: Boys.mov, Cyclers.mov, Fastslow.mov, and Finale.mov. Now click Open.

Note: *If the windows are overlapping, choose Window > Workspace > Single-Track Editing to restore the default monitor appearance.*

The four selected files appear in the Project window. For each file that you import, the Project window lists its name, media type, and duration. Other columns let you add your own descriptions or labels. You can scroll across the window or enlarge it, if necessary.

6 Before you continue, you need to name and save the project. Choose File > Save. In the Save File dialog box, type **Cycling.ppj** for the filename, and specify a location on your hard disk. Click Save.

Premiere saves the project file to your hard disk.

Creating a rough cut

For many projects, you may want to begin by creating a *rough cut* of your video program. A rough cut is simply a series of clips assembled in the general sequence you want, with little or no editing. A rough cut can quickly give you some sense of your video program's effectiveness, letting you start making decisions about where to cut, trim, and add transitions and special effects.

1 If the Timeline window is not open, choose Window > Timeline to open it. You may need to resize the Project window to see the Timeline window clearly.

The clips you imported do not become part of the video program until you place them into the Timeline. The Timeline window is where you'll construct and edit your video program—adding, copying, and moving clips, adjusting their lengths, and so on. The Timeline provides a schematic view of your work by showing where in time each clip begins and ends, as well as the relationships between clips. Changes you make in this window appear in the Program view in the Monitor window.

Note: Premiere also provides a Storyboard window in which you can quickly and easily organize a set of clips, and then move the set to the Timeline to create a rough cut. You'll learn how to create and use storyboards in Lesson 3, "Basic Editing."

One of the best things about Adobe Premiere is that there are many alternative ways to approach different tasks. Whether you are importing clips, developing a rough cut, or doing any of a variety of editing tasks, you can choose to work in the way you prefer. This Tour shows you only one approach to developing a relatively simple project. Upcoming lessons will describe alternative and more advanced approaches.

When you first open the Timeline window, it displays five separate rows, called *tracks*, underneath the time ruler. The tracks act as containers for the clips. By arranging clips within the tracks, you create sequences that become the video program you are making. This Tour introduces you to the kinds of controls available for all tracks.

2 In the Project window, select the Boys.mov clip by placing the cursor to the left of its name and dragging the clip into the Video 1 track when the cursor changes to a hand. As you drag it into the Video 1 track, the clip appears as a darkened box. Before releasing the mouse, make sure that the left end of the darkened clip box is up against the left side of the Video 1 track.

3 Next, select the Cyclers.mov clip and drag it into the Video 1 track, positioning it just after the Boys.mov clip, so that the beginning of the Cyclers clip is up against the end of the Boys.mov clip.

4 Likewise, select the Fastslow.mov clip, drag it into the Video 1 track, and position it just after the Cyclers.mov clip. Do the same with Finale.mov clip, dragging it to a position just after the Fastslow.mov clip.

Now you have four clips in your Video 1 track, forming a video program about 32 seconds in length. This is a rough cut, giving you some idea of how your sequence works and what needs to be trimmed, edited, and modified. In the next section, you'll preview this sequence. Before moving on, though, you'll change how the clips are represented in the Timeline window.

5 Click the Timeline window title bar to make sure the window is active. Choose Window > Window Options > Timeline Window Options.

6 For *Icon Size*, select the middle option. For *Track Format*, select the second format (showing graphic images on both sides of the filename) and then click OK.

The clip representations in the Timeline change size accordingly. Now, change the unit of time displayed throughout the Timeline.

7 From the Time Zoom Level pop-up menu, in the lower left of the Timeline window, choose 2 Seconds.

The clips now take up less horizontal space because you're now displaying the Timeline contents in a time unit requiring less detail.

Now, it's time to play the sequence of clips you've imported as a preview.

Previewing in the Monitor window

To see how your work is progressing, you can preview one or more clips in the Monitor window. The Dual View Monitor window displays Source and Program views.

Source view (on the left side of the window) Lets you preview a clip, trim it, and then insert it into the Timeline window. This view can store many clips at a time, but you can view and trim only one clip at a time.

Program view (on the right) Lets you preview your entire video program, at any time. This view displays the sequence of clips currently in the Timeline window. You can also use the Program view to edit your video program.

1 If the Monitor window is not already open, choose Window > Monitor.

2 In the Monitor window, click the Play button (▶) underneath the Program view, or press the spacebar on your keyboard once to play the rough cut of your video program.

Note that the *edit line* in the Timeline moves in tandem with the preview. This edit line indicates the active frame—the frame being edited or previewed.

3 To replay your video program, click the Play button again, or click the Loop button (⟳) to play the video program in a continuous loop. To stop the action, click the Stop button (■) or press the spacebar on the keyboard.

Now that you're satisfied with the rough cut of your video program, you'll trim the video clips and add audio, transitions, special effects, and superimposing to create the finished version of the Tour movie.

Trimming clips

When you shoot footage with your camera, you almost always produce much more material than you'll actually use in your video program. To create scenes, cuts, and transitions, you'll need to trim your clips to remove the parts you don't need. Trimming clips is an essential part of creating a video program, something you'll do many times. Premiere provides a number of different ways to trim clips, including quick rough-cut tools and more precise frame-by-frame views.

You'll start editing the bicycle video by trimming the Boys.mov clip (the first clip in the video program).

1 Click the Timeline window title bar to make the Timeline active.

2 In the Video 1 track in the Timeline window, double-click the Boys.mov clip.

The first frame of the Boys.mov clip appears in the Source view in the Monitor window.

Play the clip first, before you trim it.

3 Click the Play button (▶) underneath the Source view in the Monitor window, or press the spacebar.

4 As it is now, the clip is a little long, so you'll trim it somewhat. Trimming a clip involves setting a new *In point*, *Out point*, or both. An In point is the first frame at which a clip begins; an Out point is the last frame of the clip. You'll change the Out point for the Boys.mov clip.

The controls contain a shuttle slider, which lets you *scrub* clips. Scrubbing—advancing or reversing a clip manually—lets you precisely identify and mark events.

5 Under the Source view in the Monitor window, drag the shuttle slider until you see the first bike rider at the end of his ride. (The time below the shuttle slider should read between 4:20 and 5:00 seconds.)

6 Click the Mark Out point button ( ).

After you've positioned the Out point correctly, you need to apply the change to the clip in the Timeline. The Apply button is located above the clip image in the Source view in the Monitor window. This button appears whenever you mark a new In or Out point for a clip in the Timeline.

7 To apply the trim, click the Apply button.

Premiere trims the end of the clip to give the clip a new Out point. It's important to understand that the trimmed area has not been deleted; Premiere has merely hidden the trimmed frames so that they don't appear in the Timeline and will not appear when you preview or export the video program. You can easily restore any trimmed frames by resetting the Out point.

The Timeline window includes a toolbar with various tools for making adjustments to clips. In this short exercise, you will become familiar with some of these tools in the Timeline toolbar area.

Notice, that there is a black triangle in some of the tool icons to indicate that there are multiple tools nested inside that tool.

Because you have set a new Out point in the Boys.mov clip, there is now a gap in the Timeline between the first and second clips. To preserve a continuous flow from one clip to the next, you need to close this gap by moving the other clips to the left. To do this, you'll use the track selection tool (⊞) nested inside the second icon from the left in the top row of the Timeline toolbar.

8 In the Timeline window, click and hold the range select tool icon (⬚), then select the track selection tool (⊞) to select all the clips in a track to the right of where you click. (Later in this tour, you'll learn how to automatically close gaps when you trim.)

9 Click the Cyclers.mov clip in track 1. This clip, and the clips to the right, are selected.

10 Drag the selection to the left, until it is up against the end of the Boys.mov clip.

11 Click the selection tool (⬉), because you're done with track selection for now.

12 In the Program view in the Monitor window, press the Play button (▶) to preview the changes you've made.

13 Save the project.

Adding audio

Now you'll add some music to the project by importing and placing an audio file in the first audio track. The music in the audio file was recorded in a studio, digitized, and then assembled and rendered in Premiere 6.0.

1 Choose File > Import > File, and double-click the Music.aif file within the Tour folder you copied to your hard drive from the *Adobe Premiere Classroom in a Book* CD-ROM. The file appears in the Project window.

2 Drag the Music.aif icon from the Project window to the Audio 1 track in the Timeline window.

3 Click the triangle immediately to the left of the Audio 1 track label to expand your view of the audio track.

The expanded view shows the waveform of the clip. The waveform displays the volume of the audio over time. Higher peaks in the waveform indicate greater volume.

In the next section, you'll come back to the audio track to synchronize events in the video with the music. For now, you'll lock the track so it doesn't get repositioned later.

4 Click in the small box next to the speaker icon (◉) to lock the audio track. A black lock icon (🔒) appears next to the cursor arrow whenever you position it over the locked track.

5 Click the Program view title bar to make the Monitor window active, then click the Play button (▶) under the Program view to preview the video and the audio together.

As you may know, Adobe Premiere 6.0 provides a sophisticated Audio Mixer that allows you to adjust multiple audio tracks while listening to them and viewing your video in real time. You'll learn more about the Audio Mixer in upcoming lessons.

Trimming clips in the Timeline window

In addition to trimming clips in the Monitor window, you can trim clips in the Timeline window using a number of different methods. To edit more precisely in the Timeline window, it's often easier to view a wider range of frames.

Now, you'll adjust the trim you made to the Boys.mov clip so that its Out point is synchronized with the first spike in the audio track.

1 From the Timeline toolbar, click and hold the rolling edit tool icon (:‡), then click the ripple edit tool (◆) nested there.

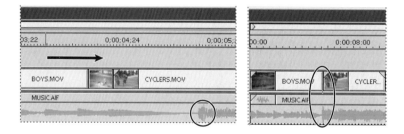

A *ripple edit* trims the specified clip, but maintains the durations of all other clips by changing the program duration. To edit the In point, drag the left edge of the clip. To edit the Out point, drag the right edge of the clip. The trim "ripples" through the project and the overall program duration is lengthened or shortened by the number of frames you added to or subtracted from the clip you are editing. The duration of the entire video program, therefore, changes.

2 Position the ripple edit tool on the Out point of the Boys.mov clip, and drag it to the right until its Out point is in line with the first spike of the waveform in the Music.aif clip. The program duration is extended or shortened to compensate for your edit, but the duration of adjacent clips remains unchanged.

Note: If the arrowhead on the ripple edit tool pointing to a clip is not visible, it means that the clip has no additional frames available. If the arrowhead on the ripple edit tool is white, it indicates that you are editing only the video or audio portion of a linked clip, because Sync mode is off.

Now you'll trim the Cyclers.mov clip so that its endpoint corresponds with an exact point in the Timeline. To trim the Cyclers.mov clip to this time, you'll use the Info palette.

1 Click the selection tool (▶) in the Timeline window.

2 Choose Window > Show Info and select the Cyclers.mov clip in the Timeline window.

The Info palette displays the name, types of clip, duration, and the starting and ending points of the selected clip. In addition, it displays the current location of the cursor. You'll use the cursor information to help you trim.

3 Select the ripple edit tool again, and move the cursor across the line where the Cyclers.mov and Fastslow.mov clips join.(Depending on your monitor, you may need to adjust the view of the Timeline window to see this clearly.)

4 Drag the ripple edit tool to the left, until the position of the cursor in the Info palette reads 0:00:08:01, and then release the mouse button.

You have trimmed the Out point of the Cyclers.mov clip. Because you trimmed the clip using a ripple edit, the subsequent clips have followed suit, shifting to the left.

5 Select the selection tool ( ) now, because you are done with ripple editing.

Now, you'll move on to applying a transition between clips.

Adding a transition

A *transition* is a change from one scene to the next, or from one clip to another. The simplest transition is the *cut*, where the last frame of one clip leads directly into the first frame of the next. By placing the first two clips together—Boys.mov and Cyclers.mov—you created a cut between them.

Premiere includes over 75 transitions, which you choose from the Transitions palette. To help you choose, you can animate icons and view brief descriptions of the available transitions. Additionally, you can preview a transition effect with actual frames from the two clips involved in the transition.

To add texture, nuance, or attention-getting special effects between scenes, you can use special transitions available in Adobe Premiere 6.0, such as dissolves, wipes, and zooms. In this Tour, you'll use the Cross Dissolve transition.

1 If the Transitions palette is not open, choose Window > Show Transitions.

The Transitions palette appears, displaying the available transitions, organized in folders by type. When you open a folder, you will see that each icon graphically represents how the transition works. Resize the palette if necessary by dragging its lower right corner.

To help you choose among the various transitions available, you can animate their icons and view brief descriptions of them. You will do that now.

2 Double click the 3D Motion folder icon to see the transitions available. You may need to make this area larger so you can see each of the transitions clearly.

3 Now, click and hold the small black arrow (▶) in the upper right corner of the Transitions palette, and choose Animate from the pull-down menu to activate the animation of the icons.

Later, if you find the animation distracting, you can turn it off by again choosing Animate from the Transitions palette menu to deselect the option. You can also view a description of each transition. You will do that now.

4 Click the Info palette if it is not active.

5 Open the Dissolve folder in the Transitions palette, and select the Cross Dissolve transition. The description of Cross Dissolve appears in the Info palette along with its animated icon. This transition is frequently used in video and film; it "dissolves" one scene into another, over a brief duration.

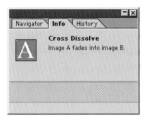

6 Now, drag the Cross Dissolve transition into the Timeline window, placing it between the Cyclers.mov clip and the Fastslow.mov clip. (You may need to shrink the Transitions palette so that Cross Dissolve is still visible, but small enough to make it easy to work in the Timeline window.)

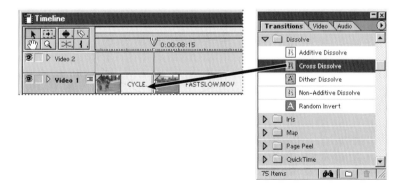

7 If the Fix Transitions dialog box appears, click OK. You will learn more about the Fix Transition in Lesson 4, "Adding Transitions" in this book.

The Cross Dissolve transition icon will now appear in the Timeline window in Video track 1, superimposed at the transition point between the two clips.

Previewing transitions and other effects

The Program view play button previews only the video clips in the Video 1 track and the audio clips but does not play transitions, effects, or superimposed clips (ones placed on the Video 2 track and higher) unless a *preview file* has been created. Once the preview file has been created, the Program view shows the additional effects.

The work area bar specifies the portion of your project that you want to preview (with transitions and other effects) or output. In this case, you'd like to preview the first three clips of your project, including the cross dissolve transition effect you just added.

To preview a transition, you can either build a preview of the section of the Timeline window containing the transition, or you can *render-scrub* it. With render-scrubbing, you can see the transition's effect quickly, but the preview doesn't get stored, so you can't replay it.

1 To render-scrub the transition: Position the cursor in the Timeline window, then drag the cursor in the time ruler over the transition, hold down the Alt key (Windows) or the Option key (Mac OS) and, when the cursor becomes a downward-pointing arrow (↓), scrub (or move the cursor into) the Timeline window's time ruler.

Dragging in this fashion provides a quick method for previewing your video program but cannot give you a precise frame rate, since you're moving it by hand. To preview effects at a specified frame rate, you need to generate a preview file.

Before you generate a preview file, you need to adjust the *work area bar*—the topmost section of the Timeline window—to span the area you want to preview.

2 To do this, position the cursor in the yellow work area bar in the Timeline window, and adjust the end points so the work area bar covers the transition and press Enter (Windows) or Return (Mac OS).

💡 *Alternatively, you can choose Timeline > Preview to build a preview of a transition that can be saved and replayed.*

3 The Cyclers.mov clip dissolves into the Fastslow.mov clip, over a duration of one second, as the preview shows.

4 To view the first three clips in their entirety, choose 1 Second from the Time Zoom Level menu in the lower left corner of the Timeline window. Now, it will be easy to extend the work area by the correct amount.

Note: *Depending on the size and resolution of your computer monitor, the 1 Second setting might not make the first three clips entirely visible; in that case, choose another setting from the Time Zoom Level pop-up menu. Doing so will not affect your ability to follow the remaining procedures in this Tour, although the illustrations may not exactly match what you see on your screen.*

5 Drag the right end of the work area bar to extend its length so that it aligns with the end of the Fastslow.mov clip. Notice that the preview status line under the work area bar changes color from red to green in the Timeline when a preview has been built for a segment that needs rendering.

6 From the Timeline window, choose Timeline > Preview or press Enter (Windows) or Return (Mac OS) on the keyboard to see the preview.

Note: Premiere displays a status dialog box as it generates a preview file. When the file generation is complete, the preview of your video program plays in the Program view in the Monitor window.

7 Because the preview has been saved, now simply press Enter (Windows) or Return (Mac OS) to replay the preview.

Splitting a clip

Sometimes you may want to superimpose only a portion of a clip. To do this, you need to split the clip to create a new and separate instance of the original clip. You can split a clip in the Timeline by using the razor tool (✑). This technique can be useful when you want to use different effects that can't both be applied to a single clip, such as different clip frame rates.

Here, you'll split the Fastslow.mov clip so that you can make a particular portion of it change speed and fade out.

1 In the Timeline window, move the edit line across the Fastslow.mov clip until you see a shot of the unobstructed bleachers (about 2 seconds into the clip). Leave the edit line positioned at this point.

2 In the Timeline window, select the razor tool (✑).

3 Position the cursor over the Fastslow.mov clip at the current edit line, and then click the mouse to split it.

Premiere cuts the Fastslow.mov clip at the point where you clicked, creating two separate clips.

Changing the speed of a clip

You can change the playback speed of a clip to make it play slower or faster. Changing the speed changes its duration without adding or removing any frames. The *speed* of a clip is the playback rate of the action or audio compared to the rate at which it was recorded. The *duration* of a video or audio clip is the length of time it plays—the difference in time between a clip's In point and Out point.

To make the bike sequence more interesting and attention-getting, you'll slow down the second portion of the clip you just cut, increasing its duration. Since you also want to fade out the same clip, which requires it to be placed in a superimpose track, you'll place it there now.

1 Click the selection tool ( ) to activate it, and then drag the second portion of the Fastslow.mov clip upward into the Video 2 track.

Make sure to keep the position of the clip at exactly the same point in time by snapping the edges of the clip to the same point in the Video 2 track.

Now you'll change the speed of the clip.

2 Select the clip you just moved (if it is not already selected), and choose Clip > Speed.

3 In the dialog box, type **30** in the New Rate box and click OK.

The playback speed of the clip is now at 30% of its original speed. Accordingly, the duration of the clip has increased proportionally, approximately tripling in length.

To change speed visually, you can select the rate stretch tool (⬌) and drag either end of the clip. The rate stretch tool is located in the toolbar of the Timeline window.

The split portion of the Fastslow.mov clip with which you have been working now overlaps some of the Finale.mov clip. Because you want the slowed-down clip to fade to black, you need to move the Finale.mov clip to the right.

4 Use the selection tool to drag the Finale.mov clip to the right until its right edge snaps to the Out point of the Music.aif clip in the Audio 1 track.

Now let's generate another preview.

5 Using the selection tool, move the Out point of the trimmed Fastslow.mov clip in the Video 2 track so that its Out point is aligned with the In point of the Finale.mov clip.

6 Drag the right end of the work area bar to the right so that it extends to the end of the Fastslow.mov clip in the Video 2 track.

7 Choose Timeline > Preview or press Enter (Windows) or Return (Mac OS) on the keyboard. To preview more than once, just repeat this step.

8 Save the project.

Changing a clip's opacity

If a clip is on the Video 2 track or higher, you can make it partially transparent by changing its opacity. The opacity option lets you fade into or out of a clip and superimpose one or more clips on top of others, so that two or more clips are visible at the same time. You'll actually superimpose clips later in the Tour: for now, you'll simply use the superimpose track to fade out a clip by manually adjusting its opacity over time.

By default, Premiere includes one superimpose track, Video 2, above the Video 1 track. You can add others, as needed. Once a clip has been placed in a superimpose track, an opacity control bar, or a "*rubberband*," becomes available. To see the bar, you need to expand the Video 2 track. By adding handles, you can adjust the opacity of a clip.

1 Click the arrow to the left of the Video 2 track label. The opacity bar shows the clip's opacity. By default, the opacity is now at 100%.

2 If the red Display Opacity rubberbands are not already selected, click the red Display Opacity rubberbands icon (◢) to display the opacity rubberband.

3 With the selection tool selected, move the cursor onto the opacity bar (now, the cursor changes into a pointing finger), and click about three-quarters of the way into the clip to create a small red box called a *handle*.

The handle divides the control bar into sections that you can adjust by dragging. A control bar includes a handle at each end to define the beginning and ending opacity settings.

4 In the Video 2 track of the Timeline window, click the rightmost handle. Keep the mouse button depressed throughout the next step.

5 Press the Shift key with a handle selected, and then drag the selected opacity handle down until the value beside the handle displays 20%.

Note: By depressing the Shift key before or after you select the handle, you will be able to see the incremental change.

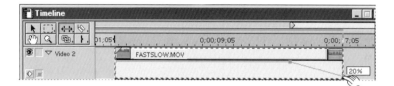

This creates a downward slope in the control bar, starting at the first handle you created. A downward slope decreases opacity. In this case, the opacity of the clip begins at 100% and decreases to 20%.

Note: You can also drag the handles without holding down Shift, but that limits you to 5% increments and does not produce a pop-up display. You can, alternatively, use the Info palette to view the opacity setting if you drag without holding down the Shift key.

6 Preview what you've done.

7 Hold down the Alt key (Windows) or the Option key (Mac OS) and slowly drag in the time ruler above the clip you just adjusted. The preview plays in the Monitor window. Because this clip is the only one playing in the Timeline, it fades into the background color, which is black.

8 Save the project.

Adding special effects to a video clip

Adobe Premiere 6.0 lets you create many different kinds of special effects. When you apply an effect (sometimes called a "filter") to a clip, the effect is listed in the Effect Controls palette. Clips that have effects applied to them appear in the Timeline window with a cyan border at the top.

Each effect has a default keyframe at the beginning and end of the clip, indicated by half-diamonds on the keyframe line in the Timeline window. The effect is listed directly above the clip's keyframe line. If an effect has adjustable controls, you can change the start or end time of the effect or add additional keyframes to create an animated effect. If you don't make any changes to the default keyframes, the settings for the associated effect apply to the entire clip.

If a clip has multiple effects applied to it, the effect pop-up menu lists them and they are rendered in order, from top to bottom in this list. You can reorder the effects in this list to change which effects are rendered first.

For the last clip in the video program, you'll add the Camera Blur effect, which blurs a clip as if it were leaving the focal range of the camera; by setting keyframes for the blur, you can simulate a subject coming into or going out of focus.

1 Select the Finale.mov clip in the Timeline window.

2 Choose Window > Show Video Effects. Double-click the Blur folder. The Camera Blur effect is listed along with other effects.

3 Drag the Camera Blur effect to the Finale.mov clip in the Timeline Window.

The effect appears in the Timeline window and in the Effect Controls palette.

4 In the Effect Controls palette, click Setup to the right of the effect name. The Camera Blur Settings dialog box appears. Drag the slider bar to zero, and then click OK. The settings you choose here apply to the first keyframe (if you change settings for other keyframes) or to the entire clip (if you make no changes to any keyframe).

To create an effect of changing focus, you can vary the Camera Blur effect over time. To do this, you set *keyframes*. A keyframe specifies a control value at a specific point in time.

Since you'd like the blurring to start about midway through the Finale.mov clip, you will move the first keyframe. Moving a keyframe scrubs the clip in the Program view in the Monitor window.

5 In the Timeline window, click the triangle to the left of the Video 1 track label to display the keyframe line. The keyframe line appears beneath the clip in the Timeline window, after you add an effect to the clip. The keyframes are the small white rectangles, appearing on either end of the keyframe line.

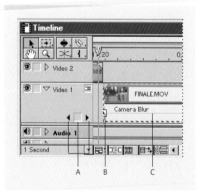

A. Keyframe navigator box B. Keyframe
C. Keyframe line

6 You create a keyframe by positioning the edit line midway through the Finale.mov clip, then select the clip and click the box between the two arrows in the keyframe navigator box. A check mark appears in the box.

With the new keyframe you just created, you'll now increase the amount of blurring.

7 In the Effect Controls palette, click Setup to access the dialog box or adjust the effect directly by moving the slider. Drag the slider until the Camera Blur is 80%, then click OK.

Note: *Since not all effects have a Setup button, the method used to change an effect's value varies depending upon the effect.*

8 Drag the keyframe you just created until the timecode in the Program view in the Monitor window reads 00:00:25:00 (25 seconds).

9 Now select the last keyframe and, once again, drag the slider bar in the Effect Controls palette until the Blur is at 80%. Click OK.

Let's briefly review what you've just done. By setting three keyframes—the first at 0%, the second at 80%, and the third at 80%—you have specified that the Camera Blur effect begins at 0% at the point in time you specified, increases to 80% at 25 seconds, and then remains at 80% for the duration of the clip.

Why not just use two keyframes—the first at 0% and the last at 80%? Premiere always creates a linear change between keyframes. So, if you use only two keyframes, the blurring would gradually increase over the duration of the clip. This isn't the effect you want; you want the blur to happen fairly quickly, and then remain at that level for its duration.

Preview your work again.

10 Drag the right end of the work area bar to the right so that it extends to the end of the Finale.mov clip.

11 Choose Timeline > Preview or press Enter (Windows) or Return (Mac OS) on the keyboard. To preview more than once, just repeat this step. Previewing may take several minutes, depending on the speed of your machine.

It's starting to look like something now!

12 Save the project.

Superimposing an image

Adobe Premiere provides 15 *keys* (methods for creating transparency) that you can apply to a clip to create transparency in many different ways. You can use color-based keys for superimposing, brightness keys for adding texture or special effects, alpha channel keys for clips or images already containing an alpha channel, and matte keys for adding traveling mattes or creative superimpositions.

In the previous section, you used the Camera Blur effect to blur the second half of the final clip. Now you'll superimpose a company logo on top of this clip, making it appear as if the camera is now focusing on the image.

1 Choose File > Import > File. Then locate and select the Veloman.eps file in the Tour folder. Click Open.

2 Position the edit line in the Timeline window at 0:00:25:00 (25 seconds).

3 From the Project window, now drag the Veloman.eps image into the Video 2 track of the Timeline window so its left end point snaps to the edit line (shown as "Starting at: 0:00:25:00" in the Info palette).

By default, the duration of a still image is set in the General Preferences at 30 frames. Because the frame rate of your Tour project is preset at 15 frames per second, the duration of the image is 2 seconds. To keep the image visible until the end of the video program, you'll need to extend its duration. Unlike a motion clip, a still image duration can be specified by stretching the clip representation in the Timeline.

4 In the Timeline window, select the selection tool and drag the right edge of the Veloman.eps image to the right until it snaps to the end of the Finale.mov clip.

The image now overlaps the Finale.mov clip in the Timeline window. The overlapping area is where the logo will be superimposed on the bike race.

Note: *Hold down the Alt key (Windows) or the Option key (Mac OS) and drag in the time ruler over the area where the two clips overlap.*

All you see is the Veloman.eps image; you don't see the Finale.mov clip at all. That's because the Veloman.eps image is still fully opaque. Now, you'll make the background of the Veloman.eps image transparent.

To specify that certain areas of a clip become transparent and other areas remain opaque, you need to use a *transparency key*. A transparency key (often referred to simply as a "key") makes designated colors (or a range of colors) in a clip transparent or partially transparent. A blue screen key, for example, makes a shade of blue transparent; in this way, an actor can be filmed in the studio against a blue screen, and then superimposed on an outdoor action scene. Creating transparency with a particular color is called *keying out* that color. To superimpose the Veloman.eps image, you need to key out the white background.

5 Select the Veloman.eps image in the Timeline window. Then, in the Effect Controls palette, click Setup next to Transparency.

The Transparency Settings dialog box shows the selected clip in the Sample area. The key you choose is applied to the clip, and the resulting effect is displayed in this area.

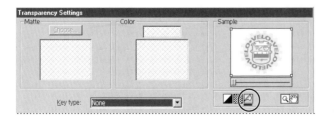

6 In the Transparency Settings dialog box, choose White Alpha Matte in the Key Type window. The White Alpha Matte key will key out any areas of alpha white in an image that contains an alpha channel.

7 Click OK to apply the settings to the clip.

8 To preview the effect, hold down the Alt key (Windows) or the Option key (Mac OS) and drag in the time ruler over the area where the superimposition occurs.

9 Save the project.

Animating a clip using keyframes

You can move, rotate, and zoom a video or still-image clip within a video program's viewable area. You can animate a clip by creating a motion path using the Motion Settings dialog box. For more information, see Lesson 10, "Adding Motion" in this book.

To add more visual interest to the Veloman.eps image, you'll make it zoom into the frame from the left.

1 If the Veloman.eps image is not still selected in the Timeline window, select it now.

2 In the Effect Controls palette, click Setup to the right of the motion effect to open the Motion Settings dialog box.

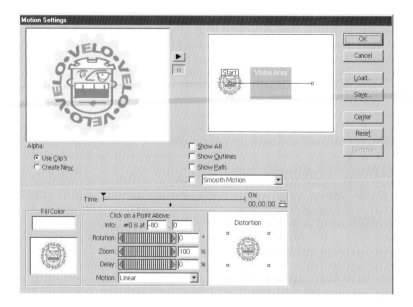

In the top left corner of the dialog box, a sample of the selected clip moves along the default motion path. The top right area shows the motion path area with keyframes indicating the beginning and the end. Notice that the default path locates the Start and Finish keyframes outside the Visible area of the video program so that the clip enters the viewable area from the left, moves across, and exits on the right.

For simple horizontal, vertical, or diagonal motion, you can drag the Start and Finish keyframes to any location within or outside the visible area. As you do so, the cursor turns into a pointing finger. You can click to add a keyframe to the path, and drag to adjust its position, creating a new segment of the path.

3 Continuing to work in the Motion path area, drag the Start keyframe to the right, so that approximately half of the image overlaps the Visible area. You can also specify the position of the image by entering coordinates. You'll do that now.

4 Click the End keyframe (Windows) or Finish keyframe (Mac OS), and then enter **26** and **-8** in the two text boxes below the line that reads "Click on a point above" in the central lower portion of the dialog box. Then, press Tab on your keyboard.

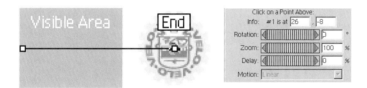

The End point (Windows) or Finish point (Mac OS) moves to the specified location.

By default, the Motion Path area provides two motion points, Start and End (Windows) or Finish (Mac OS), which you have just modified for position. You can also specify zooming, rotation, and distortion at these points, and you can create other motion points, each with particular animation values.

In order to manipulate the Veloman.eps image in an eye-catching way, you'll add a new motion point, specify new zoom values for the start and end or finish points, and, finally, apply a rotation value so that the logo spins as it appears to recede into the distance.

5 In the Motion Path area, position the cursor anywhere on the motion path. The cursor turns into a pointing finger. Click to add a keyframe to the path, and drag to adjust its position, creating a new motion point.

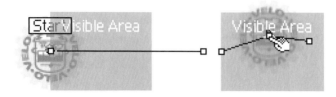

6 Move the new motion point down and to the right as shown.

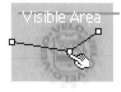

Now, you'll specify zoom values for the start and end or finish points.

7 In the Motion Path area, select the Start point.

8 In the Zoom box at the bottom of the dialog box, type **0**, and then press Tab.

9 Select the end point (Windows) or finish point (Mac OS), type **0** in the Zoom edit box, and press Tab.

The settings you just entered make the logo appear to zoom in from the left side of the frame and then recede into the distance.

10 With the end point still selected, type **720** in the Rotation text box near the bottom of the dialog box, and press Tab.

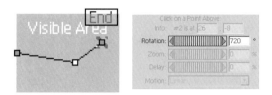

Rotation values are specified in degrees. The value of 720 (360 x 2) defines two complete circles or rotations from one point to the next.

The image now follows the motion you defined earlier as it zooms and rotates across the screen.

11 Click OK to close the Motion Settings dialog box.

Let's preview the end of the video program to see the superimposed image moving through the frame.

12 Move the work area bar to cover the last portion of your video program, where the image begins.

13 Choose Timeline > Preview or press Enter (Windows) or Return (Mac OS) on the keyboard. To preview more than once, just repeat this step.

14 Save the project.

Exporting the movie

To complete the Tour, you'll make the project into a QuickTime movie. The QuickTime format is a standard format for both Windows and Mac OS systems. When exporting to a movie (File > Export Timeline > Movie), Premiere uses settings in the Export Settings dialog boxes.

1 Activate the Timeline window.

2 Choose File > Export Timeline > Movie.

3 Click the Settings button.

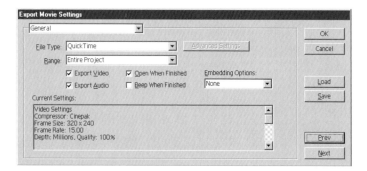

• Make sure that QuickTime is selected for File Type, and Entire Project is selected for the Range.

• Also make sure that the Export Video and Export Audio options are selected. The default values for other settings, including those for compression, are fine for this project.

4 Click Next. Change the frame size to 240 x 180 and then click OK.

5 In the Export Movie dialog box, specify a filename (be sure to add the ".mov" file extension to the end) and a location in which to store the movie, and click OK.

Premiere starts making the movie, displaying a status bar that provides an estimate for the amount of time it will take to *render* or *output* the movie. The output time always depends on the capabilities of your computer. On most systems, Premiere should finish making the movie within 7 minutes. You can cancel the output process at any time by pressing the Esc key.

When the movie is complete, it opens in its own window.

6 Click the Play button to watch the show.

Congratulations on completing the Tour!

Lesson 1

1 Getting to Know the Work Area

Premiere organizes editing functions into specialized windows. This gives you the flexibility to arrange a window layout that matches your editing style. Floating palettes give you information and quick access to any part of your video program. You can arrange windows and palettes to make the best use of your computer and television monitors.

In this introduction to the work area, you'll learn how to do the following:

- Start the Adobe Premiere program.
- Set up your workspace.
- Work with the Project window.
- Work with the Timeline window.
- Work with the Monitor window.
- Navigate to a specific time in your video program.
- Use palettes.
- Discover keyboard shortcuts.

Starting the Adobe Premiere program

Every Adobe Premiere movie starts as a project—a collection of video clips, still images, and audio that you organize along a timeline. In this lesson, you'll explore palettes and windows using a project that has already been constructed. Make sure you know the location of the files used in this lesson. For help, see "Copying the Classroom in a Book files" on page 14 of this *Classroom in a Book*.

Double-click **01Lesson.ppj** in the 01Lesson folder to open it in Premiere.

Note: Premiere 6.0 remembers the original location of each clip in a project. Because you are using the project file on a computer other than the one that created it, Premiere may prompt you to find some files when you open a lesson project. Locate and select the indicated files and then click OK.

Setting up your workspace

The arrangement of windows, features and palettes is called the workspace. There are four types of editing workspaces: A/B Editing, Single-Track Editing, Effects, and Audio. The type you will use depends on the style of editing you will be doing. You can also create custom window layouts by rearranging the Project, Monitor, Timeline, and Audio Mixer windows and changing their settings.

A/B Editing workspace   This is used if you will primarily be dragging clips from the Project window to the Timeline window. This mode resembles a conventional editing method called A/B roll editing, which uses two video tapes or rolls (A and B) and an effects switcher to provide transitions. Selecting A/B Editing sets up the following conditions:

• The Monitor window uses the Single View, displaying only the Program view window and controllers. Clips open in a separate clip window.

• The Timeline window displays the Video 1 track expanded, with the transition track showing between Video 1A and 1B. All palettes are available, with the Effect Controls, Navigator, and Transitions palettes active.

Single-Track Editing workspace   This is used for more advanced editing techniques and for work with the Video 1 track as a single track.

• The Monitor window provides the Dual View, displaying the Source view window and the Program view window, side-by-side. Clips are dragged into the Source view window for trimming and setting of In and Out points. Clips are then dragged to the Timeline window for positioning.

• The Timeline window has a single Video 1 track in which the video and transition tracks are combined. All tools act on the three subtracks as a single track for inserting and overlaying the trimmed clips. You can expand the Video 1 track to show the transition track and the upper and lower tracks of the Video 1 track. Most of the lessons in this *Classroom in a Book* are performed in this mode.

Effects workspace The Effects workspace, which provides access to both audio and video effects, uses your current workspace (Single-Track Editing or A/B Editing) with the following adjustments: The Monitor window displays in Single View, and the Effect Controls, Navigator, and Transitions palettes are active.

Audio workspace The Audio workspace, which provides access to the tools necessary for editing audio tracks, uses your current workspace (Single-Track Editing or A/B Editing) with the following adjustments: Clips open in a separate Clip window, the Audio Mixer window is open, and no palettes are displayed.

If the windows are overlapping, choose Window > Workspace, then select Single-Track Editing to restore them to their default positions.

Note: You can select a different editing workspace at almost any time while working on a project. However, it is generally not advisable to switch from A/B Editing to Single-Track Editing while working on a project, because clips can be positioned in A/B Editing in ways that are not possible in Single-Track mode.

Checking project settings

Once you start a project, you can check the project settings at any time.

1 From the Premiere title bar at the top of your screen, choose Project > Project Settings > Video. The current Video settings for the project are now displayed.

Now you'll change a Video setting temporarily to see how the Settings Viewer displays your settings.

2 Choose a Frame Rate other than the rate currently selected. For our example, choose 10 if 15 is currently selected.

3 Click Next to sequence through all of the Project Settings windows.

The project settings are organized into five categories:

General Settings   Control the fundamental characteristics of the video program, including the method Premiere uses to process video (Editing Mode), count time (Time Display), and play back video (Timebase).

Video Settings   Control the frame size, picture quality, compression settings, and aspect ratios that Premiere uses when you play back video from the Timeline.

Audio Settings   Control the characteristics of audio you play back from the Timeline.

Keyframe and Rendering Options   Control frame-related characteristics when you build (render) and play back video previews from the Timeline. These options work in combination with the Video settings.

Capture Settings   Control how Premiere transfers video and audio directly from a deck or camera. (Other Project Settings panels do not affect capturing.)

Note: Normally, you will use the preset included with your capture card software or the appropriate preset included with Premiere.

Adobe strongly recommends that if your capture card provides a preset file, you should use the preset provided; manual changes to the settings should not be made. If none of the presets available matches your video, refer to the Adobe Premiere 6.0 User Guide *for assistance in changing the settings.*

4 Click OK to temporarily accept the new Frame Rate for this project.

5 A dialog box appears indicating that the Video settings have changed. Click OK.

6 In the Premiere title bar, choose Project > Settings Viewer.

	Capture Settings	Project Settings	FERRY.MOV	Export Settings
Video				
Mode:	QuickTime Capture	QuickTime	QuickTime	QuickTime
Compressor:	Video	Video	Video	Video
Frame Size:	640 x 480	240 x 180	240 x 180	240 x 180
Frame Rate:	15.00 FPS	15.00 FPS	15.00 FPS	15.00 FPS
Depth:	Thousands	Thousands	Thousands	Thousands
Quality:	100 %	100 %	100 %	100 %
Pixel Aspect Ratio:	Square Pixels (1.0)	Square Pixels (1.0)	Square Pixels (1.0)	Square Pixels (1.0)
Audio				
Sample Rate:	8000 Hz	8000 Hz	11025 Hz	8000 Hz
Format:	8 bit – Mono	8 bit – Mono	8 bit – Mono	8 bit – Mono
Compressor:	Uncompressed	Uncompressed	Uncompressed	Uncompressed
Render				
Field Settings:	No Fields	No Fields	Unknown	No Fields

For optimal performance, Capture Settings, Project Settings and Clip Settings should be identical.

Settings Viewer from 01Lesson.ppj

You can use the Settings Viewer to review and compare all of the settings for projects and clips in your project, as well as settings used when you export or capture files. Avoid potential conflicts by matching settings for each of the four categories wherever possible. In most cases, the Capture Settings, Project Settings, and Export Settings should be the same for the different clips in your project.

Settings can vary for different clips. Observe that conflicting settings are displayed in red.

7 To resolve the Frame Rate setting conflict, click the Project Settings heading in the Settings Viewer window.

8 Locate the Video settings window in the dialog box that appears, choose the original Frame Rate setting (15), and then click OK.

9 Click OK in the Settings Viewer when you have finished comparing settings. A dialog box appears indicating that the Video settings have changed. Click OK again.

For more information, see "Specifying Project Settings" in Chapter 1 of the *Adobe Premiere 6.0 User Guide* and see Lesson 2, "About Digital Video Editing" in this book.

Getting to know your workspace

Once the project is open, the Premiere work area appears. If necessary, rearrange windows and palettes so they don't overlap one another. Throughout this book, you can follow this suggestion, by choosing in the title bar at the top of the Premiere screen > Window > Workspace > Single-Track Editing. The windows and palettes will adjust to your display without overlap.

*Sample view of 01Lesson.ppj: **A.** Project window **B.** Monitor window **C.** Timeline window **D.** Navigator, Info and History palettes **E.** Transitions, Video and Audio Effects palettes **F.** Effect Controls and Commands palettes*

Here you see the 01lesson.ppj at 00:00:00:00 with the Sailby.mov clip in the Source view in the Monitor window. The audio and video tracks are uncollapsed in the Timeline window.

A new project appears with the following windows open by default:

Project window   This window lets you import, organize, and store references to clips. It lists all source clips you import into a project, although you don't have to use every clip you import.

Monitor window   This window includes the Source and Program views. Use the Source view to see an individual video clip and the Program view to see the current state of the video program being edited in the Timeline.

Timeline window   This window provides a schematic view of your program, including all of the video, audio, and superimposed video tracks. Changes you make appear in the Program view.

The palettes are organized into tabbed groups in separate windows. All the palettes are listed in the Window menu.

This tabbed group opens by default:

Navigator palette   This palette offers a convenient way to move around the Timeline.

Info palette   This provides information about the selected clip, transition, selected area in the Timeline, or operation you are performing.

History palette   This palette lets you go back to any previous state of the project created during the current working session. Each time you make a change, a new state is added to the History palette. You can delete all edits after the selected state, return to your current state, or incrementally restore states.

This tabbed group also opens by default:

Transitions palette   This palette lets you add transitions between clips in the Timeline.

Video Effects palette   This allows you to apply a video effect to a video clip in the Video 1 track and in any superimposed track.

Audio Effects palette   This palette allows you to apply an audio effect to any audio clip in the Timeline window.

This tabbed group opens when you choose Window > Show Effect Controls: It will also open automatically whenever you apply an effect.

Effect Controls palette   This allows you to change effect settings at any time and appears when an effect has been applied to a clip.

Commands palette   This lets you create a button list of frequently used commands, and assign keyboard shortcuts to them.

For more information, see the following sections of the *Adobe Premiere 6.0 User Guide*: "Using the Navigator palette", "Using the Info palette", "Using the History palette", and "Using the Commands palette" in Chapter 1; "Using the Transitions palette" in Chapter 4; and "Working with effects" in Chapter 9.

You work with clips and assemble your program within windows; primarily working with the three windows previously described: the Source window, the Monitor window, and the Timeline window. Premiere also provides specialized windows for tasks such as capturing video and creating titles. Those windows and their uses are described later in this *Classroom in a Book*, as well as in the *Adobe Premiere 6.0 User Guide*.

Unlike windows, palettes do not actually contain the clips with which you are working. Palettes provide information and convenient access to functionality. You can change the way palettes are displayed, to best suit your working habits. For more information, see "Working with palettes" in Chapter 1 of the *Adobe Premiere 6.0 User Guide*.

Most windows and palettes in Premiere include menus, and all windows also have context menus. The commands found in window menus, palette menus, and context menus are specific to individual windows and palettes. For more information, see "Using window and palette menus" in Chapter 1 of the *Adobe Premiere 6.0 User Guide*.

Working with the Project window

The Project window is where you import, organize, and store references to clips. You can view and add information for every clip in your project. It lists all source clips you import into a project, though you don't have to use every clip you import. You can also expand the size of the Project window.

The filenames in the Project window identify the files imported into the project. Icons next to each filename indicate the file type. Video and audio files are large, so copying each one into a project would waste significant disk space. Instead, a Premiere project stores only references to the clips you import, not the clips themselves. This means that a 5 MB source clip always occupies just 5 MB on your hard disk whether you use it in one project or ten. When you edit your video program, Premiere retrieves frames from the original files as needed.

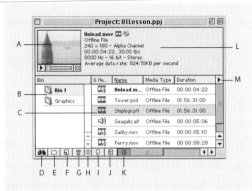

Sample of a Project window in the List view (your view may differ): **A.** *Thumbnail viewer and poster frame* **B.** *Bins* **C.** *Clips* **D.** *Search* **E.** *New Bin* **F.** *Create Item* **G.** *Delete Selected Items* **H.** *Resize Bin Area* **I.** *Icon View* **J.** *Thumbnail View* **K.** *List View* **L.** *Project window menu* **M.** *Clip information*

You can organize clips in a project using *bins*, which resemble folders on your hard drive. Bins are useful for organizing a project that contains a large number of clips; you can even organize bins within bins. You can also save a bin for use in other projects. Bins are located in the Bin area found in the left panel of the Project window. When you import clips, they are added to the currently selected bin.

Now you'll open a bin to see what's inside.

When you open your Lesson 01 project, the Bin 1 and Graphics bin icons appear in the Bin area. Bin 1 is selected by default and its contents are displayed as a list in the area to the right of the Bin 1 area.

1 If necessary, slide the Resize Bin area button (◁▷) located at the bottom of the Project window until the Bin area is the width you need to see all of the information.

2 Click the Graphics bin in the Bin area. This bin contains a single graphics file. You can organize all your graphics files in this bin.

3 Click Bin 1 again and drag Shiplogo.ptl from the Bin 1 area to the Graphics bin.

4 Click the Graphics area to view the contents of the Graphics bin. Now, there are two files in the Graphics bin.

Viewing and changing poster frames

At the top of a Project window or Bin area is the *thumbnail viewer*, which you can use to preview individual clips. When you select a clip in the Project window, the thumbnail view displays the *poster frame* associated with that clip, i.e., the frame used for the icon view of the clip and as a sample frame for titles. By default, the poster frame is the first frame of a clip, but you can change the poster frame to any frame in the clip. In addition to the poster frame, the thumbnail view also displays the clip name, media type, video information, duration, and data rate.

Now, let's view a clip and its information in the Project window:

1 Click back to Bin 1, then click the Thumbnail View button (⊞) at the bottom of the Project window.

2 Select the Ferry.mov clip in Bin 1. The clip's information appears beside the thumbnail viewer in the upper left corner of the Project window.

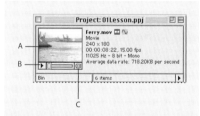

A. Thumbnail preview B. Play button
C. Set Poster Frame button

Note: *The average data rate is displayed beside the thumbnail preview for all video clips. This information is useful for analog video because maintaining a consistent data rate for all clips in a project results in smoother playback from the Timeline.*

3 View the clip by pressing the Play button (▶) on the thumbnail viewer. Press Play again to stop playback.

4 Click the List View button (▤) to change the view of the clips in Bin 1. Use the Resize button in the lower right corner of the Project window to expand the size of the file area, or scroll along the right side of the window to see all of the columns of information.

Now let's change a clip's poster frame.

5 Select the Ferry.mov clip in the Project window if it is not already selected.

6 Press the Play button (▶) until the frame you want to use as the new poster frame is displayed, then press Play again to stop the clip at this point. Alternatively, drag the play slider on the thumbnail viewer in the upper left corner of the Project window to the frame you want to use.

7 Click the Set Poster Frame button(▣)in the lower right corner of the thumbnail viewer. Alternatively, you can right-click the mouse (Windows) or press and hold the Control key and click the Set Poster Frame button (Mac OS).

8 Click the Thumbnail view or Icon view button to see the new poster frame.

Working with bins

A Project window includes a *Bin area*, which shows the bins that have been added to the project. The Bin area appears on the left side of the Project window, and can be resized or hidden. When the bins in the Bin area contain other bins, the hierarchical structure appears, much like the graphical view of folders and subfolders in your operating system.

Let's begin by creating a bin.

1 From the title bar at the top of your screen, choose File > New > Bin or click the New Bin button (◻) in the Project window. The Create Bin dialog box opens with a default name. Type **Bin 2** and then click OK.

2 Do one of the following:

• Click the Bin 1 icon in the Project window to view the contents of Bin 1.

• Alternatively, to open a Bin in its own window, you can right-click (Windows) or Control-click (Mac OS) Bin 1, and choose Open Bin in New Window. Alternatively, Option-click (Mac OS) Bin 1 will open the bin directly in a new window.

3 In the Project window, slide the Resize Bin Area button (◁▷) located at the bottom of the Bin area in the Project window until you have the width you want. You cannot make the bin view narrower than the four buttons at the bottom of the Bin area. To make the Bin area higher or wider, you may need to first make the Project window bigger.

4 Do one of the following:

• Drag the Ferry.mov clip to the Bin 2 icon.

• Alternatively, if Bin 2 is open in its own window, drag the Ferry.mov clip to the Bin area.

• Right-click (Windows) or Control-click (Mac OS) Ferry.mov, and choose Cut. Then click the Bin 2 icon and choose Paste.

5 Now, you will delete Bin 2. If you moved a video clip from Bin 1 to Bin 2 that you want to retain, move the clip back to Bin 1 *before* deleting Bin 2. Then, select Bin 2 and click the Delete Selected Items button (🗑) at the bottom of the Project window.

By default, Premiere uses the List view to display information about the clip files in the Bin area in the Project window. You can customize the way the list appears, and the settings can be unique for each window.

6 Click the Graphics bin icon in the Project window to open the Graphics Bin area.

7 Do one of the following:

• From the title bar at the top of your screen, choose Window > Window Options > Project Window Options.

• Alternatively, right-click (Windows) or Control-click (Mac OS) the Graphics bin icon, and choose Project Window Options.

8 Choose Thumbnail view from the pop-up menu at the top of the Project Window Options dialog box.

Now, you'll customize one of the four fields. In this example, you'll use the field to track the person responsible for providing the file.

9 In the Fields section, highlight the text **Label 1** in the second box and type **From** to replace the existing text. Click OK.

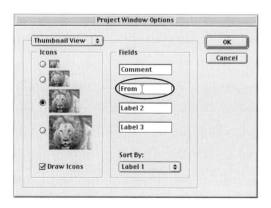

You have changed the Bin area to Thumbnail view, which lists files using large icons. You can now use the field you customized.

Note: You can change options for most windows in Premiere by choosing the first command under the window's pop-up menu, as you did here.

10 Drag the lower right corner of the Project window to the right to reveal the From column next to the Comment column.

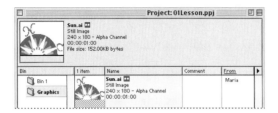

11 In the From box for the clip Sun.ai, type **Maria.**

12 Premiere can also display the list as loose icons, which you can arrange by dragging. This time, you'll use a faster method to change the view. Click the Icon View button (▫) at the bottom of the Bin area.

Click the Icon View, Thumbnail View, or List View buttons (as shown here left to right) at the bottom left of a Project or Bin area to change the view. (The same Bin area is shown, displaying the three different views.).

Comments don't appear in Icon view, but you can quickly see them by changing back to the List view or Thumbnail view.

13 Click the List View button (☰) at the bottom of the Bin area.

In List view, you can change the sort order directly. Now, you'll sort this list by name.

14 Click the Name heading just under the Thumbnail Viewer area to sort it by name.

The techniques you've learned for changing the Project window and Bin area options allow you to use these windows to manage source clips. However, you don't use the Bin area and Project window to edit the actual video program. In the following sections, you'll learn about the windows that you use for editing.

Using libraries from previous versions of Premiere

In previous versions of Premiere, you could create containers called libraries, which were used to store clips from one or several projects. A library was stored as a separate file apart from any project. Although Premiere 6.0 doesn't support libraries, you can open a library created in a previous version of Premiere. When you open it in Premiere 6.0, the library will be converted into the Bin system we've just examined.

• To import a library, choose File > Open. Locate and select the library (.PLB) file, and then click Open. The library will be converted to a bin.

• If you want to store a set of clips from a library so they are available for other projects in Premiere 6.0, save the new bin that contains the clips.

Saving and autosaving a project

Saving a project saves your editing decisions, references to source files, and the most recent arrangement of the program's windows. Protect your work by saving often. If you prefer, Premiere can save your project automatically at a specified interval. Premiere can either save the project to the same file each time or to a new file. For example, you can set Premiere to save a new archive of your project every 15 minutes.

Saving at a fixed interval produces a series of files that represent the state of your project at each interval. In this way, automatic archiving can serve as an alternate form of the Undo command, depending on how much the project changed between each save. Because project files are quite small compared to source video files, archiving many iterations of a project consumes relatively little disk space. Adobe recommends saving project files to the same drive as your application. Archived files are saved in the Project-Archive folder inside the Adobe Premiere 6.0 folder. For more information, see "Saving and autosaving a project" in Chapter 1 of the *Adobe Premiere 6.0 User Guide*.

Note: *You will not be able to save your changes to the 01Lesson.ppj project file because it is a locked file. You may want to use Save As to rename and save the Lesson as an unlocked file.*

Working with the Timeline window

The *Timeline* is a time-based representation of your program. You can assemble and edit your video in the Timeline window. When you start a new project, the Timeline is empty. In this project, clips exist in the Timeline because we've already started the project for you. The Timeline also includes a toolbox containing editing tools. In this section, you'll learn how to locate controls for navigating time and for editing.

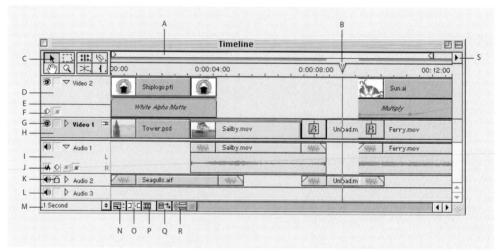

Timeline window in the Single-Track workspace: **A.** *Work area bar* **B.** *Edit line* **C.** *Tools* **D.** *Superimpose track* **E.** *Adjustable track header border* **F.** *Keyframe and Opacity icons* **G.** *Shy Video track icon* **H.** *Video track* **I.** *Audio track* **J.** *Waveform, Keyframe, Volume, and Pan icons* **K.** *Lock track icon* **L.** *Shy Audio track icon* **M.** *Time Zoom Level* **N.** *Track Options Dialog button* **O.** *Toggle Snap to Edges button* **P.** *Toggle Edge Viewing button* **Q.** *Toggle Shift Tracks Options button* **R.** *Toggle Sync Mode button* **S.** *Timeline Window Menu button*

The Timeline window displays time horizontally. Clips earlier in time appear to the left, and clips later in time appear to the right. Time is indicated by the *time ruler* near the top of the Timeline window.

The *Time Zoom Level* pop-up menu at the bottom of the Timeline indicates the time scale currently in use. You can change the time scale when you want to view time in more detail or see more of the video program.

1 Click the title bar of the Timeline window to make it active.

2 Choose 4 Seconds from the Time Zoom Level pop-up menu in the lower left corner. The Timeline changes so that four seconds of video are shown for every major division in the time ruler.

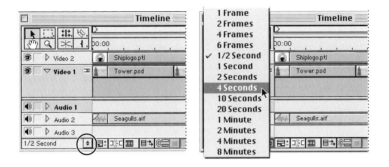

3 Choose 1 Frame from the Time Zoom Level pop-up menu.

The Timeline now changes to display one frame at every time-ruler division. Using the time scale of 1 Frame allows you to make very precise edits in the Timeline, but you can't see very much of the video program at once.

4 Click and hold the right scroll arrow at the bottom of the Timeline window to see parts of the video that are later in time. Because you're now using a highly magnified time scale, scrolling through the Timeline takes longer.

You can also use keyboard shortcuts to zoom in and out of the current time scale.

5 Press the hyphen key (-) to zoom out one level.

The Time Zoom Level pop-up menu now indicates a time scale of 2 Frames. Press the same key again to zoom out one more level. You can zoom out to a time scale of 8 minutes per time ruler division, which lets you view an entire 3-hour program at once.

6 Press the equal sign key (=) to zoom in one level. The Time Zoom Level menu changes to indicate the new time scale.

7 Press the backslash key (\) to fit the entire video within the visible area of the Timeline.

Opening a Clip window

Clips can be displayed in either the Source view (left side) in the Monitor window or in a Clip window. The most convenient way to compare several clips is to open a separate Clip window for each.

1 Press Alt (Windows) or Option (Mac OS) as you double-click the Ferry.mov clip in the Project or Timeline window or Bin area to view the clip in its own window.

2 Alternatively, double-click the Ferry.mov clip in the Project or Timeline window or Bin area to view the clip in the Source view in the Monitor window. Premiere displays the clip and adds its name to the Source menu below the Source view.

 You can choose preferences to always open a clip in its own window: Choose Edit > Preferences > General & Still Image, select Open Movies in Clip Window, and click OK.

Working with tracks

The Timeline window includes *tracks* where you arrange clips. Tracks are stacked vertically. When one clip is above another, both clips will play back simultaneously.

Tracks are divided into three sections:

• In the center of the window, the Video 1 track is the main video editing track.

• All tracks above Video 1 are for superimposing clips over the Video 1 track.

• All tracks below Video 1 are for audio.

In A/B Editing mode, the Video 1 track displays as three subtracks: Video 1A, 1B, and the transition track. But, in Single-Track Editing mode, the three subtracks are combined.

In Single-Track Editing mode, the Video 1 track can display as either collapsed or uncollapsed. When it is collapsed, all clips and transitions are combined on one track. When it is uncollapsed, the view resembles that of the A/B Editing mode, except that you cannot overlap the clips, and the separate tracks still behave as one track. In both editing modes, the Video 2 track, by default, is available for superimposing clips over the Video 1 tracks, and you can add more tracks for additional layers of superimposed video.

1 In the Timeline window, click the Track Mode button (⊐) to the right of the Video 1 track label.

Note: *In Premiere 5.0, these modes were selected using the triangle in the track header. In Adobe Premiere 6.0, the triangle is used to display or hide keyframes and fade controls.*

Premiere 6.0 expands the Video 1 track into the Video 1 (upper row), Transition, and Video 1 (lower row) tracks, so that the relationship between clips and transitions is clearer. (You'll work with transitions in Lesson 4, "Adding Transitions.")

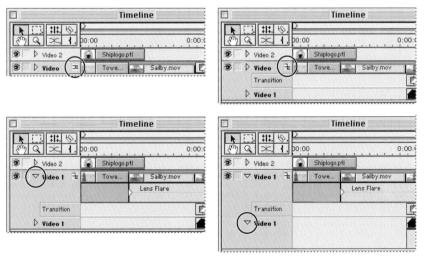

Track Mode button in Single-Track collapsed mode (top left) and Single-Track uncollapsed mode (upper right and bottom row)

2 Click the Expand/Collapse Track triangle to the left of the Video 2 track label. Premiere expands the Video 2 track.

Two clips exist on the Video 2 track:

• Shiplogo.ptl is a still image with transparency settings applied to it so that another clip, Tower.psd (on the upper track of Video 1), is visible under the Shiplogo.ptl clip. (You'll work with transparency in Lesson 9, "Superimposing.")

• Sun.ai is a still image created in Adobe Illustrator with transparency settings to reveal another clip, Ferry.mov, on the upper track of Video 1. If you double-click the file-open triangle, a red line sloping upward indicates the clip's opacity control: Sun.ai starts completely transparent and gradually becomes completely opaque.

3 Click the Expand/Collapse Track triangle to the left of the Video 2 track label to collapse the track.

Notice the red line along the bottom edge of the clip Shiplogo.ptl. This indicates that motion settings are applied to the clip. (You'll work with motion settings in Lesson 10, "Adding Motion.")

Similarly, a blue line appears along the top edge of the clip Sailby.mov. This indicates that an *effect* is applied to the clip. (You'll work with effects in Lesson 11, "Applying Video and Audio Effects.")

4 Click the Expand/Collapse Track triangle to the left of the Audio 1 track label.

Premiere expands the Audio 1 track and reveals the red fade and blue pan controls for the audio clips on that track. The red line in the audio track indicates the audio *gain level* (volume) at any point in time. (You'll work with audio in Lesson 5, "Adding Audio.")

5 Click the expand/collapse track triangle to the left of the Audio 1 track label to collapse the track.

The Timeline also includes editing tools, which are covered in more detail throughout this book. As you learn about tools, you can use tool tips to identify them and their keyboard shortcuts. See "Learning keyboard shortcuts" on page 94.

Working with keyframes

Premiere uses *keyframes* to change an effect over time. A keyframe contains the values for all the controls in the effect and applies those values to the clip at the specified time. By default, once you apply an effect to a clip, Premiere creates a beginning and ending keyframe with the same value, but by applying different values to keyframes, you can change an effect over time.

Note: Some Premiere effects cannot be changed with keyframes and cannot be animated.

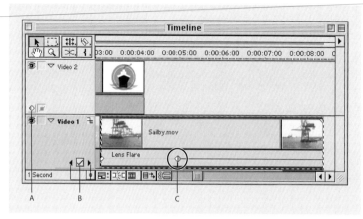

A. *Effect Keyframe button* **B.** *Keyframe Navigator button* **C.** *Keyframe line*

Each effect has a default keyframe at the beginning and the end of the clip, indicated by half-diamonds on the keyframe line in the Timeline window. If an effect has adjustable controls, you can change the start or end time of the effect or add additional keyframes to create an animated effect. If you don't make any changes to the default keyframes, the settings for the associated effect apply to the entire clip.

Note: *The cursor becomes a shaded finger when it is on a keyframe.*

Now let's set a keyframe for an effect.

1 In the Timeline window, click the triangle at the left of the Video 1 track label to expand the view and to display the keyframe line.

2 Click the Sailby.mov clip and the Keyframe Navigator box will appear to the left of the keyframe line because the Lens Flare effect has already been applied here.

3 Position the edit line at the point where you want to create a new keyframe in the Sailby.mov clip and click the keyframe navigator box ( ). A check mark will now appear in the keyframe navigator box and a keyframe diamond will appear at the precise point on the edit line that you have chosen.

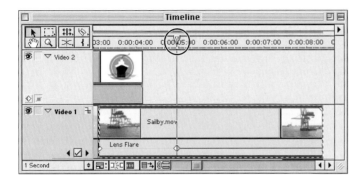

4 The Effect Controls palette allows you to adjust the effect settings, such as brightness. If effect settings are not visible, click the triangle next to the effect name to show them. (Choose Window > Show Effect Controls if the Effect Control palette is not open.)

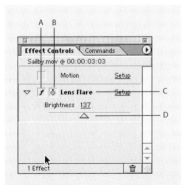

*A. Effect Enabled button **B.** Keyframing Enabled button **C.** Effect name*
D. Effect Controls slider

Note: *When you apply an effect, the first and last keyframes are automatically applied and the Effect Enabled icon ( ) appears next to the effect name in the Effect Controls palette.*

5 Adjust the brightness of the Lens Flare effect at this keyframe by moving the Effect Controls slider to the left or right.

6 To preview the change you made, Alt-drag (Windows) or Option-drag (Mac OS) the triangle at the top of the edit line in the Timeline window to see how the Lens Flare effect has changed where you added the keyframe. For more information, see "Understanding keyframes" in Chapter 9 of the *Adobe Premiere 6.0 User Guide.*

Note: *You will learn more about Effect controls later in this lesson.*

Working with the Monitor window

In addition to the Timeline, you can assemble clips in the *Monitor* window. Depending on how you want to work and the specific tasks you have to accomplish, you can choose from among a number of different view options for the Monitor window.

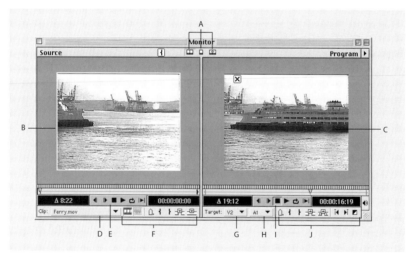

Monitor window in Dual View: **A.***View icons: Dual View icon (⊞), Single View icon (▫), Trim view icon (⊞)* **B.** *Source view* **C.** *Program view* **D.** *Source clips menu* **E.** *Source preview controls* **F.** *Source controllers* **G.** *Target video track* **H.** *Target audio track* **I.** *Program preview controls* **J.** *Program controllers*

In Single-Track Editing mode, the default for the Monitor window is the *Dual View* mode, which displays the *Source view* and the *Program view* side-by-side. It can be helpful to think of the Source view as a viewer for the Project window and to think of the Program view as a viewer for the Timeline.

The Dual View mode Displays both the Source and Program views. This is the default window display for the Single-Track Editing workspace. The Dual View icon (⊞) is located at the top center of the Monitor window.

Source view Displays the source clip with which you are currently working. When you first open a project session, the Source view is blank because you have not yet worked with any source clips. You use the Source view to prepare a clip for inclusion in the video program or to edit a clip you've opened from the video program.

Program view Displays the current state of the video program you are building. When you first open a project session, the Program view displays the first frame in the Timeline, if at least one clip was placed there in a prior session. When you play the video program in Premiere, it appears in the Program view. You can think of it as an alternate view of the Timeline—the Timeline displays a time-based view of your video program, and the Program view displays a frame-based view of your video program.

In addition to Dual View mode, you can choose from two other view modes for the Monitor window. If you want to see only the Program view, you can select *Single View*. For precise control over trimming, you can switch the Monitor window to the *Trim View*. Whichever mode you are in, the three icons at the top of the Monitor window let you toggle between the three view modes.

The Single View mode Displays only the Program view. The Single View icon (▫) is found at the top center of the Monitor window. Individual clips open in individual Clip windows. This is the default display for the A/B Editing workspace.

♡ *You may also find it convenient to use Single View if you are working in Single-Track Editing mode to save desktop space or to open individual Clip windows when you want to compare two or more clips, but you are not trimming or editing them at the time.*

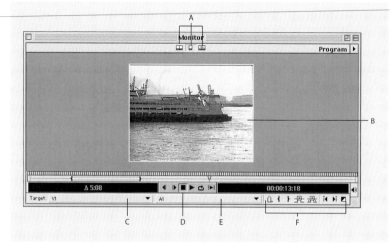

*Monitor window in Single View: **A**. View icons: Dual View icon (▢▢),*
*Single View icon (▢), Trim view icon (▦) **B**. Program view **C**. Target video track*
***D**. Program preview controls **E**. Target audio track **F**. Program controllers*

Trim view   Provides a precise way to trim clips interactively in any video track. You can
perform ripple or rolling edits on any point along the Timeline. The Trim view icon (▦)
is located at the top center of the Monitor window. When you use the Trim view, the two
views displayed represent clips in the program—the left view is the clip to the left of the
edit line; the right view is the clip to the right of the edit line. For more information on
trimming, see "Using the Trim view" in Chapter 3 of the *Adobe Premiere 6.0 User Guide*.

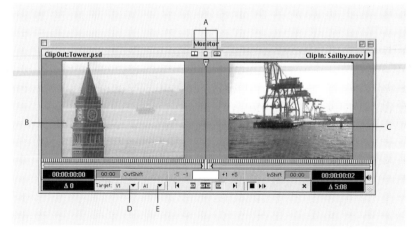

*Monitor window in Trim view: **A**. View icons: Dual View icon (▢▢), Single View icon (▢),*
*Trim view icon (▦) **B**. Program view of clip to the left of the edit line*
***C**. Program view of clip to the right of the edit line **D**.Target video **E**. Target audio*

1 In the Project window, double-click the Ferry.mov icon.

The Source view displays the clip that you selected with a double-click in the Project window. Double-clicking a clip in the Project window like this displays the uncut clip as it appears before any editing. However, if you double-click a clip in the Timeline, you see only those frames that are included in your video program. You'll try that now.

2 In the Timeline window, double-click the file Sailby.mov.

Now the Source view displays a clip that was in the Timeline. You'll do this when you want to make changes to a clip that you previously added to the Timeline.

You've viewed two clips in the Source view in this session, and Premiere remembers them in the menu below the Source view in the Monitor window.

3 Position the cursor over the Source view menu at the bottom of the Source view (next to the word "Clip") and hold down the mouse button. The two clips you've viewed in this session are listed so that you can go back to them while you have this project open.

Note: *Remember, you can also change views by clicking the Single View icon (▫), the Trim mode icon (▣), or the Dual View icon (▣) located at the top of the Monitor window.*

Because the Program window and the Timeline window offer different views of the same video program, you can edit a video using either window. If you're learning how to edit video, you may find it easier to edit in the more graphical Timeline window. Editors experienced in using high-end video-editing systems may be able to edit faster and more precisely using the Source view and Program controllers instead.

Navigating to a specific time

The *edit line* in the Timeline window indicates the frame displayed in the Program view in the Monitor window. The edit line indicates the point in time when the next edit will be applied, when you use a command or a control in the Monitor window.

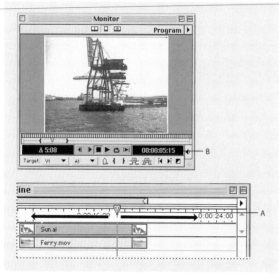

A. The edit line in the Timeline window. B. The Timecode display below the Program view in the Monitor window changes to represent the current frame.

Using the Program controller affects the Timeline, and editing the Timeline updates the Program view.

1 In the Timeline window, click in the ruler at the top of the window or drag in the ruler to move the edit line right or left (a technique called *scrubbing*). The playback speed is dictated by the speed at which you drag. Both the Program view and the Timecode display in the Navigator window below the Program view change to represent the current frame.

You may have noticed that when the Program view changed, only the basic clips are visible in the Timeline. Any effects applied to the clips, such as opacity or transitions, are not visible using the scrub method. The location of each effect in a clip is indicated by an "X" inside a square at the top left corner in the Program view in the Monitor window. If you want to see the actual effects, you need to use another method, called *render-scrub*.

2 To render-scrub while previewing, so you can see the applied effects, hold down Alt (Windows) or Option (Mac OS) as you drag the edit line in the time ruler. Now, the Program view displays frames with the opacity, transitions, and effects that have been applied to the clip.There may be a slight delay as effects are processed.

Note: *You must press and hold down the Alt (Windows) or the Option (Mac OS) key before you begin dragging in the ruler.*

Using palettes

Adobe Premiere provides several palettes to display information and to help you modify clips. By default, most of the palettes are open. You can open, close, or group palettes to best suit the way you like to work. If your operating system supports a multiple-monitor desktop and you have more than one monitor connected to your system, you can drag palettes to any monitor. Note that the palettes in Premiere work the same way as the palettes in Adobe Photoshop®, Illustrator®, and PageMaker®®.

You can change the arrangement and display of palettes and palette groups to make the best use of space on your monitor. For more information, see "Using tools and palettes" in the Overview section of the *Adobe Premiere 6.0 User Guide*.

Using the Effect Controls palette

1 Display the Effect Controls palette by choosing Window > Show Effect Controls in the Premiere title bar at the top of the screen. (If Hide Effect Controls is listed, the Effect Controls palette is already displayed).

2 Choose Hide Effect Controls from the Premiere window menu to hide the Effect Controls palette.

3 Press the Tab key to show or hide all of the displayed palettes at the same time.

4 Choose Window > Show Effect Controls again. Click the palette's Menu button, located near the upper right corner of the palette. Note that the Menu button for a specific palette identifies only the functions for that palette. Not all palettes have Menu buttons.

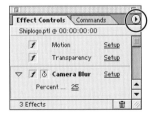

5 Click the Effect Controls Menu button again, or click elsewhere in the palette, to close the menu.

6 Click the upper left of the palette window to close the Effect Controls/Commands palette window or choose Window > Hide Effect Controls.

Using the Info palette

The Info palette displays information about a selected clip or transition. The information displayed in the Info palette may vary depending on the media type and the current window. The Info palette can be helpful in identifying the many kinds of content you can include in your project and the attributes of that content.

1 Make sure the Info palette is visible. To see it, choose Window > Show Info or press the tab key once. (The Tab key shows/hides only two palette groups: Navigator-Info-History and Transitions-Video-Audio.) You may need to click the Info tab in the window if the History or Navigator palettes are active.

2 Click the audio clip Seagulls.aif in the Timeline. The Info palette now displays the clip's name, duration, and audio attributes, its location in the Timeline, and the position of the cursor.

3 In the Timeline window, drag the audio clip Seagulls.aif to the right. As you drag it, the Info palette continuously updates the clip's position, so that you can move it precisely.

4 Choose Edit > Undo Move to return the audio clip to its original position.

If you dragged the clip multiple times, just choose the Undo command multiple times until it returns to its original position. Alternatively, you can use the History palette to return to the state you choose.

5 Now, click the clip Sun.ai in the Timeline window. (You may need to scroll across the Timeline window to see it.) Now, the Info palette identifies the clip as a still image.

6 In the Timeline window, select the gap between the first and second clips on the Video 2 track. The Info palette indicates the duration of the gap between the two clips as well as start and end times of the gap and current cursor position. Notice that no clips are listed.

Using the Navigator palette

Use the Navigator palette to quickly change your view of the Timeline by dragging a view box within a miniature representation of the Timeline. This technique is especially useful when you work with a long video program that extends far beyond the edges of the Timeline window. You can also change the level of detail displayed in the Timeline.

1 Make sure both the Timeline window and the Navigator palette are visible. If necessary, click the Navigator tab (if visible) or choose Window > Show Navigator.

The Navigator palette represents all tracks in your video program. The controls in the Navigator palette let you change the time scale at which the Timeline is displayed. Notice that the Navigator palette is color-coded to indicate various parts of the Timeline.

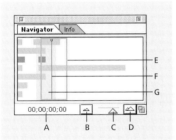

*Navigator palette: **A.** Timecode*
***B.** Zoom-out button **C.** Zoom slider*
***D.** Zoom-in button **E.** Current View box*
***F.** Edit line **G.** Current work area*

In the several numbered steps, you'll explore the Navigator palette by doing the following:

• Double-click the Timecode (A), type a new time, and press Enter (Windows) or Return (Mac OS). The edit line moves to the new time. Notice that you just type the digits for the time, you don't need to type the ":" separators. You can also use the cursor to highlight just the digits you want to change and then type in new numbers.

• Click the Zoom-out button (B) to make more of the Timeline visible.

• Drag the Zoom slider (C) left to reduce or right to magnify the Timeline.

- Click the Zoom-in button (D) to magnify the Timeline at the edit line.

- Drag the Current View box (E) to scroll the Timeline.

- Press and hold the Shift key as you drag the edit line (F) in the Navigator palette to move the edit line in the Timeline. (Notice that the hand tool changes to a triangle when you press Shift.)

- The blue area indicates the Current work area (G) that will play back during a preview.

The Navigator palette also color-codes track types to help you identify them. Video tracks are yellow, transitions are blue, and audio tracks are green.

2 Click the Zoom-in button in the Navigator palette.

The Timeline zooms in to the next higher time scale. As you do this, the Current view box (green rectangle) in the Navigator palette becomes narrower, because you're now seeing less of the video program in the Timeline.

3 Position the cursor (hand tool) anywhere inside the Current view box, then drag the green rectangle to change the visible area in the Timeline window.

4 Now, press and hold the Shift key, position the cursor over the edit line, then drag the red edit line.

This time, the edit line moves in the Timeline window, and the Program view in the Monitor window displays the frame at the new edit line.

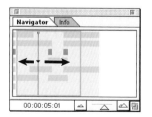

5 Deselect any clips that may be selected in the Timeline. Now, highlight the Timecode display at the bottom of the Navigator palette, type **200**, and press Enter (Windows) or Return (Mac OS). The edit line moves to frame 00:00:02:00 in the Timeline window, in the Navigator palette, and in the Timecode display in the Program view.

Using the Commands palette

The Commands palette comes with a list of preset commands that you can modify to suit your needs. You can also create a custom set of buttons for fast access to your favorite menu commands, and assign a function key to each button for instant keyboard access. You can manage command sets by first deselecting Button Mode from the Commands palette menu, and then, choosing any of the following commands from the Commands palette menu:

Play Command Executes the command for the selected button. Select the button you want to play, and click Play Command. You can also execute a command by clicking the Play Command button (▷) at the bottom of the Commands palette.

Add Command Adds a new button to the Commands palette. You can also add a command by clicking the Add Command button (▣) at the bottom of the Commands palette.

Delete Command Removes command buttons. Select the button you want to remove and click Delete. When Button Mode is off, you can delete a command by selecting it and clicking the Trash icon (🗑) at the bottom of the Commands palette.

Command Options Modifies command buttons. Select the button you want to change and select Options. When Button Mode is off, you can change command options by double-clicking a command.

Load Commands Replaces the existing buttons with a set saved on disk.

Save Commands Lets you save your commands in a file that you specify. This is useful for creating custom command sets for different purposes, such as one for video capture.

Button Mode Turns Button Mode on and off. Use Button Mode when you want to use buttons in the Commands palette. Turn Button Mode off when you want to manage buttons. Button Mode is on when the check mark is displayed next to it.

If you don't like the default keyboard shortcut for a command, you can use the Commands palette to override it; a keyboard shortcut in the Commands palette takes precedence over a corresponding built-in shortcut.

In this lesson, you'll add a button that performs the Select All command. In your own project work, you'll want to add the commands you use most frequently.

1 Make sure the Commands palette is visible: Click the Commands tab (if the Effect Controls/Commands palette group is visible) or choose Window > Show Commands.

2 Click the menu button at the top right in the Commands palette to see the menu. Now, click Button Mode to deselect it (removes its check mark).

3 Now, select Add Command from the palette menu, or click the Add Command button (▣) at the bottom of the Command palette.

4 The Command Options dialog box appears. A new, unassigned button labeled "Untitled" (Windows) or "Undefined" (Mac OS) appears next to the Name field in the Command Options window.

5 From the title bar at the top of the Premiere window, choose Edit > Select All for the command to add to the Command palette.

6 Now, the Command Options dialog box displays "Select All" in the Command field.

7 In the Name field, type **all clips**.

8 For Function Key, choose the keyboard shortcut you want to assign to your new button. The menu lists only keys that are not already assigned to other commands (Windows) or dims keys that are already assigned to other commands (Mac OS). (In our example, "F10" has been chosen).

```
                    Command Options
     Name:  all clips                        OK

  Command:  Select All                     Cancel

Function Key:  F10           ⬍

     Color:  None            ⬍
```

Note: In Windows, the F1 key is reserved for online Help by the system.

9 For Color, choose a color for the button and click OK.

10 Choose Button Mode from the palette menu to activate it.

You're ready to try your new button.

11 Click to activate a window that allows clip selection, such as the Project window or the Timeline.

12 In the Commands palette, click the "all clips" button you just created or press F10 (the keyboard shortcut). All the clips in the Timeline window are selected.

Note: You've added this command as an exercise for this lesson. It now exists in Premiere for any project you open. If you don't want to keep it, do the next two steps.

13 Choose Button Mode from the Commands palette menu to deselect it.

14 Make sure "all clips (F10)" is selected in the palette menu, choose Delete Command from the palette menu, and then click OK or Yes.

Using the History palette

Use the History palette to jump to any state of the project created during the *current working session.* Each time you apply a change to some part of the project, the new state of that project is added to the History palette.

For example, if you add a clip to the Timeline window, apply an effect to it, copy it, and paste it in another track, each of those states is listed separately in the History palette. You can select any of these states, and the project will revert to how it looked when the change was applied. You can then modify the project from that state forward.

1 Choose Window > Show History to display the History palette if it is not already open.

2 Click the name of the desired action or change in the History palette to display a state of the current project.

3 Drag the slider or the scroll bar in the palette to move around in the History palette.

Use any of the following commands from the History palette menu by clicking the menu button at the top right in the History palette:

Step Forward This command allows you to move forward through the project states listed in the History palette.

Step Backward This command allows you to move backward through the project states listed in the History palette.

Delete Use this to delete *only one* project state in the History palette menu.

Clear History This command clears *all* states in the History palette menu.

Learning keyboard shortcuts

Adobe Premiere 6.0 provides keyboard shortcuts for most commands and buttons, so it is possible to edit a video program with minimal use of the mouse. As you develop a working style, you can speed up your work by learning the keyboard shortcuts for the commands and buttons you use the most. Some experienced video editors can edit faster using the keyboard rather than the mouse. In this section, you'll learn how to find the keyboard shortcuts you need.

As in other software, if a menu command has a keyboard shortcut, you'll find it next to the command on its menu. The *Adobe Premiere 6.0 User Guide* and the *Quick Reference Card* fully document all keyboard shortcuts.

1 In the Timeline window, click any clip.

2 In the title bar at the top of your screen, click the Clip menu to view the menu commands. Notice the keyboard shortcuts to the right of most commands.

Premiere 6.0 also contains many tools and buttons, and you can find their keyboard shortcuts just as easily. Now, you'll find the shortcut for a button in the Monitors window.

3 Click the Monitors window to activate it.

4 Move the cursor over the Mark Out button (⎸) on the Source controller, and hold the cursor over the button until its tool tip appears. The keyboard shortcut appears in parentheses after the tool name.

Note: If tool tips do not appear, choose Edit > Preferences > General & Still Image and make sure Show Tool Tips is selected.

Now, you'll find a keyboard shortcut in online Help.

5 Choose Help > Keyboard (Windows) or Help > Keyboard Shortcuts (Mac OS).

Note: Your browser will open to Premiere Help, specifically to Keyboard Shortcuts.

6 Use the controls in online Help to find the shortcut you want.

Note: A complete listing of keyboard shortcuts appears on the Quick Reference Card, included in the Adobe Premiere 6.0 software package.

Review questions

1 What can you do with the Source view in the Monitors window?

2 What can you do with the Program view in the Monitors window?

3 What does a Project window Bin area show?

4 What can you do with a keyframe?

5 What are two ways to see finer increments of time in the Timeline window?

6 How can you customize a keyboard shortcut for a command?

Answers

1 You can view a clip from a Project window or Bin area, prepare a clip for inclusion in the Timeline, or edit a clip you opened from the Timeline.

2 It is used primarily for playing and reviewing an edited project in the Timeline. You can also edit the Timeline.

3 You can organize clips in a project using Bins. When you import clips, they are added to the currently selected Bin area. A Project window includes a Bin view, which shows the bins that have been added to the project.

4 A keyframe is used to change an effect over time. It contains the values for all the controls in an effect and applies those values to the clip at the specified time.

5 All of these are correct: In the Timeline window, you can choose a time scale from the Time Zoom Level menu or press the equal sign key (=). In the Navigator palette, you can click the Zoom-in button or drag the magnification slider.

6 Add a command to the Commands palette and then assign a keyboard shortcut to that command.

Lesson 2

2 | About Digital Video Editing

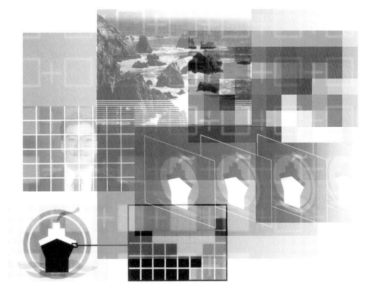

When you edit video, you arrange source clips so that they tell a story. That story can be anything from a fictional television program to a news event and more. Understanding the issues that affect your editing decisions can help you prepare for successful editing and save you valuable time and resources.

This lesson describes the role of Adobe Premiere in video production and introduces a variety of key concepts:

- Measuring video time.
- Measuring frame size and resolution.
- Compressing video data.
- Capturing video.
- Superimposing and transparency.
- Using audio in a video.
- Creating final video.

How Adobe Premiere fits into video production

Making video involves working through three general phases:

Pre-production Involves writing the script, visualizing scenes by sketching them on a storyboard, and creating a production schedule for shooting the scenes.

Production Involves shooting the scenes.

Post-production Involves editing the best scenes into the final video program, correcting and enhancing video and audio where necessary. Editing includes a first draft, or *rough cut*, where you can get a general idea of the possibilities you have with the clips available to you. As you continue editing, you refine the video program through successive iterations until you decide that it's finished. At that point you have built the *final cut*. Premiere is designed for efficient editing, correcting, and enhancing of clips, making it a valuable tool for post-production.

The rest of this chapter describes fundamental concepts that affect video editing and other post-production tasks in Premiere. All of the concepts in this section and the specific Premiere features that support them are described in more detail in the *Adobe Premiere 6.0 User Guide*.

If any stage of your project involves outside vendors, such as video post-production facilities, consult with them before starting the project. They can help you determine what settings to use at various stages of a project and can potentially help you avoid costly, time-consuming mistakes. For example, if you're creating video for broadcast, you should know whether you are creating video for the NTSC (National Television Standards Committee) standard used primarily in North America and Japan; the PAL (Phase Alternate Line) standard used primarily in Europe, Asia, and southern Africa; or the SECAM (Sequential Couleur Avec Memoire) standard used primarily in France, the Middle East, and North Africa.

Measuring video time

In the natural world, we experience time as a continuous flow of events. However, working with video requires precise synchronization, so it's necessary to measure time using precise numbers. Familiar time increments—hours, minutes, and seconds—are not precise enough for video editing, because a single second might contain several events. This section describes how Premiere 6.0 and video professionals measure time, using standard methods that count fractions of a second in frames.

How the timebase and frame rates affect each other

You determine how time is measured in your project by specifying the project *timebase*. For example, a timebase of 30 means that each second is divided into 30 units. The exact time at which an edit occurs depends on the timebase you specify, because an edit can only occur at a time division; using a different timebase causes the time divisions to fall in different places.

The time increments in a source clip are determined by the *source frame rate*. For example, when you shoot source clips using a video camera with a frame rate of 30 frames per second, the camera documents the action by recording one frame every 1/30th of a second. Note that whatever was happening between those 1/30th of a second intervals is not recorded. Thus, a lower frame rate (such as 15 fps) records less information about continuous action, while a high frame rate (such as 30 fps) records more.

You determine how often Premiere generates frames from your project by specifying the *project frame rate*. A project frame rate of 30 frames per second means that Premiere will create 30 frames from each second of your project.

For smooth and consistent playback, the timebase, the source frame rate, and the project frame rate should be identical.

Editing Video Type	Frames per second
Motion-picture film	24 fps
PAL and SECAM video	25 fps
NTSC video	29.97 fps
Web or CD-ROM	15 fps
Other video types, e.g., non-drop frame editing, E-D animation	30 fps

Note: NTSC was originally designed for a black-and-white picture at 30 fps, but signal modifications made in the mid-20th century to accommodate color pictures altered the standard NTSC frame rate to 29.97 fps.

Sometimes the time systems don't match. For example, you might be asked to create a video intended for CD-ROM distribution that must combine motion-picture source clips captured at 24 fps with video source clips captured at 30 fps, using a timebase of 30 for a final CD-ROM frame rate of 15 fps. When any of these values don't match, it is mathematically necessary for some frames to be repeated or omitted; the effect may be distracting or imperceptible depending on the differences between the timebase and frame rates you used in your project.

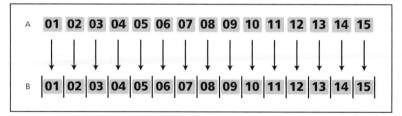

A. 30 fps video clip (one-half second shown) **B.** *Timebase of 30, for a video production When the source frame rate matches the timebase, all frames display as expected.*

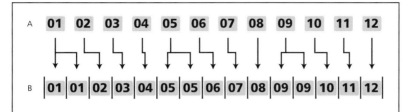

A. 24 fps motion-picture source clip (one-half second shown) *B*. Timebase of 30, for a
video production. To play one second of 24 fps frames at a timebase of 30, source frames
1, 5, and 9 are repeated.

💡 *It is preferable to capture your clips at the same frame rate at which you plan to export
your project. For example, if you know your source clips will be exported at 30 fps, capture the
clips at 30 fps instead of 24 fps. If, this is not possible (for example, DV can only be captured
at 29.97 fps), you'll want to output at a frame rate that evenly divides your timebase. So, if
your capture frame rate and your timebase are set at 30 fps (actually 29.97), you should
output at 30, 15, or 10 fps to avoid "jerky" playback.*

When time systems don't match, the most important value to set is the timebase, which
you should choose appropriately for the most critical final medium. If you are preparing
a motion picture trailer that you also want to show on television, you might decide that
film is the most important medium for the project, and specify a timebase of 24.

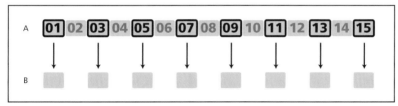

A. Timebase of 30 (one-half second shown) *B*. Final frame rate of 15, for a Web movie
If the timebase is evenly divisible by the frame rate, timebase frames are included evenly.

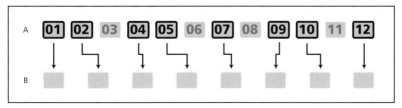

A. Timebase of 24 for a motion-picture film (one-half second shown) *B*. Final frame
rate of 15, for a Web movie. The time is not evenly divisible by the frame rate, so frames
are included unevenly. A final frame rate of 12 fps would generate frames more evenly.

The important thing to remember is this: You'll get the most predictable results if your timebase and frame rate are even multiples of one another; you'll get the best results if they are identical.

For more information, see "Measuring time and frame size" in the Adobe Premiere 6.0 Technical Guides found in the Support area on the Adobe Web site (www.adobe.com/support/ techdocs/topissuespre.htm).

Counting time with timecode

Timecode defines how frames are counted and affects the way you view and specify time throughout a project. Timecode never changes the timebase or frame rate of a clip or project—it only changes how frames are numbered.

You specify a timecode style based on the media most relevant to your project. When you are editing video for television, you count frames differently from counting frames when editing video for motion-picture film. By default, Premiere displays time using the SMPTE (Society of Motion Picture and Television Engineers) video timecode, where a duration of 00:06:51:15 indicates that a clip plays for 6 minutes, 51 seconds, and 15 frames. At any time, you can change to another system of time display, such as feet and frames of 16mm or 35mm film. Professional videotape decks and camcorders can read and write timecode directly onto the videotape, which lets you synchronize audio, video, and edits, or edit offline (see page 119).

When you use the NTSC-standard timebase of 29.97, the fractional difference between this timebase and 30 fps timecode causes a discrepancy between the displayed duration of the program and its actual duration. While tiny at first, this discrepancy grows as program duration increases, preventing you from accurately creating a program of a specific length. *Drop-frame timecode* is an SMPTE standard for 29.97 fps video that eliminates this error, preserving NTSC time accuracy. Premiere indicates drop-frame timecode by displaying semicolons between the numbers in time displays throughout the software, and displays non-drop-frame timecode by displaying colons between numbers in timecode displays.

*Drop-frame timecode uses semicolons (left)
and non-drop-frame timecode uses colons (right).*

When you use drop-frame timecode, Premiere renumbers the first two frames of every minute except for every tenth minute. The frame after 59:29 is labeled 1:00:02. No frames are lost because drop-frame timecode doesn't actually drop frames, only frame numbers.

[?] *For more information, see "Timecode and time display options" in the Adobe Premiere 6.0 Technical Guides found in the Support area on the Adobe Web site (www.adobe.com/ support/techdocs/topissuespre.htm).*

Interlaced and non-interlaced video

A picture on a television or computer monitor consists of horizontal lines. There is more than one way to display those lines. Most personal computers display using *progressive scan* (or non-interlaced) display, in which all lines in a frame are displayed in one pass from top to bottom before the next frame appears. Television standards such as NTSC, PAL, and SECAM standards are *interlaced*, where each frame is divided into two *fields*. Each field contains every other horizontal line in the frame. A TV displays the first field of alternating lines over the entire screen, and then displays the second field to fill in the alternating gaps left by the first field. One NTSC video frame, displayed approximately every 1/30th of a second, contains two interlaced fields, displayed approximately every 1/60th of a second each. PAL and SECAM video frames display at 1/25 of a second and contain two interlaced fields displayed every 1/50th of a second each. The field that contains the topmost scan line in the frame is called the *upper field*, and the other field is called the *lower field*. When playing back or exporting to interlaced video, make sure the *field order* you specify matches the receiving video system, otherwise motion may appear stuttered, and edges of objects in the frame may break up with a comb-like appearance.

Note: For analog video, the field order needs to match the field order of the capture card (which should be specified in the preset). For DV, the field order is always lower field first. Be sure to select the correct preset first; doing so will correctly specify the field order.

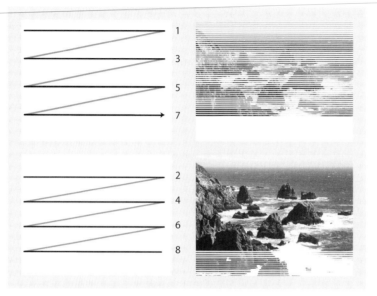

Interlaced video describes a frame with two passes of alternating scan lines.

Progressive-scan video describes a frame with one pass of sequential scan lines.

If you plan to slow down or hold a frame in an interlaced video clip, you may want to prevent flickering or visual stuttering by *de-interlacing* its frames, which converts the interlaced fields into complete frames. If you're using progressive-scan source clips (such as motion-picture film or computer-generated animation) in a video intended for an interlaced display such as television, you can separate frames into fields using a process known as *field rendering* so that motion and effects are properly interlaced.

For more information, see *"Processing interlaced video fields" in Chapter 3 of the* Adobe Premiere 6.0 User Guide *and "Interlaced and non-interlaced video" in the Adobe Premiere Technical Guides found in the Support area on the Adobe Web site (www.adobe.com/support/techdocs/topissuespre.htm).*

Measuring frame size and resolution

Several attributes of *frame size* are important when editing video digitally: pixel and frame aspect ratio, clip resolution, project frame size, and bit depth. A *pixel* (picture element) is the smallest unit that can be used to create a picture; you can't accurately display anything smaller than a pixel.

Aspect ratio

The *aspect ratio* of a frame describes the ratio of its width to its height in the dimensions of a frame. For example, the frame aspect ratio of NTSC video is 4:3, whereas some motion-picture frame sizes use the more elongated aspect ratio of 16:9.

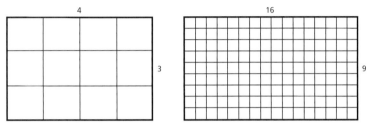

A frame using a 4:3 aspect ratio (left), and a frame using the 16:9 aspect ratio (right)

Some video formats use a different aspect ratio for the pixels that make up the frame. When a video using *non-square pixels* (i.e., pixels that are taller than they are wide, or wider than they are tall) is displayed on a square-pixel system, or vice versa, shapes and motion appear stretched. For example, circles are distorted into ellipses.

Frame with square pixels (left), frame with tall horizontal pixels (center), and center frame again displayed using square pixels (right)

Non-square pixels

Premiere provides support for a variety of non-square pixel aspect ratios, including DV's Wide screen (Cinema) pixel aspect ratio of 16:9 and the Anamorphic pixel aspect ratio of 2:1.

When you preview video with non-square pixel aspect ratios on your computer screen, Premiere displays a corrected aspect ratio on the computer monitor so that the image is not distorted. Motion and transparency settings, as well as geometric effects, also use the proper aspect ratio, so distortions don't appear after editing or rendering your video.

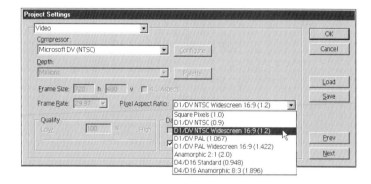

Frame size

In Premiere, you specify a *frame size* for playing back video from the Timeline and, if necessary, for exporting video to a file. Frame size is expressed by the horizontal and vertical dimensions, in pixels, of a frame; for example, 640 by 480 pixels. In digital video editing, frame size is also referred to as *resolution*.

In general, higher resolution preserves more image detail and requires more memory (RAM) and hard disk space to edit. As you increase frame dimensions, you increase the number of pixels Premiere must process and store for each frame, so it's important to know how much resolution your final video format requires. For example, a 720 x 480 pixel (standard DV) NTSC frame contains 345,600 pixels, while a 720 x 576 PAL image contains 414,720 pixels. If you specify a resolution that is too low, the picture will look coarse and pixelated; specify too high a resolution and you'll use more memory than necessary. When changing the frame size, keep the dimensions proportional to the original video clip.

💡 *If you plan to work with higher resolutions and/or you are concerned about your CPU's processing capabilities, you can specify one or more* scratch disks *for additional RAM and hard disk space. For more information, see "Setting up Premiere's scratch disks" in Chapter 1 of the* Adobe Premiere 6.0 User Guide.

Overscan and safe zones

Frame size can be misleading if you're preparing video for television. Most NTSC consumer television sets enlarge the picture; however, this pushes the outer edges of the picture off the screen. This process is called *overscan*. Because the amount of overscan is not consistent across all televisions, you should keep action and titles inside two safe areas—the action-safe and title-safe zones.

The action-safe zone is an area approximately 10% less than the actual frame size; the title-safe zone is approximately 20% less than the actual frame size. By keeping all significant action inside the action-safe zone and making sure that all text and important graphic elements are within the title-safe zone, you can be sure that the critical elements of your video are completely displayed. You'll also avoid the distortion of text and graphics that can occur toward the edges of many television monitors. Always anticipate overscan by using safe zones, keeping important action and text within them, and testing the video on an actual television monitor.

You can view safe zones in the Monitor window's Source view, Program view, or both.

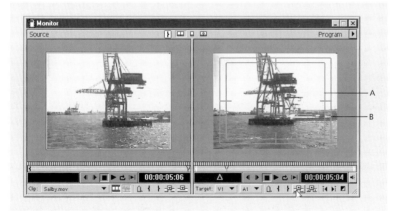

Safe zones in the Program view: **A.** *Title-safe zone* **B**. *Action-safe zone*

Safe zones are indicated by dotted lines in Premiere's Title window.

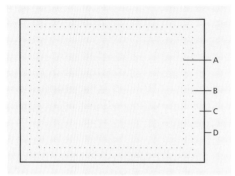

A. *Title-safe zone* **B.** *Action-safe zone*
C. *Overscan area* **D.** *Perimeter of frame*

For more information on customizing safe zones in the Monitor and Title windows, see Lesson 8, "Creating a Title" in this book.

Bit depth

A *bit* is the most basic unit of information storage in a computer. The more bits used to describe something, the more detailed the description can be. *Bit depth* indicates the number of bits set aside for describing the color of one pixel. The higher the bit depth, the more colors the image can contain, which allows more precise color reproduction and higher picture quality. For example, an image storing 8 bits per pixel (8-bit color) can display 256 colors, and a 24-bit color image can display approximately 16 million colors.

The bit depth required for high quality depends on the color format that is used by your video-capture card. Many capture cards use the YUV color format, which can store high-quality video using 16 bits per pixel. Before transferring video to your computer, video-capture cards that use YUV convert it to the 24-bit RGB color format that Premiere uses. For the best RGB picture quality, you should:

• Save source clips and still images with 24 bits of color (although you can use clips with lower bit depths).

• If the clip contains an alpha channel mask, save it from the source application using 32 bits per pixel (also referred to as 24 bits with an 8-bit alpha channel, or *millions of colors*). For example, QuickTime movies can contain up to 24 bits of color with an 8-bit alpha channel, depending on the exact format used.

Internally, Premiere always processes clips using 32 bits per pixel regardless of each clip's original bit depth. This helps preserve image quality when you apply effects or superimpose clips.

If you're preparing video for NTSC, you should keep in mind that although both 16-bit YUV and 24-bit RGB provide a full range of color, the color range of NTSC is limited by comparison. NTSC cannot accurately reproduce saturated colors and subtle color gradients. The best way to anticipate problems with NTSC color is to preview your video on a properly calibrated NTSC monitor during editing.

For more information, see "Previewing on another monitor" in the Adobe Premiere 6.0 Technical Guides found in the Support area on the Adobe Web site (www.adobe.com/support/ techdocs/topissuespre.htm).

Understanding video data compression

Editing digital video involves storing, moving, and calculating extremely large volumes of data compared to other kinds of computer files. Many personal computers, particularly older models, are not equipped to handle the high *data rates* (amount of video information processed each second) and large *file sizes* of uncompressed digital video. Use *compression* to lower the data rate of digital video to a range that your computer system can handle. Compression settings are most relevant when capturing source video, previewing edits, playing back the Timeline, and exporting the Timeline. In many cases, the settings you specify won't be the same for all situations:

• It's a good idea to compress video coming into your computer. Your goal is to retain as much picture quality as you can for editing, while keeping the data rate well within your computer's limits.

• You should also compress video going out of your computer. Try to achieve the best picture quality for playback. If you're creating a videotape, keep the data rate within the limits of the computer that will play back the video to videotape. If you're creating video to be played back on another computer, keep the data rate within the limits of the computer models you plan to support. It you're creating a video clip to be streamed from a Web server, keep an appropriate data rate for Internet distribution.

Applying the best compression settings can be tricky, and the best settings can vary with each project. If you apply too little compression, the data rate will be too high for the system, causing errors such as dropped frames. If you apply too much compression, lowering the data rate too far, you won't be taking advantage of the full capacity of the system and the picture quality may suffer unnecessarily.

Note: *DV has a fixed data rate of 3.5 megabytes per second, nominally 25 megabits per second; the DV standard compression ratio is 5:1.*

Analyzing clip properties and data rate

Premiere includes clip analysis tools you can use to evaluate a file, in any supported format, stored inside or outside a project.

1 From Premiere, choose File > Get Properties For > File. Locate and select the Sailby.mov clip from Lesson 1 and click Open.

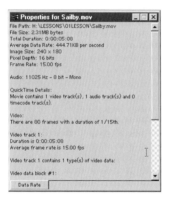

The *Properties window* provides detailed information about any clip. For video files, the analyzed properties can include file size, number of video and audio tracks, duration, average frame, audio and data rates, and compression settings. You can also use the Properties window to alert you to the presence of any dropped frames in a clip you just captured.

2 Click Data Rate to view the data rate graph for the clip.

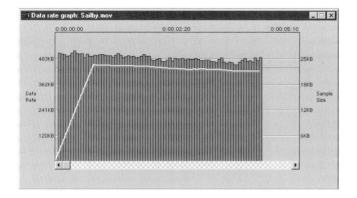

You can use the data rate graph to evaluate how well the output data rate matches the requirements of your delivery medium. It charts each frame of a video file to show you the render keyframe rate, the difference between compression keyframes and differenced frames (frames that exist between keyframes), and data rate levels at each frame.

The data rate graph includes:

- Data rate: the white line represents the average data rate.

- Sample size: the red bars represent the sample size of each keyframed frame.

If there are differenced frames, they appear as blue bars, representing the sample size of the differenced frames between compression keyframes. In this case, there are not any.

3 When you are finished, close the Data Rate Graph window and the Properties window.

For more information, see "Factors that affect video compression" in the Adobe Premiere 6.0 Technical Guides found in the Support area on the Adobe Web site (www.adobe.com/ support/techdocs/topissuespre.htm).

Choosing a video compression method

The goal of data compression is to represent the same content using less data. You can specify a compressor/decompressor, or *codec*, that manages compression. A codec may use one or more strategies for compression because no single method is best for all situations. The most common compression strategies used by codecs and the kinds of video they are intended to compress are described in this section.

Spatial compression Spatial (space) compression looks for ways to compact a single frame by looking for pattern and repetition among pixels. For example, instead of describing each of several thousand pixels in a picture of a blue sky, spatial compression can record a much shorter description, such as "All the pixels in this area are light blue." *Run-length encoding* is a version of this technique that is used by many codecs. Codecs that use spatial compression, such as QuickTime Animation or Microsoft RLE, work well with video containing large solid areas of color, such as cartoon animation.

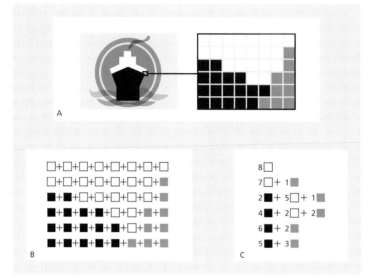

*Digital images are composed of pixels (**A**), which consume a lot of disk space when stored without compression (**B**). Applying run-length encoding stores the same frame data in much less space (**C**).*

In general, as you increase spatial compression, the data rate and file size decrease, and the picture loses sharpness and definition. However, some forms of run-length encoding preserve picture quality completely, but require more processing power.

Temporal compression Temporal (time) compression compacts the changes during a sequence of frames by looking for patterns and repetition over time. In some video clips, such as a clip of a television announcer, temporal compression will notice that the only pixels that change from frame to frame are those forming the face of the speaker. All the other pixels don't change (when the camera is motionless). Instead of describing every pixel in every frame, temporal compression describes all the pixels in the first frame, and then for each frame that follows, describes only the pixels that are different from the previous frame. This technique is called *frame differencing*. When most of the pixels in a frame are different from the previous frame, it's preferable to describe the entire frame again. Each whole frame is called a *keyframe*, which sets a new starting point for frame differencing. You can use Premiere to control how keyframes are created (see the *Adobe Premiere 6.0 User Guide*). Many codecs use temporal compression, including Cinepak. If you can't set keyframes for a codec, chances are it doesn't use temporal compression. Temporal compression works best when large areas in the video don't change, and is less effective when the image constantly changes, such as in a music video.

In this animation clip, the only change is the circle moving around the ship.

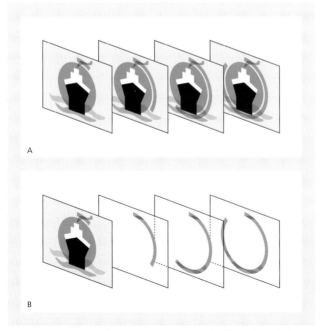

A. Storing the clip without compression records all pixels in all frames.
B. Applying temporal compression creates a keyframe from the first frame, and subsequent frames record only the changes.

Lossless compression Some codecs use *lossless* compression, which ensures that all of the information—and thus all of the quality—in the original clip is preserved after compression. However, preserving the original level of quality limits the degree to which you can lower the data rate and file size, and the resulting data rate may be too high for smooth playback. Lossless codecs, such as Animation (at the Best quality setting), are used to preserve maximum quality during editing or for still images where data rate is not an issue.

Note: To ensure smooth playback, full-frame, full-size video using lossless compression requires a very large hard disk and very fast computer system built for high data rate throughput.

Lossy compression Most codecs use *lossy* compression, which discards some of the original data during compression. For example, if the pixels making up a sky actually contain 78 shades of blue, a lossy codec set for less-than-best quality may record 60 shades of blue. While lossy compression means some quality compromises, it results in much lower data rates and file sizes than lossless compression, so lossy codecs such as Cinepak or Sorenson Video are commonly used for final production of video delivered using CD-ROM or the Internet.

Asymmetrical and symmetrical compression The codec you choose affects your production workflow, not just in file size or playback speed, but in the time required for a codec to compress a given number of frames. Fast compression speeds up video production, and fast decompression makes viewing easier; but many codecs take far more time to compress frames than to decompress them during playback. This is why a 30-second clip may take a few minutes to process before playback. A codec is considered *symmetrical* when it requires the same amount of time to compress as to decompress a clip. A codec is *asymmetrical* when the times required to compress and decompress a clip are significantly different.

Compressing video is like packing a suitcase—you can pack as fast as you unpack by simply throwing clothes into the suitcase, but if you spend more time to fold and organize the clothes in the suitcase, you can fit more clothes in the same space.

DV compression DV is the format used by many digital video camcorders. DV also connotes the type of compression used by these camcorders, which compress video right inside the camera. The most common form of DV compression uses a fixed data rate of 25 megabits per second (3.5 megabytes per second) and a compression ratio of 5:1. This compression is called "DV25." Adobe Premiere 6.0 includes native support for DV25 and other DV codecs, and can read digital source video without further conversion.

No single codec is the best for all situations. The codec you use for exporting your final program must be available to your entire audience. So, while a specialized codec that comes with a specific capture card might be the best choice for capturing source clips, it would not be a good choice for exporting clips, since it is unlikely that everyone in your audience would have that specific capture card and its specialized codec. This is a significant concern when exporting streaming media, since the three most popular streaming architectures (RealMedia, Windows Media, and QuickTime) use proprietary codecs in their players; a RealMedia stream, for example, cannot always be played back through a Windows Media player, and vice versa. So, for the convenience of audiences with diverse players set as the default in their browsers, streaming media is usually encoded in multiple formats.

For more information, see "Video codec compression methods" in the Adobe Premiere 6.0 Technical Guides found in the Support area on the Adobe Web site (www.adobe.com/support/techdocs/topissuespre.htm).

Capturing video

Before you can edit your video program, all source clips must be instantly accessible from a hard disk, not from videotape. You import the source clips from the source videotapes to your computer through a post-production step called *video capture*. Consequently, you must have enough room on your hard disk to store all the clips you want to edit. To save space, capture only the clips you know you want to use.

Source clips exists in two main forms:

Digital media Is already in a *digital* file format that a computer can read and process directly. Many newer camcorders digitize and save video in a digital format, right inside the camera. Such camcorders use one of several *DV formats*, which apply a standard amount of compression to the source material. Audio can also be recorded digitally; sound tracks are often provided digitally as well—on CD-ROM, for example. Digital source files stored on DV tape or other digital media, must be *captured* (transferred) to an accessible hard disk before they can be used in a computer for a Premiere project. The simplest way to capture DV is to connect a DV device, such as a camcorder or deck, to a computer with an *IEEE 1394* port (also known as FireWire or i.Link). For more sophisticated capture tasks, a specialized DV *capture card* might be used. Adobe Premiere 6.0 supports a wide range of DV devices and capture cards, making it easy to capture DV source files.

Analog media Must be *digitized*. That means it must be converted to digital form and saved in a digital file format before a computer can store and process it. Clips from *analog* videotape (such as Hi-8), motion-picture film, conventional audio tape, and continuous-tone still images (such as slides) are all examples of analog media. By connecting an analog video device (such as an analog video camera or tape deck) and an appropriate *capture card* to your computer, Adobe Premiere can digitize, compress, and transfer analog source material to disk as clips that can then be added to your digital video project.

Note: Video-digitizing hardware is built into some personal computers, but often must be added to a system by installing a compatible hardware capture card. Adobe Premiere 6.0 supports a wide variety of video capture cards.

If your system has an appropriate capture card, Adobe Premiere also lets you perform manual and time-lapse *single-frame video captures* from a connected camera or from a videotape in a deck or camcorder, using *stop-motion animation*. For example, you can point a camera at an unfinished building and use the time-lapse feature to capture frames periodically as the building is completed. You can use the stop-motion feature with a camera to create clay animations or to capture a single frame and save it as a still image. You can capture stop-motion animation from analog or DV sources.

Note: *Premiere 6.0 supports device control. This enables you to capture stop motion, or perform batch capture of multiple clips, by controlling the videotape from within the Capture window in Premiere. However, stop motion does not require device control within Premiere: If you don't have a controllable playback device, you can manually operate the controls on your camcorder or deck and in the Capture window.*

For more information on all the topics covered in this section on capturing video, see Chapter 2, "Capturing and Importing Source Clips" in the A*dobe Premiere 6.0 User Guide.*

Capturing DV

When you shoot DV, the images are converted directly into digital (DV) format, right inside the DV camcorder, where your footage is saved on a DV tape cassette. The images are already digitized and compressed, so they are ready for digital video editing. The DV footage can be transferred directly to a hard disk.

To transfer DV to your hard disk, you need a computer with an OHCI-compliant interface and an IEEE 1394 (FireWire or i.Link) port (standard on most newer-model Macintosh computers and on some newer Windows PCs). Alternatively, you can install an appropriate DV capture card to provide the IEEE 1394 port. Be sure to install the accompanying OHCI-compliant driver and special Adobe Premiere plug-in software that may be required. Adobe Premiere 6.0 comes with presets for a wide variety of DV capture cards but, for some, you may need to consult the instructions provided with your capture card to set up a special preset.

Adobe Premiere 6.0 provides settings files for most supported capture cards. These *presets* include settings for compressor, frame size, pixel aspect ratio, frame rate, color depth, audio, and fields. You select the appropriate preset from the Available Presets list in the Load Project Settings dialog box when you begin your project.

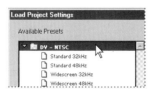

▣ *To enhance DV capture, Adobe Premiere 6.0 provides device control for an extensive range of DV devices. See the Adobe Web site for a list of supported devices (www.adobe.com/premiere).*

If you have an appropriate digital video device attached to or installed in your computer, you can do the following:

1 To specify the DV device in your computer, choose Edit > Preferences > Scratch Disks & Device Control.

2 Click the Option button in the Preferences window to see the DV Device Control Options dialog box and select your DV device. Click OK.

Capturing analog video

When capturing analog video, you need to first connect the camcorder or deck to the capture card installed in your system. Depending on your equipment, you may have more than one format available for transferring source footage—including component video, composite video, and S-video. Refer to the instructions included with your camcorder and capture card.

For convenience, most video-capture card software is written so that its controls appear within the Premiere interface, even though much of the actual video processing happens on the card, outside of Premiere. Most supported capture cards provide a settings file—a preset—that automatically sets up Premiere for optimal support for that card. Most of the settings that control how a clip is captured from a camera or a deck are found in the Capture Settings section of the Project Settings dialog box. Available capture formats vary, depending on the type of video-capture card installed.

[?] *For more information, or if you need help resolving technical issues you may encounter using your capture card with Premiere, see the Adobe Premiere Web site (www.adobe.com/ premiere) for links to troubleshooting resources.*

Using the Movie Capture window

You use the Movie Capture window to capture DV and analog video and audio. To open and familiarize yourself with the Movie Capture window, from the title bar at the top of your screen choose File > Capture > Movie Capture. This window includes:

• Preview window that displays your currently recording video.

• Controls for recording media with and without device control.

• Movie Capture window menu button.

• Settings panel for viewing and editing your current capture setting.

• Logging panel for entering batch capture settings (you can only log clips for batch capture when using device control).

To set the Preview area so that the video always fills it, click the Movie Capture window menu button and choose Fit Image in Window.

Note: When doing anything other than capturing in Premiere, close the Movie Capture Window. Because the Movie Capture window has primary status when open, leaving it open while editing or previewing video will disable output to your DV device and may diminish the performance.

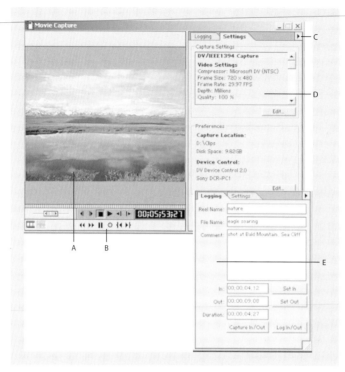

Movie Capture window: **A.** *Preview area* **B.** *Controllers*
C. *Movie Capture menu button* **D.** *Settings panel* **E.** *Logging panel*

Capturing clips with device control When capturing clips, *device control* refers to controlling
the operation of a connected video deck or camera using the Premiere Interface, rather
than using the controls on the connected device. You can use device control to capture
video from frame-accurate analog or digital video decks or cameras that support external
device control. It's more convenient to simply use device control within Premiere rather
than alternating between the video editing software on your computer and the controls
on your device. The Movie Capture and/or Batch Capture windows can be used to create
a list of *In points* (starting timecode) and *Out points* (ending timecode) for your clips.
Premiere then automates capture—recording all clips as specified on your list.
Additionally, Premiere captures the timecode from the source tape, so the information
can be used during editing.

Note: *If you're working in Mac OS, the Enable Device control button runs all the way across the bottom of the window where the image is displayed.*

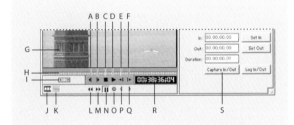

Movie Capture window with device control enabled:
A. Previous frame *B. Next frame* *C. Stop* *D. Play*
E. Play slowly in reverse *F. Play slowly* *G. Preview area*
H. Jog control *I. Shuttle control* *J. Take video* *K. Take audio*
L. Rewind *M. Fast forward* *N. Pause* *O. Record* *P. Set In*
Q. Set Out *R. Timecode* *S. Capture In to Out*

Capturing clips without device control If you don't have a controllable playback device, you can capture video from analog or DV camcorders or decks using the Adobe Premiere Capture window. While watching the picture in the Movie Capture window, manually operate the deck and the Premiere controls to record the frames you want. You can use this method to facilitate capture from an inexpensive consumer VCR or camcorder.

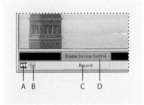

Using the Movie Capture window
without device control:
A. Take video *B. Take audio*
C. Record
D. Enable device control button

Batch-capturing video

If you have a frame-accurate deck or camcorder that supports external device control and a videotape recorded with timecode, you can set up Premiere for automatic, unattended capture of multiple clips from the same tape. This is called *batch capturing*. You can *log* (create a list of) the segments you want to capture from your tape, using the Batch Capture window. The list (called a *batch list* or *timecode log*) can be created either by logging clips visually using device control or by typing In and Out points manually. To create a new entry in the Batch List window, click the Add icon (🖺). When your batch list is ready, click one button—the Capture button in either the Batch Capture or Movie Capture window—to capture all the specified clips on your list. To open and familiarize yourself with the Batch Capture window, from the title bar at the top of your screen, choose File > Capture > Batch Capture.

Batch Capture window: **A.** *Check-mark column* **B.** *Sort by In point button*
C. *Capture button* **D.** *Add New Item button* **E.** *Delete selected button*

Note: *Batch Capture is not recommended for the first and last 30 seconds of your tape because of possible timecode and seeking issues; you will need to capture these sections manually.*

Components that affect video capture quality

Video capture requires a higher and more consistent level of computer performance—far more than you need to run general office software, and even more than you need to work with image-editing software. Getting professional results depends on the performance and capacity of all of the components of your system working together to move frames from the video-capture card to the processor and hard disk. The ability of your computer to capture video depends on the combined performance of the following components:

Video capture card You need to have a video capture card installed or the equivalent capability built into your computer to transfer video from a video camcorder, tape deck, or other video source to your computer's hard drive. A *video capture card* is not the same as the *video card* that drives your computer monitor. Adobe Premiere 6.0 software is bundled with many video-capture cards.

Note: Only supported video capture cards should be used with Adobe Premiere. There is an expansive range of choices. Not all capture cards certified for use with Adobe Premiere 5.x are certified for use with 6.x. Please refer to the list of certified capture cards found on the Adobe Web site (www.adobe.com/products/premiere/6cards.html).

Your video capture card must be fast enough to capture video at the level of quality that your final medium requires. For full-screen, full-motion NTSC video, the card must be capable of capturing 30 frames (60 fields) per second at 640 x 480 pixels without dropping frames; for PAL and SECAM, 25 frames (50 fields) per second at 720 x 576 pixels. Even for Web video that will be output at a smaller frame size and a lower frame rate, you'll want to capture your source material at the highest quality settings your system can handle. You'll be using up lots of hard-disk space, but it's better to start with high quality (more data) so you'll have more choices about what information to discard when you reach the encoding stage. If you start with low quality (less data), you could potentially regret having fewer options down the road.

Hard disk The hard disk stores the video clips you capture. The hard disk must be fast enough to store captured video frames as quickly as they arrive from the video card; otherwise, frames will be dropped as the disk falls behind. For capturing at the NTSC video standard of just under 30 frames per second, your hard disk should have an average (not minimum) access time of 10 milliseconds (ms) or less, and a sustained (not peak) data transfer rate of at least 3 MB per second—preferably around 6 MB per second.

The *access time* is how fast a hard disk can reach specific data.)

The *data transfer rate* is how fast the hard disk can move data to and from the rest of the computer. Due to factors such as system overhead, the actual data transfer rate for video capture is usually about half the stated data transfer rate of the drive. For best results, capture to a separate high-performance hard disk intended for use with video capture and editing. The state of high-end video hardware changes rapidly; consult the manufacturer of your video-capture card for suggestions about appropriate video storage hardware.

Central processing unit (CPU) Your computer's processor—such as a Pentium or PowerPC chip—handles general processing tasks in your computer. The CPU must be fast enough to process captured frames at the capture frame rate. A faster CPU—or using multiple CPUs in one computer (multiprocessing)—is better. However, other system components must be fast enough to handle the CPU speed. Using a fast CPU with slow components is like driving a sports car in a traffic jam.

Codec (compressor/decompressor) Most video-capture cards come with a compression chip that keeps the data rate within a level your computer can handle. If your video-capture hardware doesn't have a compression chip, you should perform capture using a fast, high-quality codec such as Motion JPEG. If you capture using a slow-compressing or lossy codec such as Cinepak, you'll drop frames or lose quality.

Processing time required by other software If you capture video while several other programs are running (such as network connections, non-essential system enhancers, and screen savers), the other programs will probably interrupt the video capture with requests for processing time, causing dropped frames. Capture video while running as few drivers, extensions, and other programs as possible. In Mac OS, turn off AppleTalk. See the Mac OS documentation or online Help.

Data bus Every computer has a data bus that connects system components and handles data transfer between them. Its speed determines how fast the computer can move video frames between the video-capture card, the processor, and the hard disk. If you purchased a high-end computer or a computer designed for video editing, the data bus speed is likely to be well matched to the other components. However, if you've upgraded an older computer with a video-capture card, a faster processor, or a hard disk, an older data bus may limit the speed benefits of the new components. Before upgrading components, review the documentation provided by the manufacturer of your computer to determine whether your data bus can take advantage of the speed of a component you want to add.

For more information, see "Optimizing system performance" in the Adobe Premiere 6.0 Technical Guides found in the Support area on the Adobe Web site (www.adobe.com/support/ techdocs/topissuespre.htm).

Capturing to support online or offline editing

Depending on the level of quality you want and the capabilities of your equipment, you may be able to use Premiere for either online or offline editing. The settings you specify for video capture are different for online or offline editing.

Online editing The practice of doing all editing (including the rough cut) using the same source clips that will be used to produce the final cut. As high-end personal computers have become more powerful, online editing has become practical for a wider range of productions such as broadcast television or motion-picture film productions. For online editing, you'll capture clips once, at the highest level of quality your computer and peripherals can handle.

Offline editing The practice of preparing a rough cut from lower-quality clips, then producing the final version with higher-quality clips, sometimes on a high-end system. Offline editing techniques can be useful even if your computer can handle editing at the quality of your final cut. By batch-capturing video using low-quality settings, you can edit faster, using smaller files. When you digitize video for offline editing, you specify settings that emphasize editing speed over picture quality. In most cases, you need only enough quality to identify the correct beginning and ending frames for each scene. When you're ready to create the final cut, you can redigitize the video at the final-quality settings.

Once you have completed the offline edit in Premiere, you can create a table of scene sequences called an *Edit Decision List,* or EDL. You can then move the EDL to an *edit controller* on a high-end system, which applies the sequence worked out in Premiere to the original high-quality clips.

Note: *Typically, offline editing is not employed when working with DV, because Premiere handles DV at its original quality level.*

For more information on all the topics covered in this section on capturing video, see Chapter 2, "Capturing and Importing Source Clips" in the A*dobe Premiere 6.0 User Guide.*

Understanding transparency and superimposing

Transparency allows a clip (or any portion of a clip) to reveal a second, underlying clip, so that you can create composites, transitions, or other effects. A variety of transparency types are available in Premiere. The transparency types are described in this section.

Matte or mask An image that specifies transparent or semitransparent areas for another image. For example, if you want to superimpose an object in one clip over the background of another clip, you can use a mask to remove the background of the first clip. You can use other still-image or motion graphics software (such as Adobe Photoshop or Adobe After Effects®) to create a still-image or moving (traveling) matte and apply it to a clip in your Premiere project. A mask works like a film negative; black areas are transparent, white areas are opaque, and gray areas are semitransparent—darker areas are more transparent than lighter areas. You can use shades of gray to create feathered (soft-edged) or graduated masks.

Alpha channel Color in an RGB video image is stored in three color *channels*—one red, one green, and one blue. An image can also contain a mask in a fourth channel called the *alpha channel*. By keeping an image together with its mask, you don't have to manage two separate files. (Sometimes, however, saving a mask as a separate file can be useful; such as when creating a track matte effect, because the mask must be placed in a separate track in Premiere's Timeline.

A 32-bit frame has four 8-bit channels: red, green, blue, and an alpha channel mask.

Programs such as Adobe Photoshop and Adobe After Effects let you paint or draw a mask and use the alpha channel to keep the mask with the image or movie. Premiere uses the alpha channel for compositing.

Photoshop image (left) contains an alpha channel mask (center) which Premiere uses to composite the subject against another background (right).

Keying Finds pixels in an image that match a specified color or brightness and makes those pixels transparent or semitransparent. For example, if you have a clip of a weatherman standing in front of a blue-screen background, you can *key out* the blue and replace it with a weather map.

Opacity Allows you to control the degree of overall transparency for a clip. You can use opacity to fade a clip in or out.

With Premiere, you can combine the transparency options described here. For example, you can use a matte to remove the background from one clip and superimpose it over a second clip, and then use opacity to fade-in the first clip's visible area.

Using audio in a video

Audio can play an equally important role to imagery in telling your story. In Adobe Premiere 6.0, you can adjust audio qualities in the Timeline window, or use the Audio Mixer with greater flexibility and control when mixing multiple audio tracks. For example, you might combine dialogue clips with ambient background sounds and a musical soundtrack. Mixing audio in Premiere can include any combination of the following tasks:

• Fading, (increasing or decreasing) the volume levels of audio clips over time.

• Panning/balancing monophonic audio clips between the left and right stereo channels. For example, you may want to *pan* a dialogue clip to match a person's position in the video frame.

• Using audio effects to remove noise, enhance frequency response and dynamic range, sweeten the sound, or create interesting audio distortions such as reverb.

When you import a video clip that contains audio, the audio track is *linked* to its video track by default so that they move together. Adobe Premiere 6.0 allows you to adjust and mix audio while you watch the corresponding video in real time. The Audio Mixer window, like an audio mixing console in a professional sound studio, contains a set of controls for each audio track; each set is numbered to match its corresponding audio track in the Timeline. When you edit superimposed video tracks, remember to consider the effects of your edits on the audio tracks.

For more information, see Chapter 5, "Mixing Audio," in the *Adobe Premiere 6.0 User Guide.*

Understanding digital audio

You hear sounds because your ear recognizes the variations in air pressure that create sound. *Analog audio* reproduces sound variations by creating or reading variations in an electrical signal. *Digital audio* reproduces sound by sampling the sound pressure or signal level at a specified rate and converting that to a number.

The quality of digital audio depends on the sample rate and bit depth. The *sample rate* is how often the audio level is digitized. A 44.1 kHz sample rate is audio-CD-quality, while CD-ROM or Internet audio often uses a sample rate of 22 kHz or below. The *bit depth* is the range of numbers used to describe an audio sample; 16 bits is audio-CD-quality. Lower bit depths and sample rates are not suitable for high-fidelity audio, but may be acceptable (though noisy) for dialogue. The file size of an audio clip increases or decreases as you increase or decrease the sample rate or bit depth.

Note: *DV camcorders support only 32 or 48 kHz audio; not 44.1 kHz. So, when capturing or working with DV source material, be sure to set the audio for 32 or 48 kHz.*

Keeping audio in sync with video

Be mindful of audio sample rates in relation to the timebase and frame rate of your project. The most common mistake is to create a movie at 30 fps with audio at 44.1 kHz, and then play back the movie at 29.97 fps (for NTSC video). The result is a slight slowdown in the video, while the audio (depending on your hardware) may still be playing at the correct rate and therefore will seem to get ahead of the video. The difference between 30 and 29.97 results in a synchronization discrepancy that appears at a rate of 1 frame per 1000 frames, or 1 frame per 33.3 seconds (just under 2 frames per minute). If you notice audio and video drifting apart at about this rate, check for a project frame rate that doesn't match the timebase.

A similar problem can occur when editing motion-picture film after transferring it to video. Film audio is often recorded on a digital audio tape (DAT) recorder at 48 kHz synchronized with a film camera running at 24 fps. When the film is transferred to 30 fps video, the difference in the video frame rate will cause the audio to run ahead of the video unless you slow the DAT playback by 0.1% when transferring to the computer. Using your computer to convert the sample rate after the original recording doesn't help with this problem. The best solution is to record the original audio using a DAT deck that can record 0.1% faster (48.048 kHz) when synchronized with the film camera.

Older CD-ROM titles sometimes used an audio sample rate of 22.254 kHz; today, a rate of 22.250 kHz is more common. If you notice audio drifting at a rate accounted for by the difference between these two sample rates (1 frame every 3.3 seconds), you may be mixing new and old audio clips recorded at the two different sample rates.

Note: *You can use Adobe Premiere 6.0 or a third-party application to resample the audio. If you use Premiere, be sure to turn on Enhanced Rate Conversion in Project Settings > Audio. Then, build a preview of the audio by applying an audio effect with null settings.*

Creating final video

When you have finished editing and assembling your video project, Adobe Premiere 6.0 offers a variety of flexible output options. You can:

• Record your production directly to DV or analog videotape by connecting your computer to a video camcorder or tape deck. If your camera or deck supports device control, you can automate the recording process, using timecode indications to selectively record portions of your program.

• Export a digital video file for playback from a computer hard drive, removable cartridge, CD, or DVD-ROM. Adobe Premiere exports AVI, QuickTime, and MPEG files; additional file formats may be available in Premiere if provided with your video-capture card or third-party plug-in software.

• Use Save for Web, Advanced RealMedia, or Advanced Windows Media (Windows only) export options to generate properly encoded video files for distribution over the Internet or your intranet. Adobe Premiere 6.0 exports QuickTime, RealMedia, and Windows Media formats for download, progressive download, or streaming.

• Create an EDL (Edit Decision List) so you can perform offline editing based on a rough cut, when you require a level of quality that your system cannot provide.

• Output to motion-picture film or videotape if you have the proper hardware for film or video transfer or have access to a service provider that offers the appropriate equipment and services.

For more information, see Chapter 10, "Producing Final Video" in the *Adobe Premiere 6.0 User Guide.*

Review questions

1 What's the difference between the timebase and the project frame rate?

2 Why is non-drop-frame timecode important for NTSC video?

3 How is interlaced display different from progressive scan?

4 Why is data compression important?

5 What's the difference between applying a mask and adjusting opacity?

6 What is an EDL and why is it useful?

Answers

1 The timebase specifies the time divisions in a project. The project frame rate specifies the final number of frames per second that are generated from the project. Movies with different frame rates can be generated from the same timebase; for example, you can export movies at 30, 15, and 10 frames per second from a timebase of 30.

2 Counting NTSC frames using a timecode of 30 fps will cause an increasingly inaccurate program duration because of the difference between 30 fps and the NTSC frame rate of 29.97 fps. Drop-frame timecode ensures that the duration of NTSC video will be measured accurately.

3 Interlacing, used by standard television monitors, displays a frame's scan lines in two alternating passes, known as fields. Progressive scan, employed by computer monitors, displays a frame's scan lines in one pass.

4 Without data compression, digital video and audio often produce a data rate too high for many computer systems to handle smoothly.

5 A mask, also known as a matte in video production, is a separate channel or file that indicates transparent or semitransparent areas within a frame. In Premiere, opacity specifies the transparency of an entire frame.

6 An EDL is an Edit Decision List, or a list of edits specified by timecode. It's useful whenever you have to transfer your work to another editing system because it lets you re-create a program using the timecode on the original clips.

Lesson 3

3 Basic Editing

Editing a video program is at the heart of the work you'll do with Adobe Premiere. Adobe Premiere makes it easy to trim video clips or other source files. You can then assemble the polished result for playback on a variety of media.

In this lesson, you'll learn about different ways to use Adobe Premiere 6.0 to develop your story. You'll create a 20-second video program about a horse training technique known as "dressage." You'll use these basic editing techniques:

• Developing a storyboard, using Automate-to-Timeline, then trimming clips.

• Selecting clips in a bin, using Automate-to-Timeline, then trimming clips.

• Pre-trimming clips in the Source view of the Monitor window before adding them to the Timeline.

• Previewing the video program.

• Fine-tuning the Timeline using In and Out points, ripple edit, and rolling edit.

• Exporting a project to make a QuickTime movie.

Getting started

For this lesson, you'll create a new project and then import the video clips. Make sure you know the location of the files used in this lesson. Insert the *Adobe Premiere 6.0 Classroom in a Book* CD-ROM disk if necessary. For help, see "Copying the Classroom in a Book files" on page 14 of this book.

1 Launch the Premiere 6.0 software.

2 In the Load Project Settings dialog box, choose Multimedia or Multimedia Quicktime (depending on your operating system), and click OK.

3 After you click OK, you will see the Single-Track Editing mode workspace and its three main windows (the Project window, the Monitor window, and the Timeline window) and the default palettes.

4 From the Premiere title bar at the top of your screen, choose Edit > Preferences > General & Still Image and deselect Open Movies in Clip Window if it is selected.

5 Before importing files, you should close the palettes that you don't need right now. Click the close box in the upper right corner of the Transitions/Video/Audio palette window and the Navigator/Info/History palette window, or press the Tab key to close them together.

Viewing the finished movie

To see what you'll be creating, you can take a look at the finished movie.

1 From the title bar at the top of your screen, choose File > Open and double-click the 03Final.mov file in the Final folder, inside the 03Lesson folder.

The video program opens in the Source view of the Monitor window.

2 Click the Play button (▶) to view the video program. When the movie ends, the final frame will remain visible in the Source view of the Monitor window.

Importing clips

Now you'll add files to the Project window.

1 To import the movie clips you will need, choose File > Import > File, and then open the 03Lesson folder you copied or installed from the Premiere Application CD-ROM disk. Hold down the Control key (Windows) or the Command or Shift key (Mac OS), and then select the Field.mov, Finish.mov, Logo.mov, Ride.mov, and Trot.mov files (but not the Final folder). Now click Open.

The video files are added to the Project window in Bin 1.

2 If necessary, rearrange windows and palettes so they don't overlap, by choosing Window > Workspace > Single-Track Editing.

To make your clips a little easier to see, you'll change the view somewhat.

3 Click the title bar of the Timeline window to make it active. Then, choose Window > Window Options > Timeline Window Options. Select the medium Icon Size (the second button on the left) and click OK.

4 In the Timeline window, click the Time Zoom Level menu in the lower left, and choose 2 Seconds.

Now, you'll save and name the project.

5 From the title bar at the top of your screen, choose File > Save, type **Dressage.ppj** for the filename, and choose the 03Lesson folder for the location. Click Save.

Note: In Windows, the default file extension for Premiere projects, ppj, is added to your filename automatically. In Mac OS, type the extension as part of the filename.

Methods of working in Premiere

Premiere provides several ways for you to perform tasks so you can work the way you prefer. There are many ways to accomplish the same thing. Just as there are different ways to import a clip, there are many ways to edit a video in Premiere.

Adding clips to the Timeline

A clip in your project is not actually part of your video program until you add the clip to the Timeline window. In earlier lessons in this *Classroom in a Book*, you added clips to the Timeline window by positioning the hand tool on clip icons and dragging them directly from the Bin area of the Project window to the Timeline window. In this lesson, you will use other methods to add clips to the Timeline window:

• Developing a storyboard of clips and using the Automate-to-Timeline command to add them to the Timeline.

• Selecting your clips in a bin in the Project window in a specified order and using Automate-to-Timeline to add them to the Timeline.

• Pre-trimming clips and then using the Source view of the Monitor window to add them to the Timeline window.

Developing a storyboard and using Automate-to-Timeline

Before assembling a rough-cut of a video program, editors often create a *storyboard*. A storyboard is a visual outline of the project—a collection of sketches or still shots which, in combination with descriptions, indicates the flow of the story.

In Adobe Premiere 6.0, the Storyboard window makes it easy for you to create a storyboard using poster frames to represent clips. You can easily and quickly organize a set of clips in a Storyboard window. When you are satisfied with their sequence, you can move the storyboard into the Timeline window using the Automate-to-Timeline command to create a rough cut video.

Note: The poster frames that you see for clips in the Storyboard window are the same images used to represent these clips in the Icon view of the Project window. In your own projects, it can be very useful to choose poster frames for your new clips that clearly represent them in a storyboard and distinguish similar clips from each other. (See "Viewing and Changing Poster Frames" in Lesson 1 of this Classroom in a Book.)

Now, let's create a storyboard.

1 With the Timeline window active, choose File > New > Storyboard. A blank Storyboard window opens.

2 From Bin 1 of the Project window, drag the Logo.mov clip into the Storyboard window. Then drag Field.mov to the Storyboard to the right of Logo.mov.

3 With the Storyboard window active, choose File > Import > File. Select the Trot.mov clip and click Open. The Trot.mov clip now appears in the Storyboard window after the Field.mov clip. You now have three clips in the storyboard.

In the Storyboard window, the clips are displayed in the sequence you specify. Each clip's poster frame image is assigned a number that indicates its order in the story sequence. Arrows are displayed between the poster frames to indicate the direction of flow in the sequence and an end marker indicates the end of the sequence. Basic clip information is also provided and useful tool buttons are provided at the bottom of the window.

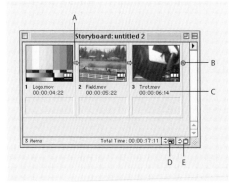

The Storyboard window includes:
A. *Sequence direction marker*
B. *End of sequence marker* **C.** *Clip information*
D. *Automate to Timeline button*
E. *Print to Video button*

4 In the Storyboard window, drag the Trot.mov clip to the left to reposition it in the sequence in front of Field.mov.

Note: *Dragging a clip to the left in the Storyboard makes it occur earlier in the sequence; dragging it to the right makes it occur later.*

5 To save the Storyboard, choose File > Save As, select the file location for Lesson 3, type **L03Story.psq** for the filename, and click Save. You have now saved the storyboard as a separate file, distinct from the project file.

Note: *The filename extension for a project is ".ppj"; the filename extension for a storyboard file is ".psq".*

Using the Automate-to-Timeline command with clips in a storyboard

Now, you'll use the Automate-to-Timeline command to add the clips from the Storyboard to the Timeline window.

1 Click the Automate-to-Timeline button (⇥📇) at the bottom of the Storyboard window to display the Automate-to-Timeline dialog box.

2 Look carefully at the dialog box. Notice that the dialog box has a section that identifies the Storyboard from which you are working and a section that pertains to the Timeline. For this step in the lesson, simply verify that Placement is identified as Sequentially, clips are to be inserted at the beginning of the Timeline, and Clip Overlap shows 15 frames. Now deselect the Use Default Transitions box.

3 Click OK. Now, the Video 1 track in the Timeline window displays the same clips and their icons in the same sequence as the Storyboard window.

4 With the Timeline or Project window active, save the project file. Remember, if the Storyboard window is active when you save, only the storyboard file is updated; not the project file.

Congratulations! You've just assembled a short rough cut. Next, you'll find out how to preview the cut.

Previewing your rough cut

Editing a video program requires a lot of previewing. You need to know how the video program looks in its current state so you can determine any necessary changes. Or, you might make a change, preview it, and then decide to undo the change because the video program looks better without it.

Premiere lets you preview your video program in a few different ways. For now, we'll preview what you've done so far in your rough cut using two simple methods:

• Dragging the edit line (also called scrubbing).

• Using the Play button.

Scrubbing in the Timeline ruler

For quick previewing, you can drag the *edit line* in the Timeline window. This method is called *scrubbing* because of the back-and-forth motion you use. This method plays your video program at the rate at which you move your hand, so it's best for a quick check of your changes, rather than as a way to accurately view your video.

1 With the Timeline window active, position the pointer in the time ruler at the point where you want to start previewing. Notice that the edit line jumps to the pointer location as soon as you click in the Timeline ruler. Now, drag the edit line to scrub. The clips appear in the Program view of the Monitor window as you scrub through them.

2 Continue scrubbing across the clips in the Timeline window until the timecode reads 00:00:07:03 in the Program view of the Monitor window.

💡 *Some steps in these lessons will direct you to make edits at an exact timecode. For convenience, first locate the general area of the Timeline described in the step, then fine-tune the edit point by using the controllers under the Program view of the Monitor window to go to the specific timecode. Using the specified timecode enables you to check your results against the figures illustrated in the procedure.*

Using the Play button

Some of the controls below the Program view are similar to those for the Source view. You use the Source view to work with individual clips; you use the Program view to work with the assembly of clips in the Timeline window. Consequently, clicking the Program view Play button plays the clips in the Timeline window.

1 To start the preview from the beginning of the project, drag the edit line from 00:00:07:03 to the left so that it is positioned at the beginning of the Timeline. (Or, click at the left edge of the timeline ruler to quickly move the edit line to the beginning.)

2 Below the Program view, click the Play button (▶). The current state of your video plays in the Program view of the Monitor window.

Selecting clips in a bin and using Automate-to-Timeline

Another way to add clips to the Timeline window is to select them in the Bin area of the Project window in a specified sequence and then use the Automate-to-Timeline command to move them all at once to the Timeline.

1 Click the Bin 1 icon in the Project window to view the contents of Bin 1.

2 Press and hold the Control key (Windows) or the Command key (Mac OS) and click the icon for the following clips in this order: Logo.mov, Trot.mov, and Field.mov. (remember to position the hand tool over the icon for the clip, not the name of the clip.) All three clips are now highlighted (selected) in the bin.

Now, let's use the Automate-to-Timeline command to add the clips to the Timeline.

3 From the title bar at the top of your screen, choose Project > Automate-to-Timeline to see the Automate-to-Timeline dialog box.

4 Make these changes in the dialog box: In the Contents field, choose Selected clips from the menu; in the Ordering field, choose Selection Order from the menu. In the Insert At field, choose End, for Clip Overlap, type 0, deselect Use Default Transitions if it is selected. Now, click OK.

5 Now, look at the Timeline window. You will see that the three clips you just added are at the end of the Timeline, after the clips you brought in from the Storyboard.

6 Now, delete the three clips you just added by clicking on each clip (a dotted box appears around the selected clip) and pressing the delete key. You should still have the clips from the Storyboard in the Timeline.

Trimming clips after they are in the Timeline

After you have clips assembled in the Timeline, you can trim them using three different methods:

• Trimming clips in the Timeline window.

• Trimming clips in the Source view of the Monitor window.

• Trimming clips in the Trim view of the Monitor window.

In this lesson, you will work with the first two methods (trimming clips in the Timeline window and in the Source view of the Monitor window). You will learn about the third method in Lesson 7, "Advanced Editing Techniques."

Trimming clips in the Timeline window

Now that you have some clips assembled in the Timeline window, you'll trim the end of the Field.mov clip to remove an extra shot.

1 Scrub in the Timeline time ruler to move the edit line through the last half of the Field.mov clip to locate the close-up of a single rider. Position the edit line so that the Program view shows the last frame of the long shot of three riders. For more precision, you can advance or go back one frame at a time using the Frame Forward (▶) and Frame Back (◀) buttons under the Program view. Each time you click one of these buttons, the clip backs up or advances one frame.

Program view in the Monitor window
A. *Program Frame Back button (left arrow)*
B. *Program Frame Forward button (right arrow)*

The edit line marks the last frame of the Field.mov clip that you want to use in your project. Now you'll trim to this point.

2 Select the selection tool ( ) in the Timeline window (if it is not already selected) and position the pointer on the right edge of the Field.mov clip so that it turns into a trim pointer ( ). Drag the trim pointer to the left until it snaps to the edit line.

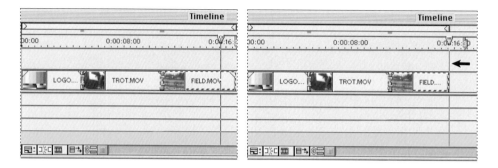

You've just trimmed Field.mov to the edit line.

Trimming in the Source view of the Monitor window

Simple trimming is easy in the Timeline window. More complex editing is easier in the Source view of the Monitor window. The Source view also provides additional tools.

1 Double-click the Logo.mov clip in the Timeline window, so that it appears in the Source view of the Monitor window.

Logo.mov is an animation created in Adobe After Effect, using Adobe Illustrator and Adobe Photoshop files. The clip contains color bars at the beginning and end. Since you don't want the color bars to appear in your video program, you need to trim them.

2 Drag the *shuttle slider* below the Source view or use the Frame Forward (▶) and Frame Back (◀) buttons to display the first frame of the logo that appears after the color bars.

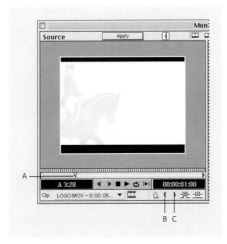

Source view of the Monitor window:
A. *Shuttle slider* **B.** *Mark In button*
C. *Mark Out button*

3 In the Source view, set the In point by clicking the Mark In button (꜀).

The In point icon appears both in the current location of the shuttle slider and in the upper right portion of the Source view title bar. In Single-Track editing mode, the Apply button appears above the Source panel in the Monitor window after you have edited a clip that is in the Timeline.

4 Drag the shuttle slider to the last frame of the actual logo image in the Logo.mov clip.

5 Click the Mark Out button (꜀) to set the Out point.

6 Click the Apply button located directly above the Source view panel to apply the edits to the clip in the Timeline window.

The Logo.mov clip in the Timeline has been trimmed to the In point and Out point you set in the Source view. Trimming this clip, however, has left two gaps in the Video 1 track. You'll now use the track select tool ( ), which enables you to select all clips to the right of any clip in a track. With this tool, you'll select the clips to the right of the Logo.mov clip and move them to close the gap between Logo.mov and Trot.mov.

7 In the Timeline window, select the track select tool by positioning the pointer on the range select icon ( ), pressing and holding down the mouse button, and then dragging right to the track select icon.

8 Position the pointer anywhere on the Trot.mov clip so that it turns into the track select pointer ( ). Drag left until the Trot.mov clip snaps to the Logo.mov clip.

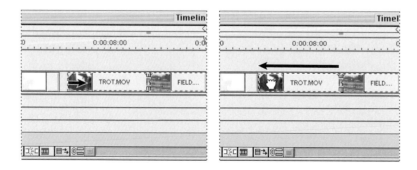

When you release the mouse, all subsequent clips move to the left.

9 To remove the gap at the beginning of the Timeline, position the pointer on the Logo.mov clip so that it turns into the track select pointer. Drag left until the Logo.mov clip snaps to the beginning of the Timeline.

All three clips in the Timeline should now be edge-to-edge, without any gap or space between them. Note that these clips are still selected in the Timeline window.

10 Click the selection tool (➤) in the Timeline window to deselect the clips you just moved. (Choosing another tool deselects the clips.)

11 From the title bar at the top of your screen, choose File > Save to save the project.

💡 *It's a good idea to get in the habit of deselecting clips when you are finished with a task so the next task doesn't affect the previously selected clips.*

Pre-trimming clips using the Source view

In the Tour, you added clips to a project by dragging them individually from the Project window into the Timeline. Earlier in this lesson, you added clips to the Timeline from a Storyboard and from a bin in the Project window using the Automate-to-Timeline command. In each case, you trimmed the clips after they were added to the Timeline.

Alternatively, you can pre-trim clips in the Source view of the Monitor window before you add them to the Timeline. (Remember that clips are included in your video program only if they are in the Timeline.)

Dragging clips to the Source view

First, you'll move two clips into the Source view.

In the Project window, select Ride.mov, and then hold down the Control key (Windows) or Command key (Mac OS) and click Finish.mov to select it also. Drag them to the Source view. Remember to drag the clip's icon, not the filename.

Both clips are copied into the Source view's Clip menu, under the clip image area. The Ride.mov clip is displayed in the Source view of the Project window.

Pre-trimming, inserting, and overlaying

Before you start trimming the clips in the Source view, let's look at the controls you'll use to add them to the program after they have been trimmed. When working in the Source view, you can add clips in two ways: inserting and overlaying. The Insert button (⊞)and the Overlay button (⊟) are at the bottom right of the Source view panel in the Monitor window.

The Insert button inserts the clip at the specified edit line by splitting any existing material into two parts; none of the existing material is replaced; it is merely displaced. In contrast, the Overlay button places a clip at the edit line by replacing any existing material for the duration of the clip you are placing.

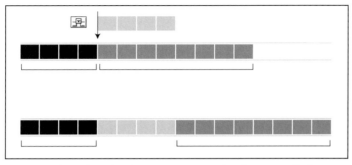

Inserting a clip makes a break in existing material and moves or displaces the existing material.

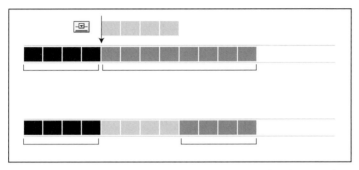

Overlaying a clip replaces a portion of the existing material with an equal amount of new video.

Now that you understand the concepts of inserting and overlaying clips, you'll trim each of the clips you dragged into the Source view using either method and add them to the video program. Let's take a look at the clip you're about to trim.

🔆 *To move and view one frame at a time in either the Source view or the Program view, use the left and right arrow keys under the image in the appropriate view.*

1 Play the Ride.mov clip by clicking the Play button (▶) below the Source view.

You'll be inserting Ride.mov at the beginning of the project, but first you'll trim it to remove some extra footage included at the end of the clip.

2 Drag the shuttle slider below the Source view to locate the point in the last half of Ride.mov at which the scene changes to an open track with a horse galloping in from the left. Locate and display the last frame of the first shot in this clip (at 04:12) using the Frame Forward (I▶) and Frame Back (◀I) buttons.

3 Click the Mark Out button (⸣) below the Source view to mark this frame as the Out point.

Now that you've set the new Out point for the Ride.mov clip, you'll insert it at the beginning of your program. This is a common editing decision—one you might make after deciding the program would work better with additional material at the beginning.

4 In the Program view of the Monitor window, drag the shuttle slider all the way to the left to display the first frame of the Logo.mov clip.

By doing this, you have positioned the edit line at the beginning of the Timeline window, which is where you want to insert the pre-trimmed Ride.mov clip.

5 In the Source view of the Monitor window, click the Insert button (玉) to place the pre-trimmed clip of the Ride.mov into the Video 1 track in the Timeline window at the specified edit line position.

The pre-trimmed Ride.mov clip is inserted at the beginning of the program because it appears at the beginning of the Timeline. You used the Insert button because you didn't want to replace any existing material. Clicking the Overlay button would have replaced some of the Logo.mov clip.

6 Preview the first few clips by dragging the edit line to the beginning of the Timeline and clicking the Play button (▶) below the Program view in the Monitor window. Click the Stop button (■) when you are finished previewing.

Now, you'll overlay the Finish.mov clip over part of the Field.mov clip at the end of the program.

7 Choose Finish.mov from the Clip menu in the lower left of the Source view panel.

The Finish.mov clip appears in the Source view. Before you can overlay this clip, you need to trim about two seconds from the beginning of it. You'll use a new method to move to a location in the project.

8 In the Source view, click the location timecode (the right set of green numbers below the Source view) to highlight all the digits, and then type **128**. Then press Enter (Windows) or Return (Mac OS) on your keyboard. Premiere interprets 128 as 01:28 (1 second and 28 frames).

The Source view advances to the specified time. Now, you'll set this as the new In point.

9 Click the Mark In button (**⊦**).

Now, you'll find the point in Field.mov at which you want to overlay the Finish.mov clip.

10 Drag the shuttle slider below the Program view to find the point in Field.mov at which the single rider moving to the left starts passing between the other two riders (at 17:00).

11 In the Source view, click the Overlay button (⊡) to place the pre-trimmed Finish.mov clip in the Timeline window in the Video 1 track.

The Finish.mov clip replaces the end of the Field.mov clip.

12 To make it easier to view the clips, choose 1 Second from the Time Zoom menu in the lower left of the Timeline window.

```
                              Timeline
        0:00:11:00          0:00:15:00         0:00:19:00

   TROT.MOV                        FIELD.MOV      FINISH.MOV
```

13 Preview this new sequence of clips by dragging the edit line to the beginning of Field.mov and clicking the Play button below the Program view in the Monitor window.

14 Save the project.

Fine-tuning in the Timeline

You will often need to adjust In and Out points after you've placed a number of clips in the Timeline window. Adjusting any clip that's part of a sequence will affect the entire video program. Special tools in the Timeline window let you specify how your adjustments will affect the other clips.

Performing a ripple edit

In this section, you'll perform what's called a *ripple edit*. A ripple edit adjusts the In or Out point of one clip and shifts other clips in or out accordingly. This method changes the total length of your video program, but preserves the duration of the other clips.

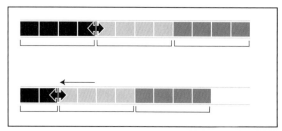

In a ripple edit, all subsequent clips move in response to the change.

Remember that this finished project should be 20 seconds long. The current duration is somewhat longer. To bring the project to 20 seconds, you'll trim Trot.mov, a clip in which the In point, Out point, and the timing are not critical.

Project duration is indicated by the *duration timecode,* the left set of green numbers marked by a delta symbol (Δ) under the Program view. If you used the exact timecodes given for edit points in the previous steps, the overall duration of the project at this point in the lesson should be 20:20. If the timecode is 20:20 on your system, the current project duration is 20 frames too long. To set the length of the project precisely, you'll trim 20 frames from the end of Trot.mov.

Note: *If your project is not exactly 20 frames too long, use the numbers appropriate for your project in place of the 20-frame value and the numbers you'll derive from it in this exercise.*

1   Use the Frame Back and Frame Forward buttons in the Program view to move the edit line to the first frame of Field.mov (at 14:01). The edit line is now at the cut between Trot.mov and Field.mov.

The location timecode (the right set of green numbers) displayed under the Program view indicates the time at the beginning of Field.mov (14:01). You'll determine where to place a new Out point for Trot.mov by subtracting 20 frames from its current Out point by positioning the edit line at the new Out point.

2   Subtract 20 frames from 14:01.

An easy way to do this is to convert 14:01 to an equivalent from which you can subtract 20 frames. Our timebase for this project is 30 fps, so 1 second = 30 frames. Borrow 1 second from 14 seconds, and add it (as 30 frames) to the frames portion of our existing timecode (:01 + :30 = :31). This gives you a timecode of 13:31, which is equivalent to 14:01. Now subtract 20 frames (:20) from 13:31. The result, 13:11, is where you'll set the new Out point for Trot.mov. (Remember the last two numbers in the timecode represent frames.)

3 In the Program view of the Monitor window, click the location timecode to highlight it, and then type **1311** and press Enter (Windows) or Return (Mac OS).

The edit line jumps to 13:11 in the Timeline.

In the Timeline window, select the ripple edit tool by positioning the pointer on the rolling edit icon (⅋), pressing and holding down the mouse button, and then dragging right to the ripple edit icon.

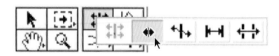

4 In the Timeline window, move the pointer to the right edge of the cut between Trot.mov and Field.mov. The pointer changes into the ripple edit pointer. Be sure the ripple edit pointer is over Trot.mov and not Field.mov. Drag left until the end of Trot.mov snaps to the edit line.

When you release the mouse button, all the other clips shift to the left, following the trim you just made to the Trot.mov clip. In a ripple edit, the total duration of your project changes. The project is now exactly 20:00 in duration.

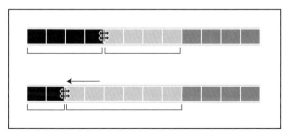

5 If you like, you can view your change by clicking the Play button (▶) below the Program view in the Monitor window.

6 Save the project.

Performing a rolling edit

Another editing method that acts on a sequence of clips is called the *rolling edit*. A rolling edit adjusts the In or Out point of one clip and also adjusts the duration of the adjacent clip, keeping the total duration of the two clips the same. As you shorten one clip, the adjacent clip is extended to maintain the total duration of the two clips. Note, however, that you can extend a clip only if the clip was previously trimmed.

Note: *You cannot make a clip longer than it its original length as captured or imported—you can only restore frames that were previously trimmed from the clip for the current project.*

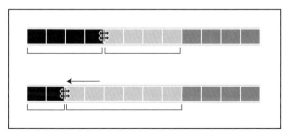

A rolling edit changes two clips at once to preserve the project's duration.

To fine-tune the last two clips, you'll now perform a rolling edit to preserve the finished duration of 20 seconds. Because you've already edited the video program length to exactly 20 seconds, you don't want to use a ripple edit as it would change the total length.

To set the new edit point, you'll look for a visual cue in the clip. Near the middle of the Finish.mov clip, the rider pats her horse. You'll use the position of her hand as a reference for setting the edit point.

1 In the Timeline window, drag in the time ruler over the Finish.mov clip. Stop dragging when the rider's left hand is at its highest point (at 17:16) in the Program view, and leave the edit line at this point.

2 In the Timeline window, select the rolling edit tool by positioning the pointer on the ripple edit icon (+I+), pressing and holding down the mouse button, and then dragging right to the rolling edit icon.

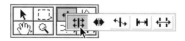

3 Position the pointer over the edit point between the Field.mov and the Finish.mov clips. The pointer changes into the rolling edit tool. Drag the pointer to the right until it snaps to the edit line, and then release the mouse button.

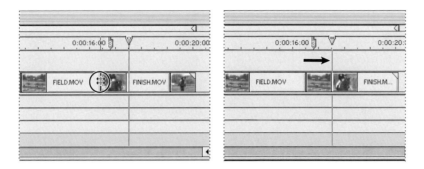

You've now performed a rolling edit on both clips, preserving the total duration.

4 Save the project.

Exporting the movie

1 Click in the Timeline window to select it.

2 From the title bar at the top of your screen, choose File > Export Timeline > Movie.

3 In the Export Movie dialog box, click Settings. Make sure QuickTime is selected for the File Type and Entire Project is selected for the Range. Also make sure that the Export Video option is selected and the Export Audio option is not selected. The default values for other settings, including those for compression, are fine for this project.

```
┌──────────────────────── Export Movie Settings ────────────────────────┐
│ ┌─────────────────────┐                                               │
│ │ General          ⬍ │                                      ┌──────┐  │
│ └─────────────────────┘                                     │  OK  │  │
│  File Type: ┌──────────────┐ ⬍  ┌Advanced Settings┐        └──────┘  │
│            │ QuickTime    │                                 ┌──────┐  │
│    Range:  ┌──────────────┐ ⬍                              │Cancel│  │
│            │ Entire Project│                                └──────┘  │
│            ☑ Export Video  ☑ Open When Finished  Embedding Options:  ┌──────┐  │
│            ☐ Export Audio  ☐ Beep When Finished  ┌None    ⬍┐        │ Load │  │
│  Current Settings:                                                    └──────┘  │
│  ┌──────────────────────────────────────────────┐          ┌──────┐  │
│  │Video Settings                                 │          │ Save │  │
│  │Compressor: Cinepak                            │          └──────┘  │
│  │Frame Size: 320 x 240                          │          ┌──────┐  │
│  │Frame Rate: 15.00                              │          │ Prev │  │
│  │Depth: Millions, Quality: 100%                 │          └──────┘  │
│  └──────────────────────────────────────────────┘          ┌──────┐  │
│                                                              │ Next │  │
│                                                              └──────┘  │
└───────────────────────────────────────────────────────────────────────┘
```

💡 *Use the Save and Load buttons in the Export Movie Settings dialog box to save and later quickly load export settings that you use frequently. Loading saved settings is particularly useful when you create several types of video files (for example, NTSC and Web video) from the same project.*

4 Click OK to close the Export Movie Settings dialog box.

5 In the Export Movie dialog box, type Dressage.mov for the name of the video program and click Save.

Premiere starts making the video program, displaying a status bar that provides an estimate for the amount of time it will take.

6 When the video program is complete, it's opened in a clip window.

Grab some popcorn, and click the Play button to watch what you've just created.

Congratulations on completing the Basic Editing lesson!

Exploring on your own

Feel free to experiment with the project you have just created. Here are some suggestions:

• Use the buttons at the bottom of the Project window to change the view of clips in the window.

• Use the rolling edit tool to change the edits between Logo.mov and Trot.mov, and between Field.mov and Finish.mov. You can choose Edit > Undo after each change to undo it.

• Use the shortcuts listed in the Premiere Quick Reference Card and in Premiere Help to position the edit line and the work area bar.

• Open the Timeline window Options dialog box by clicking the arrow icon near the upper right corner of the Timeline window. Experiment with different icon sizes and track formats.

• Read "Using Monitor window controllers" in Chapter 3 of the *Adobe Premiere 6.0 User Guide.* Experiment with Monitor window controllers and learn about the various functions, including how to jog or shuttle through frames.

Review questions

1 What are two ways to add clips to the Timeline?

2 What are two ways to create a rough cut?

3 What are two ways to preview clips in the Timeline without rendering?

4 How does the insert function differ from the overlay function?

5 The ripple edit and the rolling edit both affect a sequence of clips in some way. Which one cannot be used with untrimmed clips, and why?

Answers

1 Dragging clips into the Timeline from the Project window, using the Automate-to-Timeline command, or opening and trimming clips in the Source view and then inserting or overlaying them into the Timeline.

2 Dragging clips into the Timeline from the Project window and using the Automate-to-Timeline command from the Storyboard or Project windows.

3 Scrubbing in the Timeline ruler, or pressing the Play button (▶).

4 Inserting affects the project duration and doesn't trim any material. By contrast, overlaying trims material and preserves the project duration.

5 The rolling edit cannot be used with untrimmed clips because as one clip is shortened, the adjacent clip is extended, which can happen only if the clip has previously been trimmed to shorten it.

Lesson 4

4 **Adding Transitions**

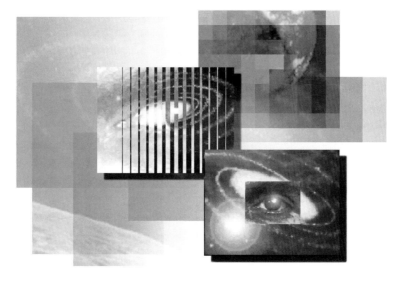

Although an instantaneous switch from one clip to another is the most common and simple way to combine video clips, Adobe Premiere also gives you dozens of options for varying the change from one clip to another. Such transitions can provide texture, nuance, and special effects.

In this lesson, you'll create a short prelude to a television program about dreams, using *transitions* between clips, special effects, and precisely trimmed clips. The *Classroom in a Book* CD includes both a sample of the final movie and the final project in the Lesson 4 folder. You may find both useful as electronic visual references as you work with the more advanced tools and perform the complex steps in the lesson. Since the subject of dreams lends itself well to the use of transitions, you'll use a variety of transitions in interesting ways. Specifically, you'll learn how to do the following:

• Place a transition using the Default transition and the Transitions palette.

• Preview transitions.

• Modify transition settings.

• Trim clips to precise timecodes for special transition effects.

• Add a special effect.

Restoring default preferences

For this lesson, it is essential that you restore the default preferences of Premiere to the factory settings before you launch the program or start the lesson. See "Restoring default preferences" on page 15 of this *Classroom in a Book*.

Getting started

In this lesson, you'll create a new project and then import the video clips and add transitions in stages. Make sure you know the location of the files used in this lesson. Insert the Premiere *Classroom in a Book* CD-ROM disk if necessary. For help, see "Copying the Classroom in a Book files" on page 14.

[?] *This lesson was written to work with the most recently updated version of Adobe Premiere 6.0 available at the time of publication. If you notice peculiar behavior with the direction of the transitions, you may need to download Premiere 6.01 or greater, which corrects these behaviors. To locate and download the updates available for your operating system, go to the Adobe Web site (www.adobe.com/support/downloads/main.html) and check the Premiere section.*

1 Launch the Premiere 6.0 software after you have restored the default preferences, and choose Single-Track Editing.

2 In the Load Project Settings dialog box, choose Multimedia or Multimedia Quicktime (depending on your operating system), and click OK.

3 After you click OK, you will see the Single-Track Editing mode workspace with its three main windows (the Project window, the Monitor window, and the Timeline window) and the default palettes. From the title bar, choose Edit > Preferences > General and Still Image and deselect Open Movies in Clip Window if it is selected.

Viewing the finished movie and a reference project file

To see what you'll be creating, you can take a look at the finished movie.

1 Choose File > Open and select the 04Final.mov file in the Final folder, inside the 04Lesson folder.

The video program opens in the Source view in the Monitor window.

2 Click the Play button (▶) in the Source view in the Monitor window to watch the video program. When the movie ends, the final frame will remain visible in the Source view in the Monitor window.

As you proceed through the lesson, you can also look at a completed project file for this movie, provided as a reference, located at Lessons > 04Lesson > Final > 04Sample.ppj. However, since you can only view or work on one project file at a time in Premiere, be sure to close the reference file and open your own, new project file to use for this lesson, as per the steps provided below. If you want to refer to the reference file while you are working through the lesson, be sure to first save your own lesson file with a different name, in order to successfully return to your work from where you left it.

Importing the clips for the project

Now you'll import the source files you need for this lesson into the Project window.

1 Choose File > Import > File, then open the 04Lesson folder you copied or installed from the *Classroom in a Book* CD-ROM disk. Hold down the Control key (Windows) or the Command key (Mac OS) or Shift key, and select the Earth.mov, Eye.mov, Solar1.mov, and Solar2.mov files (but not the Final folder). Now click Open.

The video files are added to Bin 1 and display in List view by default. Select Thumbnail view or Icon view if you prefer a different view.

2 If necessary, rearrange windows and palettes so they don't overlap, by choosing, as you did in previous lessons, Window > Workspace > Single-Track Editing.

3 Now name and save the project. Choose File > Save, type **Dream** (Windows) or **Dream.ppj** (Mac OS) for the filename, and specify 04Lesson folder for the location. Then click Save.

Note: In Mac OS, you must also type the ".ppj" extension as part of the filename to ensure compatibility for file sharing with non-Mac OS users.

About transitions

In the Tour, you were introduced to *transitions* or changes from one scene or clip to the next. The simplest type of transition is the *cut*, in which the last frame of one clip is simply followed by the first frame of the next. The cut is the most often used transition in video and film and is often the most effective. However, you will also use a variety of other types of transitions to achieve attention-getting creative effects between scenes.

In Premiere 6.0, transitions can be added to a project in a variety of ways. For example, you can select clips in the Bin area of the Project window, or create a sequence in the Storyboard window, and then use Automate-to-Timeline with a default transition. This is useful, for instance, if you want to focus on the general flow of the sequence first, and then adjust or replace some of the transitions as you fine-tune your program. You can also pre-trim clips, add them to the Timeline, and then insert a transition between them. Whichever method you prefer, Premiere makes it easy to replace or modify transitions after adding them to the Timeline.

How clips operate in transitions

Many transitions occur over time, appearing to overlap several frames from the end of one clip with frames from the beginning of the next clip. The frames at the end of the first clip that are used in the transition are called the *tail material*; the frames affected by the transition at the beginning of the next clip are called the *head material*. The way you specify the frames to be used in a particular transition instance depends on the editing mode you are using.

A/B Editing mode When you want to insert a transition in this mode, you position one clip in the Video 1A track and the other in the Video 1B track so that the clips overlap in the Timeline. The amount of overlap determines the size of the transition. You can adjust the position and duration of the overlap to change the proportion of tail and head material used from the two adjacent clips.

Single-Track Editing mode When you insert a transition in Single-Track Editing mode, Premiere repeats frames at the beginning and the ending of the two clips to create the transition or uses extra frames that you create by trimming a clip, depending on your instructions. If insufficient head or tail material is present when applying a transition, a Fix Transitions dialog box appears so you can change the duration of the transition, or of the repeat frames, and specify the placement of the transition relative to the cut between the two clips.

Note: In this lesson, you will be working in Single-Track Editing mode.

To avoid unexpected or unpredictable behavior when you export your final files, if you switch from Single-Track Editing Mode to A/B Editing Mode when working on a project, you should always save and close your project file in Single-Track Mode first; then, re-open it in A/B Editing Mode.

The Transitions palette

Adobe Premiere 6.0 includes a wide range of transitions including 3D motion, dissolves, wipes, and zooms. The transitions are grouped into folders, by type, in the Transitions palette. Each transition is listed with a unique icon to the left of its name.

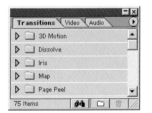

1 If the Transitions/Video/Audio palette is not visible, choose Window > Show Transitions. If necessary, click the Transitions tab to make it active and resize the Transitions palette by dragging its lower right corner.

2 Double-click the Dissolve folder or click the Expand/Collapse button to the left of the Dissolve folder to see the types of dissolve transitions available. Notice that the *Cross Dissolve* icon is outlined in red. This indicates that Cross Dissolve is selected as the *default transition*.

3 On the Navigator/Info/History palette, click the Info tab (if the Info palette is not already active), to see a description of the selected transition. As you select a transition, its description and icon appear in the Info palette.

4 Now, click and hold the small black arrow in the upper right corner of the Transitions palette and choose Animate from the menu, if it is not already selected. Animate allows you to see the style of each type of transition. If you find the animated icons distracting while you work, de-select Animate.

Transition parameters

All transitions have duration, alignment, and direction parameters. Some transitions have additional parameters such as borders, edge adjustments, and anti-aliasing. The parameters depend on the nature and complexity of the specific transition type.

Duration refers to the number of frames required for the transition. All transitions use frames from the end of the first clip—called *tail material*—and frames from the beginning of the second clip—called *head material*—to create the transition.

Alignment refers to the position of the transition in relation to the cut between the two clips. The options are Center at Cut, Start at Cut, and End at Cut.

Direction indicates how the transition operates on the two clips. Normally, the direction will be from clip A to clip B—from left to right in the Timeline. In most cases, Premiere sets the direction of the transition automatically, and you won't have to worry about it. Later in this lesson, you'll use the Track Selector and other controls to modify the direction of a transition.

About the default transition and default settings

Cross Dissolve is the factory setting for the *default transition* in Premiere 6.0 because it is so frequently used in video and films. In a Cross Dissolve, one scene "dissolves" into another over a brief duration. You can select another transition as the default at any time. The default transition and the *default effect settings* apply not just to the current project on which you are working; but to all your projects. Working with a default transition is a quick way to insert transitions between clips. You can modify or replace them after you are satisfied with the general flow of the project.

It is often useful to restore the default preferences of Premiere—including the default transition and the default effect settings—to the factory settings before you launch the program for a new project. In this way, you avoid any unintended carryover of specialized settings changes to another project. See "Restoring default preferences" on page 15.

The default effect settings for all transitions specify a duration of 30 frames with the alignment of the transition centered at the cut between the two clips. You can change both the duration and alignment of the transition in the Default Effect dialog box.

For most transitions, the default direction of the transition is from clip A to clip B (left to right in the time sequence). You alter the direction of the transition to move from clip B to clip A by double-clicking the transition icon and making changes in the transition Settings dialog box. Additional effect parameters, if they pertain to a transition, are also changed in the Settings dialog box for that transition.

Modifying the default transition settings

Now, you will modify the default effect settings of the Cross Dissolve transition before you add any clips to the Dream.ppj timeline.

1 In the Transitions palette, double-click the Dissolve folder and look at the Cross Dissolve transition icon. The icon should be outlined in red to indicate that it is the default transition. Click once on the icon to select the transition.

2 From the Transitions palette menu, click Set Selected as Default. Now the Cross Dissolve icon is still outlined in red, but the Default Effect dialog box appears so you can modify the settings of the default transition.

Default Effect

Effect Duration: `15` frames   [OK]

Effect Alignment: `Center at Cut` ▼   [Cancel]

3 Type **15** to replace 30 as the number of frames to be used for the transition's Effect Duration. Verify that the Effect Alignment is shown as Center at Cut. Click OK.

Note: *The Default Effects settings apply to all transitions, not just the transition you have specified as the default transition. So, from time to time, the Fix Transitions dialog box will appear as you work with various transitions, if the parameters of the default effects are in conflict with the number of frames available in the two clips used in the transition.*

Working with the default transition

Premiere automatically uses Cross Dissolve as the default transition, as it is one of the most commonly used transitions. If you frequently use another transition, you can set it as the default. The default transition can be added to any project quickly, without stopping to open the Transitions palette and drag the transition to the Timeline.

To specify a different transition as the default:

1. Choose Window > Show Transitions.

2. Select the transition that you want to use as the default.

3. From the Transitions palette menu, choose Set Selected as Default.

4. Type the duration that you want for the transition. (You can later change the duration for any specific transition instance in the Timeline.)

5. Choose the default alignment for the transitions: Center at Cut.

6. Click OK. These settings remain in effect for all projects until you change them.

To apply a default transition to your project in Single-Track Editing Mode:

1. Add or position two clips on the Video 1 track so that they meet.

2. Position the edit line where the two clips meet.

3. Click the Apply Default Transition button(◨) in the Monitor window, or press Ctrl+D (Windows) or Command+D (Mac OS). If extra frames are not available at the In and Out points of the involved clips, the Fix Transitions dialog box appears. If necessary, select options from this dialog box.

–From the *Adobe Premiere 6.0 User Guide*, Chapter 4

Inserting a transition

You will first use the Automate-to-Timeline feature to move two clips into the Timeline with the default transition—Cross Dissolve—between them. Later in this lesson, you will use other methods to insert clips and transitions.

Using Automate-to-Timeline and the default transition

First, make your clips and transitions a little easier to see in the Timeline.

1 Choose Windows > Window Options > Timeline Window Options. Then, select the medium-sized Icon Size if it is not already selected. Click OK.

2 From the Time Zoom Level pop-up menu at the bottom of the Timeline window, select 1 Second so you can see the action clearly, as it happens.

3 Hold the Control key (Windows) or the Command key (Mac OS) as you click first on the Solar1.mov icon and then on the Earth.mov icon in Bin 1 of the Project window to select both clips.

4 Choose Project > Automate-to-Timeline to bring both clips to the Timeline.

5 In the Automate-to-Timeline dialog box, change the Contents setting to Selected Clips, change the Ordering setting to Selection Order, and change Clip Overlap from 15 frames to 30 frames. Verify that Sequentially, Beginning, Use Default Transition, and Ignore Audio are selected in the dialog box. Click OK.

The Cross Dissolve transition appears in the Timeline window between the two clips.

6 In the Timeline window, click the Track Mode button (⊐) to the right of the Video 1 track label to display the Video 1 upper track, the Transition track, and the Video 1 lower track. This reveals the sub-structure of the Video 1 track in Single-Track editing mode. Use this expanded view of the tracks for the entire lesson.

Now the Timeline window contains two clips, starting with Solar1.mov in the upper track of Video 1 track and ending with Earth.mov in the lower track of the Video 1 track. The default transition, Cross Dissolve, has been inserted in the transition area between them.

You could also create a storyboard with the clips, use Automate-to-Timeline using the default transition, then modify or replace selected transitions as needed later. For additional information about creating a storyboard, see Lesson 3 in this Classroom in a Book.

Changing parameters of a transition instance

A transition *instance* refers to an individual occurrence of a transition in the Timeline. The default settings make the transition operate from clip A to clip B. You can change the direction for a specific instance without changing the default. You do this by changing the direction of the transition after it has been inserted into the Timeline.

1 Double-click the Cross Dissolve transition icon in the Video 1 Transition track of the Timeline. Now, the Cross Dissolve Settings dialog box appears.

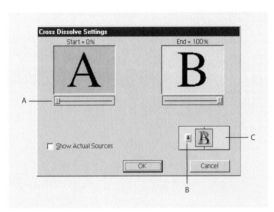

A. Start/End slider B. Transition thumbnail icon area
C. Track selector

The Cross Dissolve Settings dialog box shows the "start" clip in the upper left and the "end" clip at the upper right. By default, "A" and "B" are displayed in these clip thumbnail viewers, but you can display the actual clips instead by clicking the Show Actual Clips box below the viewers.

Now you'll explore transitions.

2 Click in the Show Actual Sources box to display the starting and ending frames of the clips used in this transition. Solar1.mov is now displayed as clip A and Earth.mov is displayed as clip B, because the direction is set for "A-to-B".

Below each clip thumbnail viewer is a *Start/End Slider* that allows you to change the initial and final appearance of the transition. You can adjust the Start sliders separately for different settings, or you can adjust them simultaneously if you want the same setting.

3 Press and hold the Shift key as you move one of the sliders to 40%. Notice that the other slider moves to the same position.

4 Put the Start and End sliders back to the original settings for this transition instance.

5 Click the track selector tool (↓) once. The track selector tool is used to set the direction of the transition, from A-to-B or from B-to-A.

6 Notice that the direction of the transition is now from clip B to clip A and the arrow faces up. Click OK.

7 In the Timeline window, select 1/2 Second from the Time Zoom Level. Now you can see the track selector tool with the Cross Dissolve transition icon.

8 Click the track selector tool once to restore the A-to-B direction for this transition instance. (The arrow now faces down).

Previewing the transition

Two preview options are useful when working with transitions: render-scrubbing in the Timeline and previewing at the intended frame rate.

Using render-scrub to preview the transition

To quickly preview the Cross Dissolve transition you have applied to the two clips:

1 Hold down the Alt key (Windows) or the Option key (Mac OS) as you drag the pointer in the Timeline ruler to move the edit line across the transition. Note that the pointer has changed into a smaller arrow, indicating that you are previewing effects. The preview plays in the Program view in the Monitor window. The motion is not smooth or precise because you are moving through the transition manually.

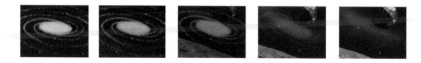

Note: *If you scrub without using the Alt (Windows) or Option key (Mac OS), you will not see any transitions or effects that have been applied, but an "x" will appear in the Program view to indicate the location of an effect.*

2 Save the project.

Previewing the transition at the intended frame rate

Although render-scrubbing in the Timeline ruler displays the transition effect, this preview method cannot show it precisely. To preview transitions (and other effects) at the intended frame rate, you need to generate a preview file. Premiere then plays this file in the Program view in the Monitor window. Before you generate a preview in this way, however, you need to set the work area bar to specify the portion of your project that you want to preview.

1 In the Timeline window, drag the arrows at the left and right ends of the yellow work area bar to cover an area slightly larger than the transition between the Solar1.mov and Earth.mov clips.

2 Choose Timeline > Preview, or press Enter (Windows) or Return (Mac OS) on the keyboard to build and play a preview file.

As Premiere generates the preview file, the Building Preview dialog box displays the status. When completed, the preview plays in the Program view in the Monitor window. You can replay this preview by pressing Enter (Windows) or Return (Mac OS).

About preview options

When you want to preview edits, transitions, and effects at the final playback speed choose to preview From Disk. When From Disk is selected, Premiere renders the preview from the hard disk.

• To enable Preview From Disk, choose Project > Project Settings > Keyframe and Rendering. Then for Preview (under Rendering Options), choose From Disk and click OK.

Alternatively, you can render a preview from memory. When render From RAM is selected, Premiere stores and processes the selected frames in RAM and creates a preview by displaying frames as they are rendered. Because frames are rendered in RAM, this process depends on the amount of RAM available. If the frame rate, frame size, or effects used require more RAM than is available, frames may be dropped during playback, or Premiere may render the preview from disk instead.

• To enable Preview from RAM, choose Project > Project Settings > Keyframe and Rendering. Then for Preview (under Rendering Options), choose From RAM and click OK.

When you want to preview edits, transitions, and effects but don't care if the preview is at final playback speed, choose to preview To Screen. When To Screen is selected, Premiere renders directly to the screen as quickly as possible. The playback speed depends on image size and resolution, the number and complexity of effects and transitions, and the processing speed of your system. This option is not recommended for previewing areas that include many effects.

• To enable Preview To Screen, choose Project > Project Settings > Keyframe and Rendering. Then for Preview (under Rendering Options), choose To Screen and click OK.

–From the *Adobe Premiere 6.0 User Guide,* Chapter 3

Pre-trimming a clip and adding a transition

Typically, a transition overlaps portions of clips that are not essential to the video program, since these portions are likely to be obscured by the effect of the transition. So it often makes sense to pre-trim your clips, in order to make sure the transition occurs where you want it to. In the next few steps, you'll pre-trim clips, add them to the Timeline, and then insert the transition.

1 Double-click Eye.mov in Bin 1 of the Project window to view it in the Source view in the Monitor window. Or, simply drag the Eye.mov clip icon to the Source view in the Monitor window.

2 Double-click the timecode under the Source view (at the right), type **114**, and press Enter (Windows) or Return (Mac OS) to locate a specific frame.

Note: The timecode needs to be in 30 Frames per Second Non-Drop Frame (00:00:01:14) format. If necessary, click the Timeline window to make it active. From the title bar, choose Window > Window Options > Timeline Window Options. In the Timeline Window Options dialog box, select 30 fps Non-Drop Frame Timecode. Click OK.

3 Now, click the Mark Out button (⊦) under the Source view to set a new Out point for the Eye.mov clip. The Clip Duration shown under the Source view (at the left) now indicates that the clip has been trimmed to 1:16 to allow the transition to operate with the eye open instead of blinking.

4 Verify that the edit line is at the end of Earth.mov clip in the Timeline.

5 Now, do one of the following:

• From the title bar at the top of the Premiere screen, choose Clip > Insert to Edit Line.

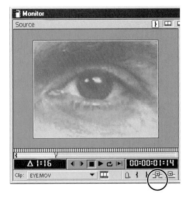

Source view with timecode and Insert to Timeline button indicated

• Click the Insert button (⊞) at the bottom of the Source view to insert the trimmed Eye.mov clip into the Timeline after Earth.mov.

• Drag the trimmed Eye.mov clip from the Source view to the Timeline at the edit line.

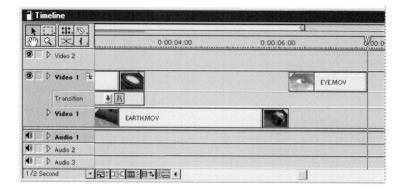

To add a transition between Earth.mov and Eye.mov, you will use the Transitions palette. But first, you'll change the duration of a transition.

Changing transition effect duration

You may remember that the default effect setting for effect duration was 30 frames, before you changed it to 15 frames earlier in the lesson. Before you add the transition from Earth.mov to Eye.mov, you need to reset the default effect setting for the effect duration.

1 Click Cross Dissolve in the Transitions palette.

2 In the upper right corner of the Transitions palette, click the menu button and choose Set Selection as Default.

Note: Even if a transition is already the designated default (icon outlined in red), you choose Set Selection as Default to change the default effect settings for the default transition and all other transitions.

3 In the Default Effect dialog box, type **30** for the effect duration. While you are looking a the Default Effect dialog box, make sure that Effect Alignment is set to Center at Cut. Click OK.

Now the default effect duration has been restored to 30 frames.

Adding a transition using the Transitions palette

1 Position the edit line in the Timeline so that it is at the end of Earth.mov (6:06).

2 In the Transitions palette, double-click the Zoom folder or click the Expand/Collapse button (▼) to see the transitions in the folder.

3 Click the Cross Zoom icon to select it.

💡 *To find a transition quickly, click the Transitions palette menu, select Find, type in the name of the transition, choose Expand folders, and click Find. Premiere will locate the transition and highlight it.*

4 Drag the Cross Zoom transition icon to the Video 1 transition track at the edit line in the Timeline window, where Earth.mov ends and the trimmed Eye.mov begins.

The Fix Transition dialog box appears.

The Fix Transition dialog box

When you insert a transition into the Timeline, but there are not enough frames available for the transition in the head material and/or the tail material of the clips, the Fix Transition dialog box appears so you can make adjustments.

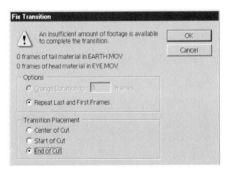

The dialog box identifies the two clips involved in the transition instance and indicates the status of the tail and head material. The default solution is to repeat frames and place the transition at the center of the cut.

1 Select or verify these options: Repeat Last and First Frames and transition placement at End of Cut.

2 Click OK.

Now, the Cross Zoom transition appears in the Timeline. Notice that grey bars appear in the affected ends of the two clips. This indicates that Premiere has repeated the last and first frames of the clips to make the transition work properly with the available footage.

Changing transitions

You can easily modify various parameters or settings for a transition, including the transition duration, alignment, direction, start and end values, border, and anti-aliasing. Frequently, you will want to modify a specific instance of a transition in your video program, but won't want to modify the general settings for that transition type. In other cases, you may want to modify the way a transition operates in general. In many cases, you may insert a particular transition into your video project, and then want to replace it with another transition.

Modifying a transition instance

The Cross Zoom you just added to the Dream project allows you to set the point in each clip where the zoom begins. You'll do that now.

1 Click the Cross Zoom transition icon in the Timeline to select it.

2 From the title bar at the top of the Premiere screen, choose Timeline > Transition Settings to see the Cross Zoom settings dialog box.

Alternatively, you can double-click the transition icon in the Timeline to bring up the settings dialog box.

3 In the settings dialog box, Select the Show Actual Sources option.

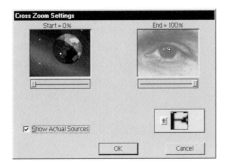

4 Leave the Start and End slider settings as they are, and make sure the track selector is pointing up (↑). When the arrow points up, the transition will start zooming into Earth.mov and then zoom out of Eye.mov.

Notice that there is a small white square in each of the clip thumbnail viewers. This square determines where the zoom ends.

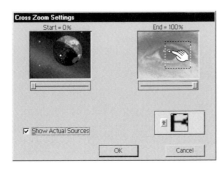

5 Drag the white square in the End clip thumbnail viewer (Eye.mov) to the reflection in the upper right area of the eye.

6 Drag the white square in the Start thumbnail viewer (Earth.mov) to the center of the sphere, so that its position is similar to the position in the eye.

7 Click OK. You now have two 1-second transitions in your project.

8 Save the Dream project.

9 Preview the Cross Zoom transition by doing one of the following:

• Render-scrub in the Timeline ruler by dragging the edit line through the transition while holding down the Alt key (Windows) or the Option key (Mac OS).

• Preview at the precise frame rate by setting the yellow work area to cover the new transition and pressing Enter (Windows) or Return (Mac OS) to generate and play a new preview file.

💡 *To preview the entire project at the precise frame rate, press Alt (Windows) or Option (Mac OS) as you click anywhere in the work area bar. This adjusts the work area bar to cover all the clips. Press Enter (Windows) or Return (Mac OS) to generate and play a new preview.*

Modifying transition settings

As you develop your own video style, or may want to modify the settings of some transition types so they have your customizations as their default settings in the Transitions palette. You'll customize Swing In now.

1 Double-click the Swing In transition icon in the 3D Motion folder of the Transitions palette to see its settings dialog box.

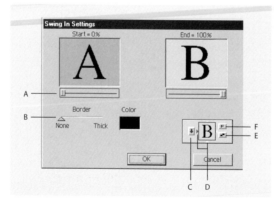

A. *Start/End slider* B. *Border thickness* C. *Track selector*
D. *Edge selector* E. *Anti-aliasing selector*
F. *Forward/Reverse selector*

2 Adjust any or all of the following settings:

• To change the initial and final appearance of the transition, use the Start and End sliders. Hold down the Shift key to move the Start and End sliders together.

• To adjust the width of the optional border on the transition, drag the Border slider.

• To select a border color, click the color swatch, select a color from the color selection window, and then click OK.

• To change the orientation of the transition, click an Edge selector on the transition's thumbnail. The Edge selectors are small triangles bordering the transition icon.

• To make the transition play forward or backward, click the Forward/Reverse selector in the upper right corner of the transition's thumbnail.

• To adjust the smoothness of the transition's edges, click the Anti-aliasing selector in the lower right corner of the transition's thumbnail. Clicking cycles through the values Low, High, and Off.

Note: *Not all of these settings parameters are available in all transitions.*

3 Click OK to change the default settings of the Swing In transition type or click Cancel to retain the factory settings for this transition.

Replacing a transition instance

You replace a transition instance by simply dropping the new transition icon on top of the old one in the Timeline. When you replace a transition instance, the *default effect settings* (duration and alignment) that apply to all transitions are preserved. However, the *transition-specific settings* (direction, borders, edges, anti-aliasing, etc.) are replaced by the transition-specific default settings of the new transition.

1 With the Transitions palette active, click the triangle next to the 3D Motion folder to expand the folder, if it is not already open.

2 Select the Cube Spin transition in the 3D Motion folder, drag its icon to the Timeline window, and place it on top of the Cross Dissolve transition between the Solar1.mov and Earth.mov clips. Now, the Cross Dissolve transition has been replaced with a Cube Spin.

3 In the Timeline, double-click the Cube Spin transition you have just inserted to see its settings dialog box. Notice that the setting options for the Cube Spin transition contain additional parameters, such as, border and color. Click OK or Cancel.

4 Choose Edit > Undo transition to restore the transition to the Cross Dissolve, in order to reproduce the 04Final.mov.

5 In the Transitions palette, choose the Cross Dissolve transition > Set Selected as Default.

6 Be sure that the Effect Duration is now set to 15 frames and the Effect Alignment is set to Center at Cut for the rest of the project.

Adding multiple transitions

To create other effects, you can string two or more transitions side-by-side. You'll do this now to give the next portion of the movie a dream-like quality. By alternating progressively trimmed clips of Eye.mov and Solar2.mov, you will produce the four successive Sliding Bands as seen in the 04Final.mov.

Conceptual view of the structure for four side-by-side multiple transitions
The clips are progressively trimmed, then the newly trimmed clips are alternated as to which is first on the Timeline.

Making the first transition

1 Position the edit line at the end of the Eye.mov clip.

2 From Bin 1, drag the Solar2.mov clip to the Source view in the Monitor window.

3 Double-click the Source view timecode, type **14** and press Enter/Return.

4 Click the Mark Out button (⊦) in the Source view to set the new Out point. The duration time of the clip now shows the new trimmed length of the clip is 0:16.

5 Do one of the following:

• From the title bar at the top of the Premiere screen, choose Clip > Insert at edit line.

• Click the Insert button (⊒) at the bottom of the Source view.

• Drag the trimmed clip to the Timeline at the edit line.

6 In the Transitions palette, scroll to the Slide folder, open the folder, scroll to Sliding Bands, and select it.

7 Drag Sliding Bands to the Timeline where Eye.mov and Solar2.mov meet.

8 The Fix Transitions dialog box appears. Click OK.

You now have a 15-frame (1/2 second) Sliding Bands transition.

9 Save the project.

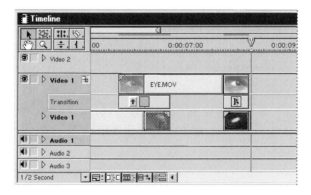

10 Preview this transition or preview the project using render-scrub or generate and play a new preview file.

The process for creating the three remaining Sliding Bands transitions for this project is similar to the first.

Trimming clips for the second side-by-side Sliding Bands transition

Now, you'll make the second trim of Solar2.mov in preparation for the second Sliding Bands transition.

1 In the Source view, change the existing Out point (at 00:00:00:14) to be the new In point by clicking on the Mark In button (ɪ) at the bottom of the Source view.

2 Still in the Source view, double-click the timecode, and type **20**, and press Enter/Return.

3 Click the Mark Out button (ɪ) in the Source view to set a new clip that is 8 frames long, as indicated by the Clip Duration display bar menu at the bottom left of the Source view.

4 In the Timeline window, move the edit line to the end of the work area at 00:00:08:08 and insert the new segment of the Solar2.mov clip (or drag it to the edit line).

Now, you'll make the second trim to Eye.mov in preparation for the second transition.

5 From the Select Source Clip pop-up menu in the Source view, select Eye.mov.

6 Double-click the timecode, type **218**, press Enter/Return.

7 Click the Mark In button (ɪ) to set the new In point.

8 Double-click the timecode once again, but this time type **224**, then press Enter/Return.

9 Click the Mark Out button (ɪ) to set the new Out point.

The result is a new trimmed clip that is 8 frames long.

10 Drag/insert the new Eye.mov segment to the Timeline, at the edit line at the end of the program (it should be 8:13).

Adding the second Sliding Bands transition

You will be using the Sliding Bands transition for this and the last two transitions.

1 Drag the edit line to the meeting point of your new Solar2.mov and Eye.mov segments.

2 Drag the Sliding Bands transition to the Timeline, where the latest Eye.mov and Solar2.mov meet.

You now have two 15-frame Sliding Bands transitions using different segments, progressively trimmed in the Source view, of the Solar2.mov and Eye.mov clips. The second transition is tinted orange.

3 Save the project.

4 Preview the two Sliding Bands transitions.

Adding the third Sliding Bands transition

To complete this portion of the lesson, you'll create two more instances of the Sliding Bands transition. But this time, you'll reverse the motion of the sliding bands, making them slide from right to left.

1 In the Source view, select the Eye.mov from the Select Source Clip menu, mark a new In point by typing **224** in the timecode, press Enter (Windows) or Return (Mac OS), and click the Mark In button.

2 Mark a new Out point by typing **300** in the timecode, press Enter (Windows) or Return (Mac OS), and click the Mark Out button.

3 Insert this newest Eye.mov segment of 8 frames at the end of the program using one of the methods you have learned.

4 Using the same process, make a new segment of the Solar.mov clip with its In point set to **20** and the Out point set to **26**.

5 Insert this newest Solar2.mov segment of 8 frames at the end of the program using one of the methods you have learned.

6 From the Transitions palette, drag the Sliding Bands transition to the Timeline between these two newest segments. Now, you have three instances of Sliding Bands in your program. (Your time will be 9:10 or close to it by a frame or two.)

You may recall from the 04Final.mov that the first two instances of Sliding Bands move from left to right and last two instances of Sliding Bands move from right to left. To make that effect, you will modify the transition settings.

7 Double-click the third Sliding Bands transition in the Timeline (the one you just added) to access the Sliding Bands Settings dialog box.

8 Click the Forward/Reverse Selector to the right of the animating icon to change the motion from Forward to Reverse. Now, an "R" should be displayed for the motion button.

Forward/Reverse Selector (in circle)

You'll notice a couple of other controls near the animating icon. Surrounding the icon itself are four triangles, called Edge Selectors; two are red and two are white. Clicking the Edge Selectors sets the orientation of the sliding bands. The Edge Selectors on the left and right sides of the icon (the red ones) specify that the sliding bands move horizontally; those on the top and bottom (the white ones) specify vertical motion. The horizontal motion arrows are already selected and displayed in red.

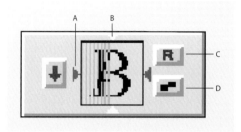

Icon controls: **A**. *Horizontal motion*
B. *Vertical motion* **C**. *Forward/Reverse*
D. *Anti-aliasing Low, High, or Off*

Below the Forward/Reverse Selector is another button. This button controls whether the transition uses *anti-aliasing*. Anti-aliasing blends the edges of the bands, smoothing the hard edges. Anti-aliasing is turned off when you see the ( ) icon; it is set to Low when you see the ( ) icon; and it's set to High when you see the ( ) icon. You'll leave it off.

Note: *These controls surrounding the icon area are only available for certain transitions.*

9 In the Setting dialog box, click OK.

Now, the third Sliding Bands transition moves with the opposite motion from the first two.

10 Save the project and preview the three Sliding Bands transitions.

Adding the fourth Sliding Bands transition

Now, you'll make more clip segments before adding the fourth Sliding Bands transition. Remember that you have been alternating the clips, so first you'll modify Solar2.mov.

1 In the Source view, select Solar2.mov from the Select Source Clip pop-up menu, mark a new In point by typing **26** in the timecode, press Enter (Windows) or Return (Mac OS), and click the Mark In button.

2 Mark a new Out point by typing **102** in the timecode, press Enter (Windows) or Return (Mac OS), and click the Mark Out button.

3 Insert this newest Solar2.mov segment of 8 frames at the end of the program using one of the methods you have learned.

4 Using the same process, make a new segment of the Eye.mov clip with its In point set to **326** and the Out point set to **402**.

5 Insert this newest Eye.mov segment of 8 frames at the end of the program using one of the methods you have learned (at approximately 9:16).

6 Drag the Sliding Bands transition once more between your newest Solar2.mov and Eye.mov segments to add the fourth side-by-side transition.

7 Double-click the fourth Sliding Bands transition. Reverse its motion by clicking on the F button in the Forward/Reverse area.

8 Save the project.

Let's briefly look at what you've done. You've created four instances of the same transition, The motion for the last two is the reverse of the motion of the first two. You should preview it at the precise frame rate.

9 From the Time Zoom level menu in the Timeline window, choose 1 Second, if it is not selected. This will make it easier to find the work area bar.

10 Drag the ends of the yellow work area bar to cover the entire length of the Solar2.mov and Eye.mov clips. Then press Enter or Return.

11 Premiere generates the preview file and then plays it in the Program view.

12 To watch it again, press Enter (Windows) or Return (Mac OS).

Notice that the preview plays in the Program view immediately because you have made no new changes since your most recent preview file was generated.

Adding the final effect

To complete the project, you'll add a Zoom effect with the last segments of Eye.mov and Solar2.mov. The Zoom is implemented differently from the Cross Zoom. While the Cross Zoom "zooms" in or out on one element within the clip, the Zoom motion effect zooms an entire clip into or out of another clip, playing both at the same time. You'll use the Effect Controls palette to make this sequence, creating a centered inset of the eye inside the stars.

1 With Eye.mov in the Source view, the final segment needs a duration of 02:04, beginning at 03:26 and ending at 05:28.

2 Locate the current end of the program at the last frame of the fourth Sliding Bands transition at approximately 09:21 and drag the edit line there.

3 The last trimmed portion of Eye.mov gets placed in the Timeline on the Video 2 track. Do that now so that its In point snaps to the edit line in the Timeline.

4 To create the final Zoom effect, from the Premiere menu, choose Window > Show Effect Controls. Select the Eye.mov clip in the Video 2 Track.

5 In the Effect Controls palette, click the Setup link to the right of the word Motion. The Motion Settings dialog box opens.

6 Click the Pause button (▪▪) in the upper left Alpha viewing area of the Motion Settings box to stop the motion preview.

7 Locate the text entry area at the bottom of the dialog box, where you see the words "Click a Point Above." The second line reads: "Info #0 is at <-80>, <0>. Change -80 to 0 to center the clip at the In point. Click or tab to another field in the box to set the new input of 0.

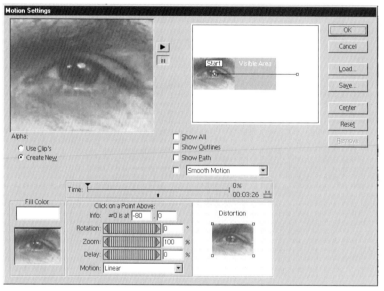

Motion Settings dialog box in Windows operating system. Mac OS differs slightly.

8 Similarly, to center the clip on the Out point, first click in the upper right area of the dialog box that has a gray rectangle containing the works Visible Area. Click the little white square to the right of the gray rectangle. This represents the Out point, designated by Premiere as either End or Finish. Now return to the text box that shows <-80> and change it to <0>. Click or tab to another field to set the new input of 0.

9 Click or tab to Zoom text entry box and change 100% to 30% and click OK.

10 Preview the effect.

You'll see the final Eye.mov clip zooming away from the camera as the footage plays.

The final effect of this project is completed with Solar2.mov. The concluding footage of the Solar2.mov has a lens flare special effect built into it. The trimming of the clips and their placement at the edit line will synchronize the lens flare with the sparkle gleaming in the reflection in the eye at the end of the Eye.mov.

11 In the Source view, from the Select Source Clip pop-up menu, choose Solar2.mov.

12 In the Source view timecode, type **124**, then press Enter (Windows) or Return (Mac OS). Use the Mark In ( ) button to set this as the In point.

13 In the Source view timecode, type **328**, then press Enter (Windows) or Return (Mac OS). Use the Mark Out button ( ) to set this as the Out point. This creates a clip segment with a duration of 02:06.

14 Drag this new Solar2.mov segment to the Timeline onto Video 1 track directly beneath the last Eye.mov clip, so that its In point snaps to the edit line.

15 Save the project.

16 To preview the end of the project, hold down the Alt key (Windows) or the Option key (Mac OS) and render-scrub in the Timeline ruler across the final portion.

17 Set the work area bar to cover the entire project and generate and play a new preview of the entire movie.

Enjoy the satisfaction of having performed a professional-level digital video editing session.

Exporting the movie

1 Click in the Timeline window to select it.

2 Choose File > Export Timeline > Movie.

3 In the Export Movie dialog box, click the Settings button. Make sure QuickTime is selected for the File Type and Entire Project is selected for the Range. Also make sure that the Export Video option is selected and the Export Audio option is not selected. The default values for other settings, including those for compression, are fine for this project.

Q *Use the Save and Load buttons in the Export Movie Settings dialog box to save and later quickly load export settings that you use frequently. Loading saved settings is particularly useful when you create several types of video files (for example, NTSC and Web video) from the same project.*

4 Click OK to close the Export Movie Settings dialog box.

5 In the Export Movie dialog box, type **Dream.mov** for the name of the video program. Click Save (Windows) or OK (Mac OS).

Premiere starts making the movie, displaying a status bar that provides an estimate for the amount of time it will take.

6 When the video program is complete, it's opened in a Clip window. Click the Play button (▶) to watch what you've just created. You may notice that some frames are dropped during playback. This depends on the system you are using and also the frame rate at which the movie was exported.

Congratulations on completing the Transitions Lesson!

Exploring on your own

Feel free to experiment with the project you have just created. Here are some suggestions:

• Change the direction of a transition (click the Track Selector), and then preview the results.

• Open the settings dialog box for one of the transitions (double-click the transition) and see how the options affect the transition.

• Look at the differences in the appearance of transition icons when you change the icon size in the Timeline Window Options dialog box (make the Timeline window active and then, from the title bar, choose Window > Window Options > Timeline Window Options).

• Look at the difference in the appearance of the transition icons when you change the Time Zoom Level to 1/2 Second and then to 1 Second.

• Practice using the shortcuts listed on the Premiere Quick Reference Card and in Premiere Help to preview in the Monitor window and the Timeline window.

Review questions

1 What are two ways to preview transitions?

2 What does the Track Selector button do in a transition?

3 What is the purpose of the anti-aliasing feature available in a number of transitions?

4 What does the Forward/Reverse button do in a transition?

5 What are two ways to get more information within the Transitions palette about the function of a specific transition?

Answers

1 Render-scrubbing in the Timeline ruler while holding down the Alt key (Windows) or the Option key (Mac OS), or generating a preview of the work by pressing Enter (Windows) or Return (Mac OS).

2 The track selector tool sets the direction of the transition between the two clips.

3 Anti-aliasing smooths the edges of an effect, reducing the rough appearance of the edge. This can be useful for transitions that have angled or curved edges.

4 The Forward/Reverse button sets the direction of the effect used in the transition. For example, in the Zoom transition, F zooms in and R zooms out.

5 Select (check) Show Hidden in the Transitions palette menu, or select (check) Animate in the Transitions palette menu.

Lesson 5

5 Adding Audio

The right music or sound effects add
impact to your video program. Adobe
Premiere makes it easy to add additional
audio, mix the sound, and carefully
control the volume for maximum effect.

To learn about working with sound in Premiere, you'll create a promotional spot for a film festival, using a number of basic audio techniques. Specifically, you'll learn how to do the following:

• Place audio clips.

• Synchronize audio and video tracks.

• Adjust audio fades and volume levels.

• Adjust volume levels using the cross-fade and fade adjustment tools.

Restoring default preferences

For this lesson, it is essential that you restore the default preferences of Premiere to the factory settings before you launch the program or start the lesson. See "Restoring default preferences" on page 15 of this *Classroom in a Book*.

Getting started

Because you'll need to listen to audio clips in this lesson, first make sure that your computer's speakers or headphones are set up to play sounds at an appropriate volume. Make sure you know the location of the files used in this lesson. Insert the Premiere *Classroom in a Book* CD-ROM disk if necessary. For help, see "Copying the Classroom in a Book files" on page 14.

1 Start Premiere.

2 In the Load Project Settings dialog box, choose Multimedia or Multimedia Quicktime (depending on your operating system), and click OK.

3 After you click OK, you will see the Single-Track Editing mode workspace and its three main windows (the Project window, the Monitor window, and the Timeline window) and the default palettes.

4 Choose Edit > Preferences > General & Still Image and deselect Open Movies in Clip Window if it is selected. Click OK.

5 Click the close box on the Navigator/Info/History palette. Leave the Transitions/Video/Audio palette open, as we'll be using it in this lesson.

Viewing the finished movie

If you'd like to see what you'll be creating, you can take a look at the finished movie. Because parts of the lesson let you make your own editing decisions, your video program may be slightly different.

1 Choose File > Open and double-click the 05Final.mov file in the Final folder, inside the 05Lesson folder.

The video program opens in the Source view in the Monitor window.

2 Click the Play button (►) to view the video program.

Importing and organizing clips

Now you're ready to import source files to the Project window. To keep things organized, you'll create a separate bin for sound files, and then move the audio files into the sounds bin.

1 To import the video and audio clips you will need for this lesson, choose File > Import > File, and then open the 05Lesson folder you copied or installed on your hard drive, from the Adobe Premiere 6.0 *Classroom in a Book* CD-ROM disk. Hold down the Control key (Windows) or the Shift key (Mac OS), and then select the Danger.aif, Door.mov, Feet1.mov, Feet2.mov, and Hall1.mov, Hall2.mov, Horror.aif, Man.mov, Shadow.aif, Suspense.aif, Woman1.mov, and Woman 2.mov files (but not the Final folder). Now click Open.

The video and audio files are added to the Project window in the Bin 1 folder.

2 If necessary, drag the Resize Bin Area button located at the bottom of the Project window until the Bin area is the size you want. If necessary, rearrange windows and palettes so they don't overlap, by choosing Window > Workspace > Single-Track Editing.

Now you'll create a bin for the sound files.

3 With the Project window active, choose File > New > Bin or click the New Bin button (⌷) in the Project window. Type **Sounds** for the Bin Name and click OK.

4 Click the Bin 1 icon in the Project window to view the contents of Bin 1.

5 In the Project window, hold down the Control key (Windows) or Command key (Mac OS), and click the Danger.aif, Horror.aif, Shadow.aif, and Suspense.aif icons to select them.

6 Then drag the icons to the Sounds Bin folder. You will see the list of files displayed in the Project window, in List View, by default.

7 Click the Sounds Bin in the Project window.

To make the clips in the Sounds Bin easier to identify, let's change the view for the window.

8 Choose Window > Window Options > Project Window Options, select Thumbnail View from the menu at the top of the dialog box, and then click OK or click the Thumbnail View button (⊞) at the bottom of the Project window.

Finally, you'll save and name the project.

9 Choose File > Save, type **Mystery.ppj** for the name, and select 05Lesson folder for the location. Then click Save.

In Windows, the default file extension for Premiere projects, ppj, is added to your filename automatically. In Mac OS, type the extension as part of the filename.

Creating an L-cut

Video and film editors often use a technique called a *split* edit to create an audio transition between scenes. In a split edit, the audio that belongs to one clip extends into one or both adjacent clips.

The audio from a quiet forest scene, for example, could extend into the scene of a crowd. One specific type of split edit, called an *L-cut* or a *six-point edit*, extends the audio (only) from one clip into the following clip. In an L-cut, the audio Out point is later than the video Out point. The result is that the audio from the first clip continues to play after the video from the next clip has begun to play.

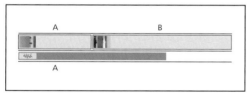

*An L-cut allows the sound from one clip (**A**) to extend into the next clip (**B**).*

Unlinking the video and audio

Typically, when you shoot a scene with your camera, you capture both video and audio at the same time. When you digitize the footage, the video and audio are linked together in one file. In Premiere, this is known as a *hard link*. You can break these links to replace or edit audio and video independently. In a later lesson, you'll temporarily override linked clips instead of breaking the link (see "Creating a split edit" on page 252).

When you add a clip containing video and audio to the program, and you've specified adding both the video and audio portions, the video portion appears in a video track and the audio portion appears in an audio track. The video and audio portions of the clip are *linked* so that when you drag the video portion in the Timeline window, the linked audio moves with it. If you split the clip, the video and audio are still linked within the two resulting clips. Video can only be linked to audio—a video clip cannot be linked to another video clip.

In many situations it is useful to link or unlink clips manually. For example, you might want to move previously unlinked audio or video clips together, or edit the In or Out point of the video or audio portion of a clip independently. You don't have to unlink clips if you only want to delete one clip or the other.

You'll start by assembling the first two video clips of the project.

1 Choose Window > Window Options > Timeline Window Options. Select the medium-sized icon for the Icon Size and then click OK.

2 Click and hold down the Timeline menu button—the small black triangle in the upper right corner of the Timeline window—and deselect Sync Selection if it is selected.

3 In the Project window, click Bin 1 and drag Door.mov into the Video 1 track, placing it at the starting point of the Timeline. Here, you have placed the clip in the Video 1 track because later you will be overlaying clips in the Video 2 track.

When you place a clip in the Video 1 lower track, the audio portion of the clip is automatically placed in the Audio 1 track. Notice that as you move the video clip in the Timeline, the audio portion moves with it.

4 Drag Hall1.mov from the Project window into the Video 1 track, placing it so that it snaps to the end of Door.mov.

Let's take a look at what you've assembled so far.

5 Make the work area bar cover all contiguous clips by pressing Alt (Windows) or Option (Mac OS) as you click the work area bar. Then press Enter (Windows) or Return (Mac OS).

The audio plays along with the video. Because the audio in Hall1.mov was recorded further from the door than the audio in Door.mov, it is difficult to hear the door being opened. Instead, you'll delete the Hall1.mov audio and let the audio from Door.mov extend into this clip.

6 Click the audio portion of Hall1.mov to select it.

7 Press the Delete key on your keyboard to delete the audio.

The Door.mov clip you added to the Timeline window contains linked audio and video. In this lesson, you will unlink the audio and video to edit them separately.

8 Do one of the following:

• Choose Timeline > Sync Selection. Then select either the video or the audio portion of the Door.mov clip and choose Clip > Unlink Audio and Video. A white marker is added to the Door.mov audio clip and to the Door.mov video clip. If you wish to realign these clips after they are moved independently, drag the Door.mov audio clip's marker to the Door.mov video clip's marker or vice versa.

• Select the link/unlink tool (). Click the Door.mov video clip and then click the Door.mov audio clip to unlink the video and audio.

Because the video and audio portions of the Door.mov clip are no longer linked, they can be moved and trimmed separately.

For more information, see "Linking video and audio clips in the Timeline," in Chapter 3 of the *Adobe Premiere 6.0 User Guide*.

Trimming the video

Next, you'll trim the first clip so that the action matches that in the Hall1.mov that follows it. This will also permit you to extend the audio from Door.mov into the second clip.

1 In the Monitor window, drag the shuttle slider underneath the Program view to find the frame in Door.mov just before the man's coat starts to obscure the door knob (at 2:03).

2 In the Timeline window, select the ripple edit tool.

3 In the Timeline window, position the pointer on the end of the Door.mov video clip. The pointer turns into the ripple edit tool.

4 Trim the video portion by dragging it to the left until it snaps to the edit line.

You have just completed an L-cut, in which the audio from one clip extends into the following clip.

5 Select the selection tool (➤) to deselect the ripple edit tool.

Now you'll add a new video clip.

6 Drag the Feet1.mov clip from Bin 1 of the Project window into the Timeline window, just to the right of the Hall1.mov clip in the Video 1 track.

7 Make the work area bar cover all contiguous clips by pressing Alt (Windows) or Option (Mac OS) as you click the work area bar. Then press Enter (Windows) or Return (Mac OS) to preview the video.

8 Save the project by choosing File > Save.

Using markers to synchronize clips

When working with audio clips that are not linked to video, you'll occasionally encounter situations where you need to synchronize the audio to the video clip. In this part of the lesson, you'll cut together two clips of a man walking, filmed from different angles. One clip doesn't have audio, so you need to position it so that the footsteps in it match the sound of footsteps in the audio portion of the other walking clip. The most straight-forward method of synchronizing these clips is to insert markers at matching events in both clips.

Using markers

Markers indicate important points in time and help you position and arrange clips. The Timeline and each clip can individually contain its own set of up to ten markers numbered from 0 to 9 and up to 999 unnumbered markers. Markers are only for reference and do not alter the video program (except for markers set up as Web links).

In general, add a marker to a clip in Source view or the Clip window for important points within an individual clip; the added marker and any existing markers in the master clip are included with the clip when you add it to the Timeline or create a duplicate clip. Add a marker to the Timeline or the Program view for significant time points that affect multiple clips, such as when you need to synchronize video and audio on different clips; the added marker appears in both the Timeline and in the Program view, but is not added to any master clips. Timeline markers can also include a comment, a Web link, or a chapter link.

——From the Adobe Premiere User Guide, Chapter 3

You'll start by marking a footstep in the clip that will be overlaid.

1 Double-click the Feet2.mov clip in the Project window to display it in the Source view in the Monitor window.

2 Play the clip by clicking the Play button (▶).

3 Drag the shuttle slider under the Source view to locate the first footstep of the man's right foot at approximately 1:04. Find the first frame in which the right heel makes contact with the floor.

Now you'll mark this position. Premiere lets you use numbered or unnumbered markers. Numbered markers are convenient because they let you quickly jump to the marker by pressing Control (Windows) or Command (Mac OS) followed by the marker number. Each clip can have up to ten numbered markers.

4 Mark this point in the clip by selecting Clip > Set Clip Marker > 0. The marker appears at the top of the image in the Source view.

Note: You can also set a clip marker by clicking the Marker button (⌂) at the bottom of the Monitor window.

Now you'll insert a marker into the Timeline, using the Program view of the Feet1.mov clip as a guide.

💡 *To quickly locate or synchronize sounds in an audio clip, view the clip as a waveform. Simply expand the audio track by clicking the arrow to the left of the track label. Sounds are visible as pulses in the waveform displayed at the bottom of the audio track.*

5 Drag the shuttle slider below the Program view until the Source and Program views display the same moment in the action from a different camera angle (at approximately 14:11 below the Program view). In the Program view, click the Frame Forward (▶) and Frame Back (◀) buttons to find the frame in which the right heel contacts the floor. (You can also use the left and right arrow keys on your keyboard.)

6 Mark this point in the Timeline by selecting Timeline > Set Timeline Marker > 0.

A marker appears in the Timeline at the edit line and on the clip in the Program view. It doesn't matter what number you choose from the Set Marker menu as long as you haven't already used that number in the same clip. Choosing a marker number previously used in the same clip moves that marker to the current frame.

Note: To insert markers while a clip or the Timeline plays, play the clip and press the asterisk key (*) on the numeric keypad, whenever you want to insert a marker. You can also insert a numbered marker by pressing its keyboard shortcut as a clip or the Timeline plays.

Now you can synchronize the two clips by lining up the markers. You'll do this by placing the Feet2.mov clip in the Video 2 track. Any video in the upper tracks covers or hides video in the lower tracks, except when a higher track has a Transparency setting. Here, you'll place a clip in the Video 2 track to cover a portion of the video in the Video 1 track. (Because the overlaid clip has no sound, the underlying audio is unaffected.) The result is similar to that of using the Overlay button. An advantage of this method is that it is easier to locate and position your overlaid clips.

7 In the lower left corner of the Timeline window, choose 1 Second from the Time Zoom Level pop-up menu.

8 Drag the Feet2.mov clip from the Source view into the Video 2 track of the Timeline.

9 Position the pointer over the marker in the Feet2.mov clip and drag the clip so that the marker in the clip snaps to the edit line, which is on the other marker in the Timeline.

```
Timeline
▶ ◀ ◆ ◉
🖑 🔍 ✂ ↕           W:00:15:00        0:00:19:00
◉  ▷ Video 2              FEET2.MOV
◉  ▷ Video 1 ⊒    FEET1.MOV
◀)) ▷ Audio 1    FEET1.MOV
◀)) ▷ Audio 2
1 Second         ◆ ▦ ▥ ▦ ▤ ◉
```

10 Press Enter (Windows) or Return (Mac OS) to preview your work.

The footsteps in the Feet2.mov clip should match the audio track of the Feet1.mov clip. If your markers were not placed correctly, however, the video and the audio may be slightly out of sync. You can easily correct this.

11 If the sound of the footstep occurs before or after the heel contacts the floor, move the Feet2.mov clip slightly one way or the other and preview it again.

To move a clip in the Timeline one frame at a time, click the clip to select it, and then press the left or right arrow key on your keyboard to move the clip in the desired direction. Each time you press an arrow key, the clip moves one frame.

12 When you're satisfied that the clip is in sync with the audio, save the project.

To jump to a numbered marker, press and hold down Control (Windows) or Command (Mac OS), and then press the number key that corresponds to the marker number.

Overlaying video without sound

Now that you have positioned and synchronized the second walking clip to the audio, you'll overlay additional clips that don't need to be synchronized and that don't have audio linked to them. As before, you'll place clips in the Video 2 track. The audio from Feet1.mov will continue to play underneath.

1 Set the edit line in the Timeline window to the Out point of Feet2.mov (at approximately 16:02 in the Program view).

2 In the Project window, hold down the Control key (Windows) or the Command key (Mac OS) and click Hall2.mov, Man.mov, Woman1.mov, and Woman2.mov, to select them all. Then drag them to the Source view in the Monitor window.

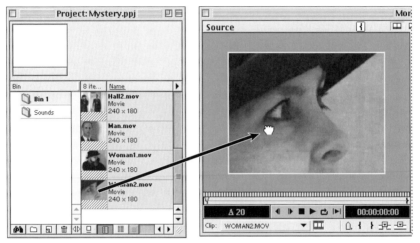

When making a selection in the Project window, click the Poster Frame image for the clip you want.

💡 *A clip in the Timeline can include the clip name, but it may not be displayed if the clip is too short or if you select the track format that does not include a name. To see the name of a clip in the Timeline, click the Timeline title bar to activate it, if necessary, and then simply position the pointer on the clip.*

3 From the Clip menu below the Source view, select Woman1.mov.

The Woman1.mov clip appears in the Source view.

4 Click the Play button (▶) to preview the clip.

5 Drag the Timeline scroll bar to display the center of the Feet2.mov clip.

6 In the lower left corner of the Timeline window, choose 1/2 Second from the Time Zoom Level pop-up menu.

7 Drag the Woman1.mov clip from the Source view into the Video 2 track, so that it ends at the beginning of the Feet2.mov clip you inserted earlier.

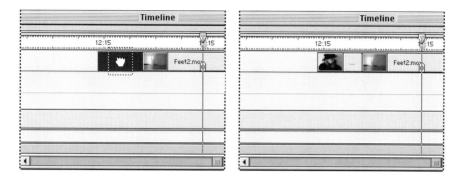

8 From the Clip menu below the Source view in the Monitor window, select Woman2.mov, and then click the Play button to preview it.

9 Drag the Woman2.mov clip from the Source view into the Video 2 track, positioning it at the end of the Feet2.mov clip.

You now have three clips covering part of Feet1.mov. At this point, you want to let some of Feet1.mov "show through," so you'll place the next clip so that it starts a few seconds after the end of Woman2.mov.

10 From the Clip menu below the Source view in the Monitor window, select Hall2.mov, and then click the Play button to preview it.

11 Drag the edit line in the Timeline to 19:00.

12 Drag the Hall2.mov clip into the Video 2 track so that its In point snaps to the edit line.

```
┌─────────────────────────────── Timeline ─────────────────────────┐
│  □                                                          [日][目] │
│  [▶][⊡][◆][✎]                                                   ▶  │
│  [✋][Q][✂][↕] 0        0:00:14 0       0:00:18:00 ▽      0:00:22:00 │
│  👁  ▷ Video 2        [🖼️🖼️]△FEET2.MOV              [🖼️]         │
│                              0                                     │
│  👁  ▷ Video 1  ⊐                    FEET1.MOV           [🖼️]      │
│  ◀)  ▷ Audio 1                       FEET1.MOV          〜〜〜    │
│  ◀)  ▷ Audio 2                                                    │
└───────────────────────────────────────────────────────────────────┘
```

You can now insert the last clip of the video.

13 Select Man.mov from the Clip menu below the Source view, and then preview it.

14 Drag the Man.mov clip into the Video 2 track at the end of the Hall2.mov clip.

```
┌─────────────────────────────── Timeline ─────────────────────────┐
│  □                                                          [日][目] │
│  [▶][⊡][◆][✎]                                                   ▶  │
│  [✋][Q][✂][↕] 0        0:00:14 0       0:00:18:00 ▽      0:00:22:00 │
│  👁  ▷ Video 2        [🖼️🖼️]△FEET2.MOV              [🖼️🖼️]    ▲ │
│                              0                                   ▼ │
│  👁  ▷ Video 1  ⊐                    FEET1.MOV           [🖼️]      │
│  ◀)  ▷ Audio 1                       FEET1.MOV          〜〜〜    │
│  ◀)  ▷ Audio 2                                                    │
└───────────────────────────────────────────────────────────────────┘
```

Now let's look at a preview of the entire project.

15 Make the work area bar cover all contiguous clips by pressing Alt (Windows) or Option (Mac OS) as you click the work area bar. Then press Enter (Windows) or Return (Mac OS).

16 Save the project.

Adding audio clips

In addition to the synchronous audio that is recorded when you shoot your video, you can also import and add audio-only files. These files might include narration, music, or sound effects that you've recorded or purchased from a music library. In this part of the lesson, you'll add some audio clips containing music and effects. The audio clips you'll be using are in the Sounds Bin.

Earlier in this lesson you saw that adding clips to the Video 2 track obscured the video clips beneath it in the Video 1 track. However, when you add audio to different tracks, the result is different. Rather than covering the audio beneath it, audio on all tracks is mixed so that you can hear all audio tracks together.

1 In the lower left corner of the Timeline window, choose 1 Second from the Time Zoom Level pop-up menu.

The first sound you'll add is an effect to set the mood for this spot.

2 In the Project window, click the Sounds Bin.

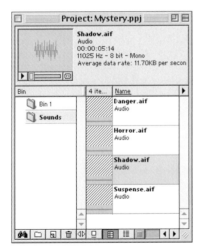

3 Double-click Shadow.aif.

The clip opens in the Source view in the Monitors window, represented by an icon.

4 To play the audio clip, click the Play button (▶).

5 Select Shadow.aif from the Sounds Bin and drag it into the Audio 2 track, positioning it at the beginning of the Timeline window.

6 Resize the work area bar so that it spans the duration of the Shadow.aif audio clip, and then press Enter (Windows) or Return (Mac OS).

The audio from the first video clip is mixed with the audio clip you just inserted.

The next audio clip you'll add will be a sound effect. You'll position it slightly before the man turns, as if he is turning in response to this sound.

7 Drag the edit line in the Timeline to a point several frames before the man starts to turn to his right in the Feet1.mov clip (at roughly 10:20).

8 Click to select Danger.aif from the Sounds Bin.

9 Drag Danger.aif from the Sounds Bin into the Audio 2 track so that it is approximately centered on the edit line of the Timeline.

Because the time interval between the effect and the man turning is critical to making the man's reaction look natural, you'll now fine-tune the sound's position.

10 Click the arrow next to the Audio 2 track to expand it. This lets you see the sound displayed as a waveform.

11 Drag the top portion of Danger.aif so that most of the noise (represented by the large pulse in the waveform) comes before the edit line, just before the man turns.

12 To preview your work, drag the work area bar so that it extends from the start of the Timeline to beyond the end of the audio clip you just inserted. Then press Enter (Windows) or Return (Mac OS).

If the man appears to be turning too soon before or too long after he hears the sound, you may want to reposition the audio clip slightly.

13 To simplify the Timeline, click the arrow next to Audio 2 track to collapse it.

Now you'll add the last two audio effects clips by placing them in the Audio 3 track. If necessary, you could add additional audio tracks (up to 99 total), but you won't need to do that for this project.

14 Drag the edit line in the Timeline so it is at the start of the Feet1.mov clip.

15 Select Suspense.aif from the Sounds Bin and drag it into the Audio 3 track, so that it is positioned at the edit line of the Timeline.

16 Select Horror.aif from the Sounds Bin and drag it into the Audio 3 track, so that its In point snaps to the Out point of the Suspense.aif clip.

17 In the Timeline window, click the Time Zoom Level pop-up menu and choose 2 Seconds.

Because you want all audio to end at the end of the last video clip, you'll need to trim the Horror.aif audio clip.

18   Move the edit line to the End point of the Man.mov clip in the Video 2 track.

19   Move the pointer to the end of the Horror.aif clip, and then drag to trim until it snaps to align with the edit line at the end of the Man.mov clip.

20   Save the project.

21   Preview your work to see and hear the suspense movie you've created. Make sure the yellow work area bar in the Timeline covers the entire video program, and then press Enter (Windows) or Return (Mac OS).

Getting to know the Audio workspace

In Adobe Premiere 6.0, you can edit, add effects, and mix up to 99 tracks of audio, and there are several ways to process an audio clip. You can control volume and pan/balance settings of audio tracks directly within the Timeline, or use the Audio Mixer window to make changes in real time.

You can select the Audio workspace at almost any time while working on a project. The Audio workspace uses your current workspace (Single-Track Editing) with the following adjustments: the Audio Mixer is open, and no palettes are displayed.You customize the audio workspace by rearranging the windows and changing their settings. Saving a workspace preserves the locations of the Project, Monitor, Timeline, and Audio Mixer windows.

Let's begin by opening the Audio workspace.

1 Choose Window > Workspace > Audio. The Audio Mixer window appears, along with the Project, Monitor, and Timeline windows.

Note: *If the Audio Mixer window is ever closed or hidden, you can choose Window > Audio Mixer to display it again.*

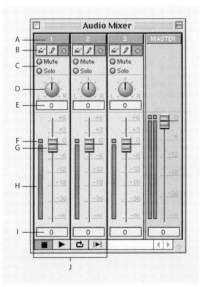

A. Audio track number B. Automation buttons
C. Mute/Solo buttons D. Pan/Balance control
E. Pan/Balance indicator/entry field
F. Clipping indicator G. Volume fader control
H. VU meter I. dB level indicator/entry field
J. Transport controls

The Audio Mixer window, like a professional, sound studio-style audio mixing console, contains a set of controls for each audio track, numbered according to the corresponding audio track in the Timeline.

In addition, in the Audio Mixer window, you can adjust the volume level and pan/balance of multiple audio tracks while listening to them and viewing the video tracks. Premiere uses automation to record these adjustments and then to apply them as the clip plays back. You'll learn more about automating the mixing process later in this lesson.

Now, adjust the volume level with the Volume Fader in the Audio Mixer window.

2 In the Timeline window, click the triangle to the left of the Audio 3 track to expand it.

3 In the Audio Mixer window, locate the Audio 3 mixer track, which corresponds to the the Audio 3 track in the Timeline window.

4 Do one of the following:

• Using the mouse, drag the volume fader up to increase volume level.

• Set a level by typing a decibels (dB) value from +6 to –95 in the box displayed directly below the volume fader.

Note: Audio level is represented graphically by a segmented VU meter to the left of the volume fader. The small indicator at the top of the VU meter turns red when the level is high enough to cause clipping, or distortion. To avoid clipping, adjust the volume so that the VU meter to the left of the volume fader does not display red.

Let's now adjust the gain uniformly throughout a clip.

Setting the gain is useful to balance the gain levels of several clips or to adjust a clip's audio signal when it is too high or too low.

5 In the Timeline window, select the Suspense.aif audio clip in the Audio 3 track.

6 Choose Clip > Audio Options > Audio Gain.

7 Do one of the following:

• Type a Gain value. A value above 100% amplifies the clip. A value below 100% *attenuates* the clip, making it quieter.

• Click Smart Gain to have Premiere set an automatic maximum gain value, up to 200%. This value represents the percentage of amplification necessary to boost the loudest part of the clip to full strength (the loudest sound your system can reproduce).

8 Click OK.

By default, the Audio Mixer window displays both the audio tracks and the master fader. At any point, you can modify the Audio Mixer window so that you see only the audio tracks or only the master fader, or both.

9 Right-double-click (Windows) or Control-double-click (Mac OS) the title bar of the Audio Mixer window to open the Audio Mixer Window Options dialog box, and do one of the following:

• To display the audio tracks without the master fader, choose Audio Tracks Only.

• To display the master fader without the audio tracks, choose Master Fader Only.

• To display both the audio tracks and the master fader together, choose Audio Tracks and Master Fader.

Adjusting audio levels in the Timeline

When you expand the Audio track in the Timeline, you'll notice that an audio clip is represented by a waveform. Running through the center of the waveform is a red line, called the *red volume rubberband*, which allows you to adjust the volume level of a clip at any point. Clicking on the red line creates a small red square, called a *handle*, on the rubberband, which breaks the rubberband into separate segments. The volume for a segment can be adjusted separately.

A handle is included at the beginning and ending of a *rubberband segment*, and you can drag the handle up or down to change the audio level. All audio clips include two handles that you can't remove—one at the beginning of the clip, and another at the end.

You can also *cross-fade* two audio clips automatically so that one fades out as another fades in. The rubberband in the Timeline corresponds to the volume fader in the Audio Mixer window, and serves the same purpose. To create fades in the Timeline, you visually adjust levels. For each track in the Timeline, there is one volume rubberband per clip.

First, let's fade out the end of the audio track linked to the Feet1.mov video clip.

1 In the Timeline window, click the triangle to the left of the Audio 1 track to expand it and locate the Feet1.mov audio clip.

2 In the lower left corner of the Timeline window, click the Time Zoom Level pop-up menu and choose 8 Frames.

3 If the red volume rubberband is not displayed in the clip, click the red Volume Rubberband icon (▰) in the Audio 1 track.

4 With the selection tool selected, position the pointer over a part of the red volume rubberband at a point that corresponds to the middle of the Hall2.mov video clip to create a new handle. The pointer changes to a pointing finger with red plus and minus signs.

5 Click the red line to create a handle and a small red square appears.

6 Position the pointer over the handle at the end of the Feet1.mov audio clip.

7 Press and hold down the Shift key, as you drag the volume handle down as far as it will go. A numeric display appears next to the pointing finger indicating the current volume level. As long as you continue to hold the Shift key, you can drag the handle outside of the audio track in order to obtain the necessary volume level, which in this case is 0%.

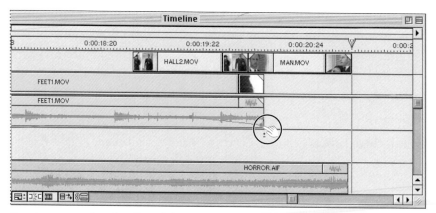

Creating a new volume handle and the result of dragging it down to decrease volume

You've just created a downward slope at the end of the Feet1.mov audio clip. A downward slope fades out the audio. Because you dragged the handle as far down as possible, the audio fades out to no sound at all.

Note: *If you activate the Info palette before you drag, you can watch the volume level update in the Info palette as you drag.*

The audio in the Horror.aif clip starts too abruptly. You will increase the volume at the end of the Horror.aif clip to build suspense. To make these changes, you'll fade in the audio by creating two separate handles.

8 Click the Horror.aif clip in the Audio 3 track to select it.

9 Click the red line of the volume rubberband about 1/2 second from the In point.

10 Press and hold down the Shift key, as you drag the handle at the In point all the way down. You may need to drag the handle below the Audio 3 track in order for the numeric display to read 0%.

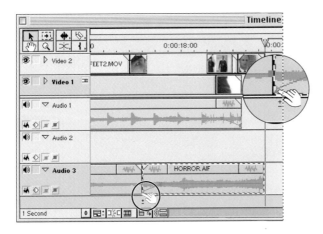

You've just created an upward slope at the beginning of the Horror.aif clip that fades in the audio. Now let's slowly raise the volume.

11 Position the pointer over a part of the red volume rubberband in Horror.aif at a point that corresponds to the handle you created in the Feet1.mov audio clip in the Audio 1 track. The pointer changes to a pointing finger with red plus and minus signs.

12 Click the red line in the Horror.aif clip to create a new handle.

13 Click the handle at the Out point of the Horror.aif audio clip. Press and hold the Shift key, as you drag the volume handle up as far as possible. You may need to drag the handle above the Audio 3 track, until the numeric display next to the pointing finger reads 200%.

The volume in this audio clip will now fade in to full-level, maintain that level for about two seconds, and then slowly rise to an even higher level at the end of the clip.

Let's preview this.

14 Make sure the yellow work area bar covers the entire video program, and then press Enter (Windows) or Return (Mac OS).

As the video plays, you can see the changes in the volume level reflected in the Audio Mixer window.

In about the middle of the piece, you may have noticed that the man calls out a name, but the volume is too low for it to be heard clearly. You'll need to boost just that portion of the audio clip by creating two sets of two handles and then adjusting them.

15 In the lower left corner of the Timeline window, click the Time Zoom Level pop-up menu and choose 4 Frames.

16 In the Audio 1 track of the Timeline window, position the edit line to locate the pulse that forms the word "Marilyn" in the audio portion of the Feet1.mov clip at 11:12. With the selection tool, create a new handle at the edit line in the audio portion of the Feet1.mov clip, by clicking on the red line in the Feet1.mov audio clip.

17 Position the edit line at 12:03 and click the red line in the Feet1.mov audio clip to create a second new handle.

18 Position the selection tool just to the right of the 11:12 handle. Click and drag upward to create and move the handle in one step.

Timeline

Video 2

Video 1 — FEET1.MOV

Audio 1 — FEET1.MOV

Audio 2

Audio 3 — SUSPENSE.AIF

4 Frames

19 Position the selection tool just to the left of the 12:03 handle and drag upward to create and move the handle in one step.

Timeline

11:06   0:00:11:22   0:00:12:

FEET1.MOV

FEET1.MOV

SUSPENSE.AIF

You can achieve the same action by using the fade scissors tool (✂). Click the volume rubberband at the 11:12 and 12:03 points. This creates two handles side-by-side. Select the selection tool (▸). Drag upward on each of the two inner handles that the fade scissors tool created while positioning to the left or the right.

Check the sound level by playing this part of the project.

20 Make sure the work area bar covers the area of the clip you just changed, and then press Enter (Windows) or Return (Mac OS).

The sound effect we added before the man turns is a little too loud. You'll use a technique to adjust the volume in two handles simultaneously.

21 If the Audio 2 track is collapsed, click the triangle to the left of the Audio 2 track label to expand it. Locate Danger.aif in the Audio 2 track.

22 Select the fade adjustment tool (‡).

23 Position the fade adjustment tool between the two handles in the Danger.aif clip. Press and hold down the Shift key, as you drag the segment downward until the volume display indicator reads about –5 db.

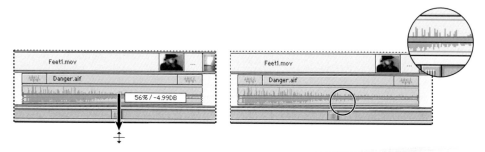

The entire segment moves, adjusting its volume.

The red volume rubberband in the Timeline corresponds to the volume fader in the Audio Mixer window, and serves the same purpose. To create fades in the Timeline, you visually adjust levels. For each track in the Timeline, there is one volume rubberband per clip.

Finally, let's *cross-fade* two audio clips automatically so that one fades out as another fades in.

24 If necessary, click the triangle to the left of the Audio 2 track and the Audio 3 track to expand the audio tracks.

25 Make sure to choose two audio clips that overlap and are staggered in the Timeline, such that one clip ends later than the other. For example, choose Shadow.aif in the Audio 2 track and Suspense.aif in the Audio 3 track. Two clips cannot overlap on the same track, so earlier in this lesson, you were instructed to place audio clips that overlap in time on different audio tracks.

26 Select the cross-fade tool (✕).

27 Click the clip you want to fade in.

28 Click the clip you want to fade out. Premiere automatically creates and adjusts volume handles on both clips.

Note: When creating a cross-fade, the clip that is selected first will fade in. The second clip selected will fade out.

29 To preview the project, make sure the yellow work area bar covers all your clips. Then press Enter (Windows) or Return (Mac OS).

30 Save the project.

Automating the mixing process

In the Audio Mixer window, you can adjust the volume level and pan/balance of multiple audio tracks while listening to them and viewing the video tracks. Premiere uses automation to record these adjustments and then to apply them as the clip plays back. You can start and stop recording automation changes at any point in the audio track using the transport controls at the bottom of the Audio Mixer window.

For each audio track, three buttons determine the automation state during the mixing process:

Automation Write (✎) Reads the stored level and pan/balance data for an audio track and records any adjustments you make to these settings using the volume and pan/balance controls in the Audio Mixer window. These adjustments are stored as new handles on the Volume and Pan/balance rubberbands in each clip in the Timeline track. In Automation Write mode, the function of the track controls is determined by the Automation Write Options selections in the Audio Mixer Window Options dialog box.

Automation Read ( ) Reads the stored volume and pan/balance data and uses it to control the audio level of the track during playback.

Automation Off (⊘) Ignores the stored volume and pan/balance data during playback. Automation Off is the default mode for Premiere, allowing real-time use of the mixer controls without interference from the rubberbands in the Timeline.

First, let's specify which tracks are monitored during playback in the Audio Mixer window.

1 In the Audio Mixer window, select Solo on the Audio 1 and Audio 2 tracks to monitor those tracks.

2 In the Audio Mixer window, select Mute on the Audio 3 track to silence the Audio 3 track, if it is not muted already.

Note: *If neither button is selected on any track, then all the tracks will be audible.*

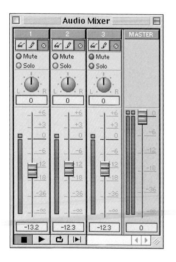

Next, let's *gang* the audio tracks so you can adjust the volume for more than one track at a time.

3 To gang the Audio 1 and Audio 2 tracks click and press down the Audio 1 volume fader and right-click (Windows) or Control-click (Mac OS).

4 Choose a gang number from the context menu.

5 Repeat this process for the Audio 2 volume fader, assigning each the same gang number.

6 In the upper portion of the Audio 1 and Audio 2 panels, click the Automation Write button ( ) for the Audio 1 and Audio 2 tracks.

7 Choose Window > Window Options > Audio Mixer Window Options

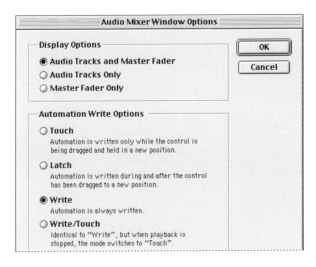

8 Set your Automation Options to Write to modify the stored volume level and pan/balance data based on the current position of the audio track controls and click OK. As you adjust a volume fader on any one of the ganged tracks, the change is applied to all ganged tracks.

Note: *To ungang the audio tracks, right-click (Windows) or Control-click (Mac OS) each ganged volume fader and choose No Gang. You can also temporarily override the ganging by holding the Shift key while dragging the volume fader.*

Now, let's adjust audio levels in the Audio Mixer window using automation.

9 Drag the edit line to the point where you want to start recording automation changes.

10 If the Audio Mixer window is not open choose Window > Audio Mixer.

11 In the Audio Mixer window, locate the Audio 1 mixer track which corresponds to the Audio 1 track in the Timeline window.

Note: *Because we have previously ganged the Audio 1 and Audio 2 tracks, we make volume changes to both of these tracks at once. However, you cannot operate each volume fader independently.*

12 If it is not already selected, click the Automation Write button (∅) at the top of the Audio 1 mixer track.

13 Click the Play button (▶) in the Audio Mixer window to start recording. You can also click the Loop button (↻) to play the program in a continuous loop or click the Play In to Out button (⏮) to play from the In point to the Out point.

14 In the Audio 1 track of the Audio Mixer window, drag the volume fader up to increase the volume level or down to decrease the volume level.

15 To stop recording, click the Stop button (■).

16 To prevent accidently overwriting automation that has already been applied, you must click the Auto Read button (☞) for the track you just recorded.

17 To preview your volume changes, drag the edit line in the Timeline window to the beginning of your changes and press Enter (Windows) or Return (Mac OS).

18 Once the adjustments have been applied, fine-tune your changes directly in the Timeline by dragging the handles on the volume rubberbands in each clip. In order to see the volume rubberbands, click the triangle to the left of the Audio track to expand it.

Now let's pan a monophonic clip or balance a stereo clip in the Audio Mixer window using automation. You'll need to change the project settings from mono to stereo.

19 Choose Project > Project Settings > Audio. In the Format field, choose 8Bit-Stereo and click OK.

20 In the Timeline window, click the triangle to the left of the Audio 1 track to expand it.

21 Drag the edit line to the point where you want to start recording automation changes.

22 Click the Auto Write button (∅) in the Audio 1 mixer channel.

23 Select an option from the Automation Write Options section.

24 Click the Play button (▶) in the Audio Mixer window to start recording.

25 Click the pan control and drag outside it, and then drag clockwise to pan or balance right, or counterclockwise to pan or balance left. Dragging outside the pan control gives you greater precision in adjusting it.

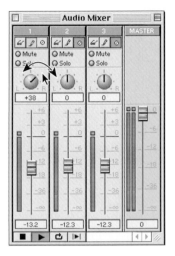

26 To stop recording, click the Stop button (■).

27 To preview your changes, choose the Auto Read button (⚟) to prevent accidentally overwriting applied automation, drag the edit line to the beginning of your changes, and click the Play button (▶).

28 Save the project.

Exporting the movie

You've finished editing, but your video program is still composed of several video and audio files and a Premiere project file. In order to distribute it as a single file, you need to export it to a movie file.

1 Choose File > Export Timeline > Movie.

2 In the Export Movie dialog box, click the Settings button. Make sure QuickTime is selected for the File Type and Entire Project is selected for the Range. Also make sure that the Export Video and Export Audio are selected. The default values for other settings, including those for compression, are fine for this project.

Use the Save and Load buttons in the Export Movie Settings dialog box to save and later quickly load export settings that you use frequently. Loading saved settings is particularly useful when you create several types of video files (for example, NTSC and Web video) from the same project.

3 Click OK to close the Export Movie Settings dialog box.

4 In the Export Movie dialog box, specify the 05Lesson folder for the location and type **Mystery.mov** for the name of the video program. Click Save.

Premiere starts making the movie, displaying a status bar that provides an estimate for the amount of time it will take. When the movie is complete, it opens in its own window.

5 Click the Play button (▶) to play the movie you've just created.

Exploring on your own

Feel free to experiment with the project you have just created. Here are some suggestions:

• See the "Understanding nonlinear volume changes" section in Chapter 5, "Mixing Audio," in the *Adobe Premiere 6.0 User Guide* and experiment with making nonlinear and linear volume changes.

• See the "Stereo channel" sections in Chapter 5, "Mixing Audio," in the *Adobe Premiere 6.0 User Guide* and experiment with muting one channel of a stereo clip or swapping stereo channels in the Timeline window.

Review questions

1 What major advantage does a numbered marker have over an unnumbered marker?

2 What are the two different ways to fade audio in Premiere 6.0?

3 What must you do to see the waveform of an audio clip?

4 Which command might you need to use before editing a video clip containing linked sound?

Answers

1 You can jump to a numbered marker by pressing and holding down Control (Windows) or Command (Mac OS) while pressing the number key that corresponds to the marker number.

2 You can fade audio by:

• Creating new handles by clicking the red Volume Rubberband icon in the track header and positioning the pointer over a part of the red volume rubberband. Click to create a new rubberband segment and then drag the volume handle up or down.

• Using the cross-fade tool (✳) to cross-fade two audio clips automatically so that one fades out as another fades in.

3 You must expand the track by clicking the arrow to the left of the audio track name.

4 Choose Clip > Unlink Audio and Video or select the link/unlink tool (▦) to unlink a video clip from an audio clip before editing the video clip.

Lesson 6

6 Additional Editing Techniques

Complex editing situations demand specialized tools. This lesson provides the tools and techniques you need to whip your projects into shape.

In this lesson, you'll fine-tune a segment for a documentary on glassblowing. In editing this segment, you'll learn the following techniques:

- Making three-point and four-point edits.
- Targeting video and audio tracks.
- Linking, unlinking, and synchronizing video and audio clips.
- Creating a split edit using the link override tool.
- Closing a gap with the Ripple Delete command.

Getting started

For this lesson you'll open an existing project with the clips roughly assembled in the Timeline. Make sure you know the location of the files used in this lesson. Insert the *Classroom in a Book* CD-ROM disk if necessary. For help, see "Copying the Classroom in a Book files" on page 14.

1 Restore the Adobe Premiere 6.0 default preferences as you have in previous lessons. Then, launch the Premiere 6.0 software and choose Single-Track Editing mode

2 In the Load Project Settings dialog box, choose Multimedia or Multimedia Quicktime (depending on your operating system), and click OK.

3 Choose Edit > Preferences > General and Still Image and deselect Open Movies in Clip Window if it is selected.

4 Double-click 06Lesson.ppj in the 06Lesson folder that you copied to your hard disk to open it in Premiere.

5 If necessary, rearrange windows and palettes so they don't overlap, by choosing Window > Workspace > Single-Track Editing.

6 When the project opens, choose File > Save As, open the appropriate lesson folder on your hard disk if necessary, type **Glass1.ppj**, and press Enter (Windows) or Return (Mac OS).

Viewing the finished movie

To see what you'll be creating, take a look at the complete movie.

1 Choose File > Open and double-click the 06Final.mov file in the Final folder, inside the 06Lesson folder.

The movie opens in the Source view in the Monitor window.

2 Click the Play button (▶) under the Source view in the Monitor window to view the movie.

Viewing the assembled project

Let's take a look at the project as it has been assembled so far. Because there are no transitions, filters, or other effects used in this project, you do not need to generate a preview to view the project.

1 Ensure the edit line is at the beginning of the Timeline. To move it to the beginning, click the Timeline window title bar and then press the Home key on your keyboard.

2 To view the project, click the Play button (▶) under the Program view in the Monitor window.

The project plays in the Program view. Although the assembled project looks much like the finished movie you viewed earlier, you may notice some small problems that could be solved by further editing. In this lesson, you'll use some editing tools that are especially useful in fine-tuning a project.

Much of this lesson deals with editing techniques that preserve the length or duration of a project or of a range of frames.

Understanding three-point and four-point editing

In some situations, you may want to replace a range of frames in the program with a range of frames from a source clip. In Premiere, you can do this using a three-point edit or a four-point edit; both are standard techniques in video editing.

In previous lessons, you have worked with *source In and Out points*—the first and last frames of a clip that will be added to the video program. In addition, it's important to understand *program In and Out points*—the location in your video program where you will apply some editing technique. Being able to specify In and Out points for both the source and the program gives you more control, so your edits are as precise as possible. You'll need to set source and program In and Out points for the three- and four-point editing exercises in this lesson.

Three-point editing Use three-point editing when at least one end point (In or Out) of the source material or the program material it replaces is not critical. The three-point edit is more common than the four-point edit because you set only three points and the ranges do not have to be the same duration. Premiere automatically trims the point you don't set so that the source and program material are the same length. This is called a three-point edit because you specify three points: any combination of In and Out points in the program material being replaced and in the source material being added.

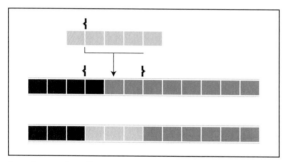

In a three-point edit, you set three points and Premiere sets the fourth point.

Four-point editing Use four-point editing when you want to replace a range of frames in the program with a range of frames of equal duration in the source. This is called a four-point edit because you specify all four points: the In and Out points both for the source material being added and for the program material being replaced.

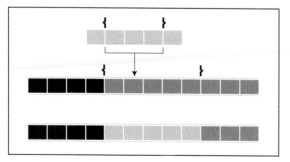

In a four-point edit, you set all four points. If source and target material have different lengths, you can tell Premiere to make the source material fit the target area (as shown above).

If the source material you've selected is not exactly the same duration as the material you're replacing, Premiere gives you one of two options for completing the replacement, depending on the situation: *fit to fill* or *trim source*. If you select Fit to Fill, the duration and speed of the source frames change to fit into the duration of the frames being replaced. If you select Trim Source, Premiere changes the Out point of the source frames, effectively making this a three-point edit instead of a four-point edit.

In the next exercise, you'll make a three-point edit.

Making a three-point edit

You'll use a three-point edit to overlay a scene with linked sound, Talk.mov, replacing parts of Shape.mov and Heat-1.mov in the program. As part of this edit, you'll also eliminate some unwanted camera movement at the beginning of Talk.mov. First, you'll open the source clip in the Source view and preview it.

1 In the Navigator palette, use the Zoom-out (⌃) button or the Zoom-in (⌃) button or use the Time Zoom Level pop-up menu to set the Time Zoom Level (in the Timeline window) to 1 Second.

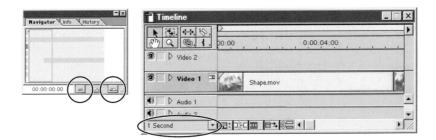

2 In the Project window, double-click Talk.mov, so it appears in the Source view in the Monitor window.

3 Preview a bit of the clip by clicking the Play button (▶). Notice the camera movement at the beginning of the clip.

You'll set the In point in Talk.mov to remove the camera movement.

4 In the Source view in the Monitor window, double-click the location timecode (the right set of green numbers), or click and drag to highlight all the digits, type **516**, and press Enter (Windows) or Return (Mac OS).

5 In the Source view in the Monitor window, click the In button (￤) to set the In point in Talk.mov.

Now you'll indicate where you want to place this clip in the program by setting the program In point within Shape.mov and the program Out point within Heat-1.mov.

6 In the Navigator palette, drag the green box all the way to the left so that the first two clips are visible in the Timeline.

7 Double-click the location timecode under the Program view to highlight it; if necessary, click in the Program view first. Type **625**, and press Enter/Return.

8 In the Program view in the Monitor window, click the In button (￤) to set the In point. An In icon appears in the Timeline time ruler, which may be obscured by the edit line, and the Program view shuttle bar.

9 Under the Program view, double-click the location timecode, type **1018**, and press Enter (Windows) or Return (Mac OS).

10 Click the Out button (￤) to set the Out point in the Program view. An Out icon appears in the Timeline time ruler and the Program view shuttle bar.

At this point, the duration timecode (Δ) in the Program view should read 3:23, which is the duration from program In point to program Out point in the Program view.

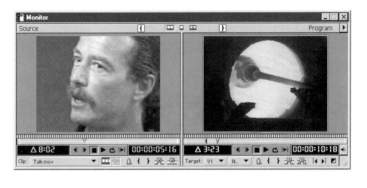

Whenever you add clips to the Timeline using the keyboard or Monitor window controls (as you're about to do), you need to tell Premiere which tracks you want to use. To do that, you'll use the targeting controls immediately below the Source view panel in the Monitor window. Because a sound file already exists in the Audio 1 track, you need to tell Premiere to put the Talk.mov audio in the Audio 2 track so as not to disturb Audio 1.

11 Under the Program view in the Monitor window, select A2 for Target, in the right side pop-up window.

Now that you have specified a source In point and program In and Out points (for a total of three points) and set the target tracks for your edits, you are ready to replace the program material with the source material.

12 In the Source view in the Monitor window, click the Overlay button (⬚).

The range of frames marked in Shape.mov and Heat-1.mov is replaced with an equal duration of Talk.mov.

Result of targeting Talk.mov audio to Audio Track 2

13 Save the project.

For more information about how to specify source and target tracks, see "Specifying source and target tracks" in Chapter 3 of the *Adobe Premiere 6.0 User Guide.*

Using the Toggle Shift Tracks Options

Premiere 6.0 allows you to control the manner in which clips are shifted along the Timeline, regardless of the Sync mode setting. It is useful to remember that Sync mode specifies which portion of a clip is edited, and the On Insert options specify which clips are shifted in response to an edit. The Toggle Shift Tracks Options button, located along the bottom of the Timeline window, allows you to specify whether a specific edit, such as a ripple edit, a rolling edit, or an insert shifts clips on all tracks or just the clips on the edited track. Click the Toggle Shift Tracks Options button (⬚) at the bottom of the Timeline window to alternate between these two options.

A. Shift Material in All Tracks
B. Shift Material Only in Target Tracks

Another way to set up the Toggle Shift Track Options is from the Timeline window menu.

1 In the top right of the Timeline window, hold down the menu button (small black triangle), and choose Timeline Window Options. The Timeline Window Options dialog box appears.

2 In the Options section, select one of the following in the On Insert field:

• Select *Shift Material in All Tracks* if you want all tracks to move when you insert a clip into the Timeline. All tracks are rippled in response to an edit.

• Select *Shift Material Only in Target Tracks* if you want only the target tracks to be moved when you insert a clip, which could offset the sync of linked clips, depending on which tracks were selected as target tracks.

3 Click OK.

Linking and unlinking clips

In Premiere, you can link a video clip to an audio clip, in order to move the two clips together. When you drag the video portion in the Timeline, the linked audio portion moves with it. Linked clips are easily identified, appearing in light green.

You can also override a link temporarily to edit linked clips without breaking the link. When you want to work with linked clips individually, you temporarily turn off synchronized behavior by using the Toggle Sync Mode button. When Sync mode is on, both clips of a linked pair behave as a single unit. In this mode, all Timeline tools act on both clips in a linked pair, and both clips are affected when you select, trim, split, delete, move, nudge, or change the duration or speed of either clip. When Sync mode is off, linked clips can be edited independently, as if they were not linked.

Sound recorded on a video camera can be captured and imported into a Premiere project already linked to its video clip. Breaking a link is useful when you want to replace linked audio. Or you may want to break a link to edit In or Out points independently. You used this technique in the previous lesson to create an L-cut, see "Creating an L-cut" on page 205.

In this exercise, you'll perform three separate tasks. First, you'll link a video clip with an audio clip. Then you'll resynchronize a pair of linked clips. Finally, you'll use the link override tool to create a *split edit*. As you may remember from Lesson 5, a split edit (also known as an L-cut or a 6-point edit) extends the audio only, from one clip into an adjacent clip. In this case, the audio will begin to play before the associated video appears.

Linking clips

You'll start by aligning an audio clip to a video clip, and then you'll link them. You want Music.aif to start at the beginning of Oven.mov.

💡 *To quickly display or hide open palettes, press the Tab key.*

1 Use the Zoom-out (⌃) button or the Zoom-in (⌃) button in the Navigator palette or the Time Zoom level pop-up menu to set the Time Zoom level (in the Timeline window) to 2 Seconds. Scroll to the beginning of the Timeline window.

2 In the Program view in the Monitor window, click the Next Edit button (▸ɪ) until the edit line moves to the beginning of Oven.mov.

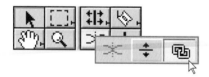

3 Drag Music.aif from the Project window into the Audio 2 track so that it snaps to the edit line, which is at the beginning of Oven.mov.

4 In the Timeline window, select the link/unlink tool (🔗).

5 Click Oven.mov and then click Music.aif with the link/unlink tool (🔗).

Oven.mov and Music.aif flash momentarily and then appear light green, indicating they are linked. In the next exercise, you'll see the effect of linking more clearly.

A shortcut to linking clips without selecting the link/unlink tool is to click one clip and then hold down the Shift key while clicking the other clip. This works only when the selection tool is selected.

Note: *To prevent unintentional edits, always deselect a tool (other than the selection tool) when you are finished using it. The easiest way to deselect a tool is to select the selection tool.*

6 In the Timeline, select the selection tool (▸).

The action in the clips you just linked takes place at the beginning of the process of making the glass platter, so let's reposition them.

You want to move the Oven.mov scene and its linked audio, Music.aif, to the beginning of the program.

7 In the Timeline, drag Oven.mov to the beginning of the project.

Music.aif is automatically added to the Audio 1 track when you move Oven.mov to the beginning of the Timeline.

During the shifting process, directional arrows will appear, indicating that Premiere will need to make space for Oven.mov linked to Music.aif in Audio 2.

Notice what happened: All of the video clips shifted to the right the length of the Oven.mov clip, leaving a gap the size of Oven.mov. Don't worry about the gap created by moving Oven.mov—you'll fix that later.

The results of shifting Oven.mov linked to Music.aif are gaps the size of Oven.mov; and Music.aif has shifted to the Audio 1 track from the Audio 2 track.

8 Save the project.

Handling unsynchronized linked clips

For video clips that have audio linked to them when they are imported into a project, Premiere stores sync information, and attempts to keep these clips synchronized.

In the Project window, for instance, observe that Talk.mov has its own audio track. When they are moved out of sync, both clips display a red triangle at the In point to indicate the out-of-sync condition.

When in the process of resyncing, clicking and holding the red triangle causes a box to appear at the In point of the out-of-sync clip. This box displays the amount of time the clip is out of sync with its accompanying video or audio clip.

In some situations, clips may be accidentally shifted out of sync during an edit. When this happens, it is an easy matter to resynchronize them.

In order to produce an out of sync condition, you'll unsync the video and audio portions of Talk.mov, which were linked together upon import into the Project window.

1 At the Timeline, select either the Talk.mov audio or video clip, and both will be selected because they are linked.

2 Choose Clip > Unlink Audio and Video. White markers appear in both the Talk.mov audio and video clips.

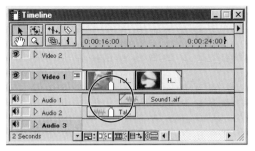

A white marker is added to each unlinked clip.

To double-check that the clips have been unlinked, click the selection tool ( ), then click the Talk.mov audio clip. Only the audio clip will be selected, because it has been unlinked from its video track.

3 Toggle the Sync Mode button to the Sync Off state.

A. *Toggle Sync button on state* **B.** *Toggle Sync button off state*

4 Move the Talk.mov audio clip to the left about half of its own length.

5 In the Timeline window, select the link/unlink tool ( ).

6 Click the Talk.mov video clip and then click the Talk.mov audio clip. The clips flash momentarily and red triangles appear at the In point of each clip indicating that Talk.mov audio and video are now out of sync.

Resynchronizing linked clips

To relink clips that were moved out of sync:

1 Click and hold the red triangle that appears at the In point of the Talk.mov audio clip. The cursor changes into a red pointer and a dialog box displays the amount of time you have moved it out of sync.

2 Drag inside the box and release the mouse.

The audio portion of Talk.mov moves back into sync with the video portion, and the red triangles disappear. To ensure video and audio are now in sync, you'll preview Talk.mov.

💡 *To set the start of the work area bar, press and hold Control + Shift (Windows) or Command + Shift (Mac OS) and then click just below the Timeline window title bar. To set the end of the work area bar, press and hold Control + Alt (Windows) or Command + Option (Mac OS) and then click the just below the Timeline window title bar.*

3 Resize the work area bar to span Talk.mov, and then press Enter (Windows) or Return (Mac OS) to preview it. You can see that the clips are in sync if you watch the man's lips as he speaks and listen to the audio clip.

The audio ends prematurely. That's because, in the lesson material provided, the Talk.mov clip was trimmed. You'll restore the clip's full audio in the next exercise.

4 Save the project.

Creating a split edit

In Lesson 5, "Adding Audio," you created a split edit, also known as an L-cut or a 6-point edit, by breaking the link between the video and audio clips. Here, you'll use a new technique to create a split edit, temporarily overriding a link using the Toggle Sync Mode button. In this split edit, you'll extend the audio both before and after the video clip to which the sound is synchronized.

1 Choose 4 Seconds from the Time Zoom Level pop-up menu in the Timeline window.

2 Make sure the Toggle Sync Mode button along the bottom of the Timeline window is set to turn off Sync mode. This will allow you to edit the audio clip independently of its linked video.

*Toggle Sync Mode button linking on (A) and
Toggle Sync Mode button linking off (B)*

3 In the Timeline, select the selection tool (↖).

4 Position the pointer over the left end of the audio portion of Talk.mov in the Audio 2 track, and extend the clip by dragging left as far as it will go.

5 Position the pointer over the right end of the audio portion of Talk.mov and extend the clip by dragging right as far as it will go.

6 In the Timeline, click the Toggle Sync Mode button again to restore Sync mode.

7 Save the project.

Closing a gap with the Ripple Delete command

Earlier in this lesson, you moved Oven.mov, leaving a gap in the video track between Heat-1.mov and Blow-2.mov. You'll use the Ripple Delete command to remove this gap. The Ripple Delete command eliminates the selected gap by moving all clips that are on the right of the gap. Unlike the ripple edit tool, you must select either a gap or one or more clips in the Timeline before choosing the Ripple Delete command.

It's important to understand that you can use the Ripple Delete command only on one or more clips or a gap—you cannot use it to delete a range of frames marked by In and Out points as you can with the Extract button (discussed in the next lesson). Also, the Ripple Delete command has no effect on clips in locked tracks.

Because the audio in Audio 1 and Audio 2 tracks extend into the portion of the program that will be affected by the Ripple Delete command, you need to lock these audio tracks to keep them from being affected. Locking a track prevents further changes until the track is unlocked.

1 Click the box next to the speaker icon on the far left of the Audio 1 track; the white lock icon changes to a black lock icon (🔒) to indicate that the track is now locked. Repeat for Audio 2 track.

2 In the Timeline, select the gap between Heat-1.mov and Blow-1.mov.

3 Choose Timeline > Ripple Delete.

Once the space is deleted, all clips on the track shift to close the gap; Blow-1.mov is moved left, next to Heat-1.mov.

Now, you'll close the gap on the Audio 1 track

4 Unlock the Audio 1 track by clicking on the lock icon on the far left to deselect it.

5 Lock the Video 1 track by clicking the box next to the speaker icon on the far left of the Video 1 track.

6 In the Timeline window, select the gap between the Music.aif and Sound1.aif clips in the Audio 1 track.

7 Choose Timeline > Ripple Delete. The space is deleted between the two audio clips.

8 Unlock the Video 1 track by clicking on the lock icon on the far left of the Video 1 track. Unlock the Audio 2 track.

In order to align the sound and video of your video program, you may need to move the Out point of Sound1.aif to the left if it extends past the final video clip in the Video 1 track.

9 Position the pointer over the right end of the Sound1.aif clip and drag left until it aligns with the Out point of Top.mov in the Video 1 track.

10 Alt-click (Windows) or Option-click (Mac OS) just below the Timeline title bar to extend the work area bar over all clips. Then press Enter (Windows) or Return (Mac OS) to preview your work.

11 Save the project.

Exporting the movie

Now that you've finished your editing, it's time to generate a movie file.

1 If you turned off audio previewing earlier in the lesson, make sure you turn it on again by clicking the icon at the left edge of each audio track so that it changes to the speaker icon (◀).

2 Choose File > Export Timeline > Movie.

3 In the Export Movie dialog box, click the Settings button. Make sure QuickTime is selected for the File Type and Entire Project is selected for the Range. Also make sure that Export Video and Export Audio are selected. The default values for other settings, including those for compression, are fine for this project.

4 Click OK to close the Export Movie Settings dialog box.

5 In the Export Movie dialog box, specify the 06Lesson folder for the location and type **Glass1.mov** for the name of the movie. Click Save (Windows) or OK (Mac OS).

Premiere starts making the movie, displaying a status bar that provides an estimate for the amount of time it will take. When the movie is complete, it opens in the Source view.

6 Click the Play button (▶) to play the movie you've just created.

Printing to video

When you want to print your finished movie to video tape, you use the Print to Video option. This option lets you display the movie at full screen on your computer monitor. If your movie is not in full screen resolution (640 x 480) you can zoom the movie to fill the screen, or you can display it at its smaller resolution with a black border.

1 In the Timeline window, drag the work area bar over the portion of the video program that you want to record and press Enter (Windows) or Return (Mac OS) to build a preview file.

2 Make sure that the video program preview plays to your deck or camera. If it does not, review the steps for preparing a digital video program for videotape recording in the documentation for your device.

3 Make sure that your video recording device is on and that the tape is cued to the point where you want to start recording.

4 Choose File > Export Timeline > Print to Video.

5 Enter 1 second for Color Bars, 1 second for Play Black, and then select Full Screen (Windows) or Zoom Screen (Mac OS).

Note: For the Play Black option, make sure that you enter a long enough time for the speed of the video recording device to stabilize before the video starts.

6 Click OK, and start the video recording device.

The movie plays at full screen on your computer or peripheral monitor. Because the movie created in this lesson is not full resolution (640 x 480), it appears pixelated or jagged.

7 Choose File > Export Timeline > Print to Video again and don't select Full Screen (Windows) or Zoom Screen (Mac OS). Now the movie plays in high resolution at its smaller size.

Exploring on your own

Feel free to experiment with the project you have just created. Here are some suggestions:

• Move the edit line in the Timeline by pressing Shift and dragging the red line in the Navigator palette representing the edit line.

• Perform a four-point edit, but make the source material shorter than the program material. Experiment with the options Premiere gives you to complete the edit.

• Experiment with the History palette by applying a change to some part of the project, and then observing that the new state of that project is added to the History palette. For example, if you add a clip to the Timeline window, apply an effect to it, copy it, and paste it in another track, each of those states is listed separately in the palette. You can select any of these states, and the project will revert to how it looked when the change was applied. You can then modify the project from that state.

Review questions

1 In addition to the Timeline window, which two Premiere windows let you move the edit line?

2 What is one advantage of using a three-point edit?

3 To edit linked video and audio clips separately without permanently destroying the link, what tool would you need to use before you begin editing?

4 What is one easy step that helps prevent accidental edits?

Answers

1 You can move the edit line from the Monitor window using the Program view controls, and from the Navigator by pressing the Shift key and dragging.

2 In a three-point edit, Premiere trims the unspecified point for you.

3 Use the Toggle Sync Mode button to temporarily break the link between video and audio clips.

4 Deselecting a tool prevents using it accidentally. Locking a track is another way to prevent accidental edits.

Lesson 7

7

Advanced Editing Techniques

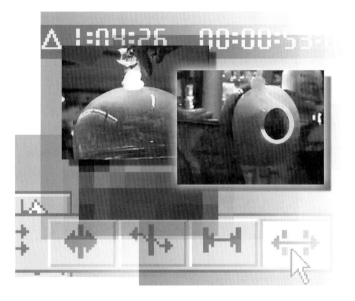

Finishing a project can mean fine-tuning edits while preserving the duration of individual clips and the overall program. The techniques covered in this lesson will help prepare you for the detailed editing needed to polish a project.

Now, you'll complete the introductory segment for a documentary on glassblowing that you started in the previous lesson. This segment must be kept to a finished length of 60 seconds. In editing this segment, you'll learn the following techniques:

- Removing frames using the Extract and Lift buttons.

- Pasting a clip using the Paste Custom command.

- Using the slip and slide tools to adjust edits.

- Editing in the Trim View.

- Changing a clip's rate.

Getting started

For this lesson you'll open an existing project with all of the necessary files imported. Make sure you know the location of the files used in this lesson. Insert the *Classroom in a Book* CD-ROM disk if necessary. For help, see "Copying the Classroom in a Book files" on page 14.

1 Restore the Adobe Premiere 6.0 default preferences as you have in previous lessons. Then, launch the Premiere 6.0 software and choose Single-Track Editing mode.

2 In the Load Project Settings dialog box, choose Multimedia or Multimedia Quicktime (depending on your operating system), and click OK.

3 Choose Edit > Preferences > General and Still Image and deselect Open Movies in Clip Window if it is selected. Click OK.

4 Double-click 07Lesson.ppj in the 07Lesson folder that you copied to your hard disk to open it in Premiere.

5 If necessary, rearrange windows and palettes so they don't overlap, by choosing Window > Workspace > Single-Track Editing.

6 Choose File > Save As, open the folder on your hard disk where you have saved your lessons, type **Glass2.ppj**, and press Enter (Windows) or Return (Mac OS).

Viewing the finished movie

To see what you'll be creating, take a look at the finished movie.

1 Choose File > Open and double-click the 07Final.mov file in the Final folder, inside the 07Lesson folder.

The movie opens in the Source view in the Monitor window.

2 Click the Play button (▶) to view the movie. When the movie ends, the final frame will remain visible in the Source view in the Monitor window.

Viewing the assembled project

Let's take a look at the project as it has been assembled so far. Because there are no transitions, filters, or other effects used in this project, you do not need to generate a preview file to view the project. You can preview by scrubbing.

Note: This project is a continuation of the project you worked on in Lesson 6, "Additional Editing Techniques." The project you just opened reflects the tasks covered in Lesson 6 with several clips added.

1 Ensure that the edit line is at the beginning of the Timeline. To do this, make sure the Timeline window is active and that no clips are selected. Then, do one of the following:

• Press the Home key, if your computer keyboard has one.

• Drag the edit line in the Timeline ruler all the way to the left to the start of the Timeline

• In the Navigator palette, drag the green current view rectangle all the way to the left.

• In the Program view, timecode entry box, type 0 and press Enter/Return.

2 To view the project, click the Play button (▶) under the Program view in the Monitor window. The project plays in the Program view.

Although the assembled project looks much like the final movie you viewed at the beginning of this lesson, you may notice some small problems that could be solved by further editing—such as correcting a cut where the action is not synchronized. You'll also make some changes to improve the look of the project; for example, you'll add a close-up to show detail.

In this lesson, you'll use some editing tools that are especially useful for fine-tuning a project. Much of this lesson deals with editing techniques that tune edits to match action while preserving the length or duration of clips.

Understanding the extract and lift functions

Premiere 6.0 provides two methods for removing a range of frames or a gap from the Timeline: *extracting* and *lifting*.

Extracting Removes frames from the Timeline, closing the gap like a ripple deletion. These frames can be within a single clip or can span multiple clips, but it is important to understand that extracting removes the selected range of frames *from all unlocked tracks.* You can also extract a gap from the Timeline. This feature works only with a range of frames that have been marked with In and Out points in the Program view.

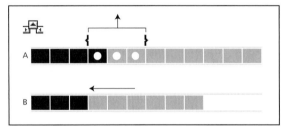

Frames are marked in the Program view with In and Out points (A). The marked portion of the program is deleted and the gap is closed up (B).

Lifting Removes a range of frames from the Timeline, leaving a gap. The frames removed can be within a single clip or can span multiple clips and are removed *only from the target track.* As in extracting, you select the frames you want to remove by setting In and Out points in the Program view in the Monitor window. The Lift button does not affect the duration of the other clips in the Timeline.

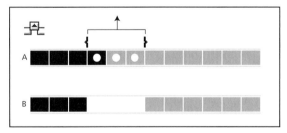

Frames are marked in the Program view with In and Out points (A). The marked portion of the program is deleted, leaving a gap (B).

Removing frames with the Extract button

Here, you'll use the extract feature to remove some camera movement in the middle of the Top.mov clip. Extracting the frames will split the clip into two separate clips.

*Top.mov before (**A**) and after (**B**) extracting frames*

To begin, you'll set In and Out points in the Program view to define the portion of Top.mov you want to extract from the Timeline. But first you'll use the Locate Clip command to find Top.mov in the Timeline.

1 Select Top.mov in the Project window and choose Edit > Locate Clip. Premiere selects the clip in the Timeline and displays the Find Next Clip dialog box. Click Done.

2 Scrub in the Timeline ruler to preview Top.mov, noting the camera movement near the beginning of the clip. Leave the edit line where the movement starts.

3 Under the Program view, use the controls to locate the frame just before the sphere and the camera start moving (at 35:12).

4 In the Program view, click the Mark In button ({) to set the In point for the frames you will extract.

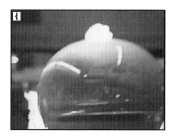

5 Find the frame in which the camera has stopped moving, the image is in focus, and the tool doesn't obscure the sphere (at 42:10).

6 Click the Mark Out button (⬥) to set the Out point.

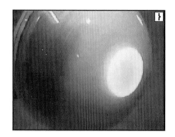

7 To prevent deletion of the audio, lock the Audio 1 and Audio 2 tracks by clicking once in the box to the right of the speaker icon on the left of each track label in the Timeline so the lock icon appears.

Now, you'll extract the frames you've just marked.

8 In the Program view in the Monitor window, click the Extract button (⬛).

The portion of Top.mov that you previously marked is now removed. This step breaks Top.mov into two clips. The gap in the track is closed, shortening the program.

9 Preview the video you just edited.

10 Save the project.

💡 *To turn off audio previewing temporarily, make audio tracks "shy" by clicking the speaker icon (◀)) at the left edge of any audio track that contains audio clips.*

Removing frames with the Lift button

You'll use the Lift button in the Program view in the Monitor window to remove the middle portion of Closeup1.mov, making two clips. You'll set the In and Out points to keep specific frames in the two remaining clips. Later, you'll fill the gap with a similar scene taken from a different point of view with a second camera.

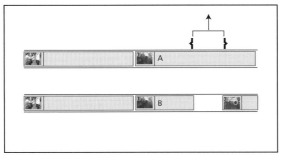

Closeup1.mov before (A) and after (B) lifting frames

First, you'll define the range of frames you want to remove.

1 In the lower left corner of the Timeline window choose 2 Seconds from the Time Zoom Level pop-up menu. Alternatively, use the Navigator palette to obtain the 2 Seconds position.

Now you'll locate Closeup1.mov in the Timeline window.

2 Select Closeup1.mov in the Project window, choose Edit > Locate Clip, and click Done.

Premiere selects the clip in the Timeline.

3 Scrub in the Timeline ruler to preview Closeup1.mov.

4 Use the controls under the Program view to locate the point several seconds before the molten glass meets to form a circle (at 55:28). This is where you'll cut to a new scene. Click the Mark In button (∤) to set the In point in Closeup1.mov.

5 Use the controls under the Program view in the Monitor window to find the frame just before the glob of molten glass meets the left edge of the frame (at 56:27). This is where you'll cut back to this scene. Click the Mark Out button (✎) to set the Out point.

Now that you've defined the range of frames you want to remove, you'll lift this range of frames from the Timeline.

6 In the Program view in the Monitor window, be sure the V1 track is shown as the target, then click the Lift button.

The portion of Closeup1.mov that you marked is removed—leaving the other clips in the track undisturbed and preserving the program's duration. In the next exercise, you'll use Paste commands to fill this gap.

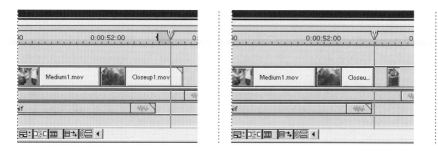

To prevent confusion, let's give a new name, or *alias*, to the fragment of Closeup1.mov to the right of the gap.

Note: *Giving an alias to an* instance *(a copy of a clip in the Timeline) doesn't affect the* master clip *in the Project window or other instances of the clip.*

7 Select the second fragment of Closeup1.mov and choose Clip > Set Clip Name Alias.

8 When prompted, type **Closeup2** (Windows) or **Closeup2.mov** (Mac OS) and click OK.

9 Save the project.

Pasting into a gap

You can rearrange existing clips in the Timeline by cutting and pasting. If you simply paste a clip, Premiere inserts it at a selected area in the Timeline by either trimming the clip's Out point to allow it to fit into a gap between two other clips or placing the entire clip. If you want another result, you can control exactly what happens to the clips at the edit point when you paste. This kind of control is most useful when you are pasting a clip of one duration into a selected space of a different duration.

If you have applied settings to a clip and want to use the same settings in another clip, you can easily copy the settings. For example, you might want to apply identical color correction to a series of clips captured in the same session.

There are a number of ways to insert material into a gap in the project, including using 3-point and 4-point edits. Before pasting the copy into the gap, you'll need to determine which of the four points involved in this procedure can be moved without negatively affecting the edit. Because you want to use frames near the end of this clip, moving the In point in the copy makes the most sense in this case. The position of this new In point is not critical here; you'll fine-tune it later. Premiere adjusts the duration of this clip to fit the gap when you paste it.

In this exercise, you'll use Paste Custom to paste a copy of Medium1.mov into the gap you just created with the Lift button. Medium1.mov, Closeup1.mov, and Closeup2 contain the same scene shot with two cameras.

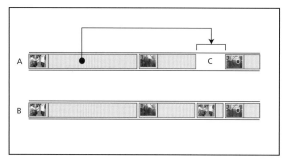

*The gap between Closeup1.mov and Closeup2.mov before (**A**)*
*and after (**B**) pasting a copy of Medium1.mov into the gap (**C**)*

Now, you'll make a clip fit into a selected space when you paste it.

1 In the Timeline, select Medium1.mov, and then choose Edit > Copy.

2 Using the selection tool, select the gap created when you lifted a portion of Closeup1.mov.

3 Choose Edit > Paste to Fit.

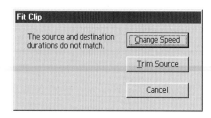

4 When the Fit Clip dialog box appears, click one of the following options:

• Click Change Speed to slow down or speed up the clip to fit it into the designated space.

• Click Trim Source to adjust the duration to fit by keeping the source In point and setting a new source Out point.

5 Click Edit > Undo Paste to clear the gap to use another method for pasting a clip.

6 Use the slider or zoom buttons in the Navigator palette or use the pop-up menu in the lower left of the Timeline window to set the Time Zoom Level to 1 Second.

7 In the Timeline, select Medium1.mov and then choose Edit > Copy.

8 Use the selection tool to select the gap created when you lifted a portion of Closeup1.

9 Choose Edit > Paste Attributes, and make sure that Content is selected.

Notice that the selected/default option, Normal (under Content), is shown in animation.

10 From the pop-up menu, select Move Source In Point.

An animated representation of the option appears in the Content section to help you determine if the selected option is appropriate.

This option does not change either the gap duration or the Out point of the source clip.

11 Click Paste to paste the copy of Medium1.mov into the gap.

Now assign an alias to the copy of Medium1.mov you just pasted.

12 Select the copy of Medium1.mov and choose Clip > Set Clip Name Alias.

13 Type **Medium2** (Windows) or **Medium2.mov** (Mac OS) and click OK.

14 Preview the project by scrubbing in the Timeline ruler.

All the clips in the project are now in the proper order and are trimmed to about the right length. In the next exercise, you'll start fine-tuning some critical edits.

15 Save the project.

Fine-tuning your edits

The remaining exercises in this lesson involve adjusting edits to match the action between scenes. When fine-tuning a project, it's often necessary to preserve the duration of a clip or of the entire project. In this project, we want to preserve the duration of Closeup1.mov, Closeup2.mov, and the gap between these clips because we'll be cutting between scenes shot with two cameras, and we'll be matching action between those scenes. In the exercises that follow, you'll use the slide tool, the slip tool, and the Trim view to put the finishing touches on your project.

In the exercises that follow, you'll adjust the last three edits, working from left to right.

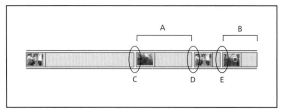

*To preserve the In and Out points and durations of Closeup1.mov (**A**) and Closeup2.mov (**B**), you'll refine the last three edits using the slide tool on the first (**C**), the slip tool on the second (**D**), and the Trim view on the third (**E**), working from left to right.*

Understanding the slide and slip tools

Premiere provides two tools for adjusting a clip in the Timeline while preserving its duration: the slide tool and the slip tool.

Slide tool Adjusts the duration of the two clips adjacent to the target clip, while preserving the In and Out points of the selected clip. This tool also preserves the duration of the project. You can think of this as a rolling edit with a clip between the two clips being trimmed. The slide tool also preserves the duration of the selected clip. As you drag the selected clip, the location of the clip moves left or right in the Timeline.

Note: *The slide tool can be used only when (and to the extent that) the adjacent clips have been trimmed so that extra frames are available in those clips.*

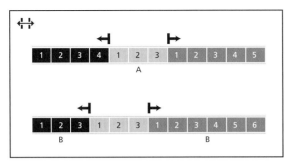

*The slide tool preserves the duration of the sliding clip (**A**)
while changing the In or Out points of the adjacent
clips (**B**), but only if those two clips have trimmed
frames available.*

Slip tool Adjusts a clip's In and Out points while preserving its duration. As you drag in the clip with the slip tool, the clip's In point and Out point shift simultaneously in the same direction, while the duration of the clip remains unchanged. You can think of this as slipping the clip one way or the other behind a fixed window in the track. The location of the clip in the Timeline does not change.

Note: You can use the slip tool only on trimmed clips so that additional frames are available beyond the current In and Out points.

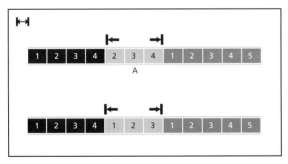

*The slip tool changes the In and Out points of a clip (**A**)
while preserving its duration, provided the clip has
trimmed frames available.*

When you hold down the mouse button with either the slide tool or the slip tool selected, the Monitor window changes to show the four critical frames: the last frame of the adjacent clip on the left, the first and last frames of the selected clip, and the first frame of the adjacent clip to the right.

Note: You can't use the slip and slide tools directly on audio clips. But, when you use the slip and slide tools on video clips, any audio clips linked to those video clips will be adjusted to match the video clips.

Using the slide tool

You'll use the slide tool to match the action in the close-up shot (Closeup1.mov) to the same action in the medium shot (Medium1.mov). Because you want to preserve the In point and Out point of Closeup1.mov, you'll trim only the Out point of Medium1.mov. Performing this edit shortens one adjacent clip while extending the other.

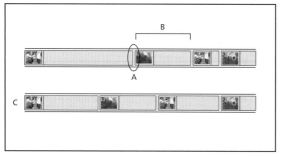

*The slide tool will be used to match action at the edit point (**A**) between Medium1.mov and Closeup1.mov, while preserving the In and Out points and duration of Closeup1.mov (**B**). The result can be seen in (**C**).*

1 In the Timeline, choose 2 Seconds from the Time Zoom Level pop-up menu.

2 In the Timeline, select the slide tool (⟷).

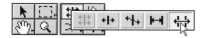

3 Position the pointer on Closeup1.mov, and then press and hold down the mouse button.

When you hold down the mouse button with the slide tool selected, the view in the Monitor window changes to show critical frames of three clips. It displays four frames: the Out point of the adjacent clip on the left (Medium1.mov), the In point and the Out point of the clip under the tool (Closeup1.mov), and the In point of the adjacent clip on the right (Medium2.mov).

While synchronizing the action, you'll be comparing the two frames in the left half of the Monitor window.

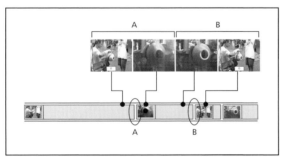

*You can view the edit between Medium1.mov and Closeup1.mov (**A**) and the edit between Closeup1.mov and Medium2.mov (**B**). Here, you'll fix the first edit (**A**).*

With the mouse button still held down, notice the flash of light on the right edge of Closeup1.mov (the second frame from the left in the Monitor window). You want to synchronize this flash with the corresponding flash in Medium1.mov.

4 Drag left in the Timeline to trim Medium1.mov until you see the flash in the first frame (Medium1.mov Out point). This moves the Out point of the Medium1.mov and the In point of the Closeup1.mov earlier in time. The numeric display in the first frame should show -122, indicating you have moved Closeup1.mov 122 frames earlier.

Note: Changing the Time Zoom level may make it easier to obtain precise results.

5 Release the mouse button. Select the selection tool (➤) to deselect the slide tool.

When you release the mouse button, Premiere updates the In and Out points for the adjacent clips, displaying the result in the Monitor window and maintaining the Closeup1.mov clip and the program duration. You have changed only the clip's position in the Timeline.

*Match the action between Medium1.mov (**A**) and Closeup1.mov (**B**), ignoring the other two frames.*

6 Preview the change by scrubbing.

The action in the first and second frames should match.

7 Save the project.

Using the slip tool

You'll use the slip tool to match the action between Closeup1.mov and Medium2.mov. To do this, you'll move the In point of Medium2.mov while preserving the clip's duration. The In and Out points of Medium2.mov will appear in the two middle frames in the Monitor window as you use the slip tool.

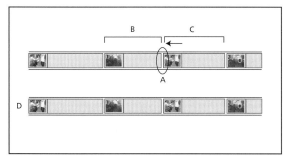

*Use the slip tool to match action at the edit point (**A**)
between Closeup1.mov (**B**) and Medium2.mov (**C**). The tool
changes the In and Out points of Medium2.mov while
preserving its duration. Adjacent clips, such as Closeup1.mov,
are unaffected. The result can be seen in (**D**).*

1 In the Timeline, select the slip tool (⊢⊣).

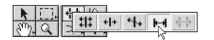

2 Position the pointer on the Medium2.mov clip in the Timeline, and then press
and hold down the mouse button.

As it did when the slide tool was activated, the Monitor window changes, this time showing the Out point of Closeup1.mov, the In and Out points of Medium2.mov, and the In point of Closeup2.mov.

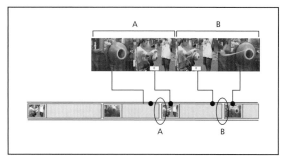

*You can see the edit from Closeup1.mov and Medium2.mov (**A**) and the edit between Medium2.mov and Closeup2.mov (**B**). Here, you'll fix the second edit.*

3 Drag left until the action in the third frame (the Out point of Medium2.mov) matches the action in the last frame (the In point of Closeup2.mov). The read out boxes will register -43 frames. This creates new Timeline In and Out points that reflect footage appearing earlier in the source clip.

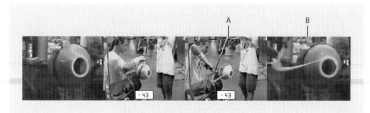

*Match the action between Medium2.mov (**A**) and Closeup2.mov (**B**), ignoring the other two frames.*

4 Release the mouse button. The Monitor window changes back to the usual configuration.

5 Select the selection tool ( ) to deselect the slip tool.

6 Preview the change.

The action in the third and fourth frames should match. Premiere updates the source In and Out points for the clip, displaying the result in the Monitor window and maintaining the clip and program duration. Adjacent clips are unaffected.

7 Chose Edit > Undo Slip to return the Timeline to its status after you used the slide tool.

Note: It essential to do this now because you will approach this again in the next exercise. If you don't undo at this time, your finished project will not match the finished movie.

8 Save the project.

Understanding the Trim view

The Trim view is used to trim individual frames on either side of an edit while viewing those frames, so you can view the edit as you work. The Trim view provides the same function as the ripple tool, but it provides finer control and a better view of program material. When you select Trim Mode in the Monitor window, the Source and Program views are replaced by two views in which 1, 3, or 5 frames of adjacent clips are displayed. Both views in the Monitor window represent clips in the program—the left view displays the clip to the left of the edit line, and the right view displays the clip to the right of the edit line.

Being able to see frames on either side of the edit line enables you to precisely trim each clip. You can also perform a rolling edit in Trim view. This view is useful for fine-tuning the edit between two clips in which the action must match or for which the timing is critical. The Timeline updates as you perform the edit.

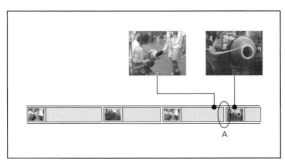

*The Trim view provides a frame-by-frame ripple edit function and a view of each clip at the edit point (**A**).*

Editing in the Trim view

At this point, the action in Medium2.mov and Closeup2.mov is not synchronized because you saved the edit you performed with the slide tool, but did not save the edit you practiced with the slip tool.

Now, you'll use the Trim view to match the action in these clips so that the action at the Out point of Medium2.mov is the same as at the In point of Closeup2.mov. First, you'll trim Medium2.mov to match the action in Closeup2.mov. Then, you'll use a rolling edit to move the edit point between them for the most effective edit. The rolling edit preserves the combined duration of the two clips.

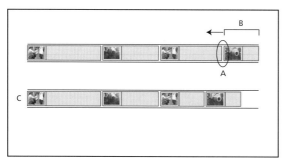

*The Trim view will be used to match action at the edit point (A)
between Medium2.mov and Closeup2.mov while preserving the
In and Out points and duration of Closeup2.mov (B).
The result can be seen in (C).*

1 In the controller area under the Program view, use the controls to set the edit line between the last two clips in the program: Medium2 and Closeup2 (at 56:27).

2 In the Monitor window menu, choose Monitor Window Options.

3 Under Trim Mode Options, ensure that the mode on the left is selected; then, click OK.

For more information about customizing Trim view options, see "Using the Trim view" in Chapter 3 of the *Adobe Premiere 6.0 User Guide*.

4 Select Trim mode by choosing Trim Mode from the Monitor window menu.

Note: You can also select Trim mode by clicking the Trim Mode button (⊞) at the top of the Monitor window.

In the Trim view, Premiere displays two frames: the Out point of Medium2.mov on the left and the In point of Closeup2.mov on the right.

You'll notice some new buttons in the Trim view.

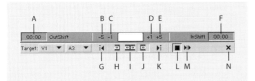

*A. Outshift **B.** Trim Left n frames -5 (shift + left arrow)*
*C. Trim Left -1 (left arrow) **D.** Trim Right +1 (left arrow)*
E. Trim Right n frames +5 (shift + left arrow)
*F. Inshift **G.** Previous Edit **H.** Set Focus Left*
*I. Set Focus Both **J.** Set Focus Right **K.** Next Edit*
*L. Stop **M.** Play Edit **N.** Cancel Edit (all edits)*

Now you'll sync up the action in Closeup2.mov to the matching action in Medium2.mov. When you select one of the views in the Trim view, the color of the timecode below it changes to green.

5 In the Monitor window (which is now in Trim view), click in the left frame (Medium2.mov) to select it and then click the Trim Right *n* Frames button (+5) and Trim Right button (+1) to adjust Medium2.mov until the action in the Medium2.mov Out point matches that in the Closeup2.mov In point. If you go too far, use the Trim Left *n* Frames button (-5) and Trim Left button (-1) buttons to reverse the trim.

💡 *To undo edits made in the Trim view, click the cancel Edit button (✖).*

The action in both clips is now in sync. Next, you'll move the edit between the clips using a rolling edit in the Trim view.

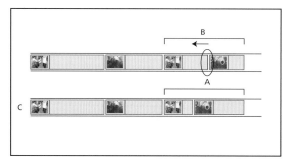

*You'll use a rolling edit in the Trim view to move the edit (**A**) between Medium2.mov and Closeup2.mov while preserving the combined duration of both clips (**B**). The result can be seen in (**C**).*

Now, you'll change the edit to the close-up to show a better look at the instrument pulling away from the rim.

6 In the Monitor window (which is in Trim view), do one of the following:

• Click the Set Focus Both button (![icon]).

• Position the pointer in the space between the clip windows to activate both the clips to the left and right of the edit line.

7 Do one of the following:

• Perform an interactive rolling edit by dragging the tool icon left until the instrument just starts to pull away. Use the illustration below as a guide.

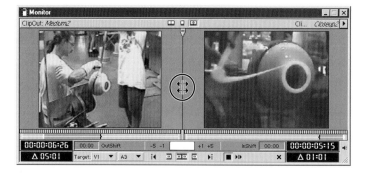

• Click the Trim Left button (◂|) to remove one frame from the left clip and add one frame to the clip on the right.

• Perform a rolling edit numerically by typing a negative number (to move left)—or typing a positive number (to move right)—in the space between the buttons, and then pressing Enter (Windows) or Return (Mac OS).

8 Scrub in the Timeline ruler to preview the change. Scrubbing automatically exits Trim Mode and returns the Monitor window to its normal view.

Note: You can also exit Trim Mode by choosing Trim Mode from the Monitor window menu to remove the checkmark from the command.

9 Preview the last four clips.

10 Save the project.

For more information about performing a rolling edit in Trim view, see "Using the Trim view" in Chapter 3 of the *Adobe Premiere 6.0 User Guide.*

Changing a clip's rate

To polish the end of this project, you'll change the frame rate of the last two clips to create a slow motion effect. At the same time, you'll use the change in clip duration to make the project duration exactly 60 seconds (1:00)—the specified length for this segment of the documentary. To do this, you'll use the Clip Speed dialog box to make the Closeup2.mov clip play at exactly one-quarter speed. Then, you'll obtain the required program length.

1 Restore the Monitor window to Dual view.

2 Click the Zoom-in (⌂) button in the Navigator palette, or use the Time Zoom Level pop-up menu in the Timeline window, to set the Time Zoom level to 1/2 Second. Then drag the green current view box in the Navigator palette to view Medium2.mov and Closeup2.mov in the Timeline.

3 Click Closeup2.mov and choose Clip > Speed to open the Clip Speed dialog box.

Clip Speed

New Rate: [100] %

New Duration: [0:00:02:04]

OK   Cancel

4 To change the rate, type **50** in the New Rate box, and then click OK.

Closeup2.mov now plays at one-quarter speed, which means it is four times as long as it was originally. Now, you'll move the edit line to 01:00:00 (60 seconds)—where you want the project to end.

5 Double-click the location timecode under the Program view, type **10000**, and press Enter (Windows) or Return (Mac OS).

6 Use the Slider or Zoom buttons in the Navigator palette or use the Time Zoom Level pop-up menu to set the Time Zoom Level to 1 Second.

7 Drag Closeup2.mov until the end snaps to the edit line.

8 Preview Closeup2.mov at its new frame rate.

9 Save the project.

For more information, see "Changing clip duration and speed" in Chapter 3 of the *Adobe Premiere 6.0 User Guide.*

Exporting the movie

Now that you've finished your editing, it's time to generate a movie file.

1 If you temporarily turned off audio previewing earlier in the lesson, make sure you turn it on again by clicking once in the small box to the far left the left of each audio track. When audio is turned on, the speaker icon (🔊) is visible in this box.

2 Choose File > Export Timeline > Movie.

3 In the Export Movie dialog box, click the Settings button.

4 Make sure QuickTime is selected for the File Type and that Entire Project is selected for the Range.

5 Also, make sure that both Export Video and Export Audio are selected. The default values for other settings, including compression, are fine for this project.

6 Click OK to close the Export Movie Settings dialog box.

7 In the Export Movie dialog box, select the 07Lesson folder as the file location and type **Glass2.mov** for the name of the movie. Click Save (Windows) or OK (Mac OS).

Premiere starts making the movie, displaying a status bar during its generation and estimating the amount of time it will take. When the movie is complete, it opens in the Source view in the Monitor window.

8 Click the Play button (▶) to play the movie you've just created.

Exploring on your own

Feel free to experiment with the project you have just created. Here are some suggestions:

• Try changing the name of a clip in the Project window without using Clip > Set Clip name Alias. Here's a hint: You don't need to use any menu items, icons, or buttons, but the Project window must be in List View. Once you've changed the name, observe what effect it has on instances in the Timeline.

• Try using a freeze frame on Closeup2.mov at the end of this lesson instead of changing the frame rate. Set marker 0 on the frame you want to freeze and then choose Clip > Video > Hold Frame. Experiment with extending a hold frame to see how it differs from a still image.

• Replace the middle of Closeup1.mov with Medium2.mov using a three-point edit instead of using the Lift button and Paste to Fit.

Review questions

1 The Ripple Delete command and the Extract button provide similar functions. What is the main difference between them?

2 Which tool would you use to change the In and Out points of a clip while preserving the clip's duration?

3 What features does the Trim Mode offer that make it well suited to fine-tuning edits?

4 What are two ways to change the frame rate of a clip?

Answers

1 Ripple Delete works on one or more whole clips or on a gap; the Extract button works on a range of frames in one or more clips.

2 The slip tool changes the In and Out points of a clip while preserving its duration.

3 The Trim Mode enables you to trim individual frames on either side of an edit point, while viewing those frames.

4 You can change a clip's frame rate using either the Clip Speed dialog box (choose Clip > Speed) or the rate stretch tool (↔).

Lesson 8

8 Creating a Title

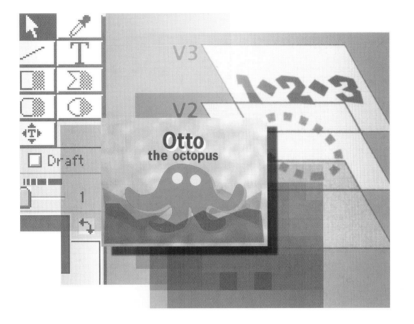

Text and graphics play an integral role in conveying information in a video program. The Title window in Premiere lets you create text and graphics that you can import and superimpose over existing video.

In this lesson, you'll use the Title window in Premiere 6.0 to create a 14-second cartoon for a children's educational Web site. You'll create three different titles using text, rolling text, and graphic tools. Then, you'll superimpose the titles over a movie clip in the project Timeline. Specifically, you'll learn how to do the following:

- Enter text and change text attributes.

- Kern text.

- Add shadows and color.

- Create graphics.

- Apply opacity to graphics and text.

- Create and preview rolling type.

- Add titles to a project.

- Superimpose a title over a video clip.

- Edit titles.

Restoring default preferences

For this lesson, you should restore the default preferences of Premiere to the factory settings before you launch the program or start the lesson. See "Restoring default preferences" on page 15 of this *Classroom in a Book*.

Getting started

For this lesson, you'll open an existing project in which the necessary files are already imported. Then, you'll add titles. Make sure you know the location of the files used in this lesson. Insert the CD-ROM disk if necessary. For help, see "Copying the Classroom in a Book files" on page 14. Also, make sure you have installed the News Gothic font. For help, see "Installing the Classroom in a Book fonts" on page 14.

1 After you have restored the default preferences, launch the Premiere 6.0 software, and choose Single-Track Editing.

2 In the Load Project Settings dialog box, choose Multimedia or Multimedia Quicktime (depending on your operating system), and click OK.

3 Choose Edit > Preferences > General and Still Image and deselect Open Movies in Clip window if it is selected.

4 Click OK.

Opening the existing project file

1 To open the existing file, double-click 08Lesson.ppj in the 08Lesson folder that you previously copied to your hard disk.

2 If necessary, rearrange windows and palettes so they don't overlap, by choosing Window > Workspace > Single-Track Editing.

3 Choose File > Save As, select the **08 Lesson** folder location on your hard disk, type **Cartoon.ppj** for the new project name, and press Enter (Windows) or Return (Mac OS).

Viewing the finished movie

To see what you'll be creating, you'll first take a look at the finished movie.

1 Choose File > Open and select the 08Final.mov file in the Final folder, inside the 08Lesson folder.

The video program opens in the Source view in the Monitor window.

2 Click the Play button (▶) in the Source view in the Monitor window to watch the video program. When the movie ends, the final frame will remain visible in the Source view in the Monitor window.

About titles

Titles include text, lines, shapes, and rolling credits. Titles are separate files that you work with just like other types of source clips. A title becomes part of your video project only when you add it to the Timeline for that project. Titles can be edited using cuts and transitions. Titles can also be superimposed over other clips. You can also create a title using a graphics or title application, save it in a format compatible with Premiere, such as pict (.pct), TIFF (.tif), Photoshop (.psd), Illustrator (.ai or .eps), and import the title file into your Premiere project.

The Title window

Use the Title window in Premiere to create title files with text and simple graphic images to be used only in Premiere projects. You can use the Title window when you first launch Premiere—with an untitled Project window open—or you can create them with an existing or new project open. You can also have more than one Title window open.

1 Choose File > New > Title to open the Title window.

Title window A. Tools B. Draft button C. Line Width slider
D. Object and Shadow colors E. Gradient and Transparency settings
F. Shadow Offset control G. Title-safe zone H. Action-safe zone

2 Reposition the Title window so that it does not obscure the Project window.

3 Resize the Title window if you like by dragging the lower right corner of the window.

The main work area is bounded by two dotted-line boxes. The inner box represents the *title-safe zone*; the outer box represents the *action-safe zone*. Text placed outside the title-safe zone may appear blurry or distorted on some television monitors. Graphic images beyond the action-safe zone may not be visible on some television monitors. Various *tools* are grouped at the upper left in the Title window. Notice that some tools have more than one function, depending on where you click the tool icon.

You can specify that a title is a draft by clicking the Draft button under the tool area. Availability of the *Line Width Slider* depends on the tool selected. *Object and Shadow colors* can be specified in the Title window, as can the *Gradient and Transparency settings* and the *Shadow Offset*.

When you open the Title window, Premiere adds the *Title menu* to the title bar at the top of the Premiere screen. The Title menu contains the commands for setting the font, size, style, alignment, orientation, rolling title options, and shadow options.

4 Click Title and review the available menu items and current defaults.

💡 *You can also access the menu items directly from the Title window if you right-click (Windows) or Control-click (Mac OS) anywhere in the Title window.*

Some Title window settings require the use of the Title Window Options dialog box. These include size (specified in pixels), background color, aspect ratio, and settings for show safe titles, NTSC color, and opacity.

5 Access the Title Window Options dialog box by doing one of the following:

• Choose Window > Window Options > Title Window Options

• Right-click (Windows) or Control-click (Mac OS) in the title bar in the Title window and click again on Title Window Options.

6 Click Cancel to close the dialog box.

> ### Importing graphics and titles
>
> *You can import graphics to use in titles from other software such as Adobe Photoshop (3.0 or later) and Adobe Illustrator. You can import entire title sequences created in other software, such as Adobe After Effects. You can also import an individual layer from a multilayer Photoshop file. Note that Premiere 6.0 supports 8-bit TIFF images, but does not support 16-bit TIFF images created in Photoshop or other graphic applications.*
>
> *For more information on importing graphics and animations for titles, see Chapter 2, "Capturing and Importing Source Clips," in the* Adobe Premiere 6.0 User Guide.
>
> *An alpha channel is a fourth channel in an RGB image that defines which parts of the image are transparent or semitransparent. Many programs, such as Adobe Illustrator and Photoshop, use alpha channels. Premiere preserves alpha channels when you import graphics that include them.*
>
> *For more information on using alpha channels in titles, see "Adding a title to a project" in Chapter 6, and "Using the Alpha Channel key" in Chapter 7 of the* Adobe Premiere 6.0 User Guide.
>
> *You can use the Edit Original command in Premiere to open a clip in its original application, such as Adobe After Effects, so that you can edit it and then have those changes automatically incorporated into the current project without exiting Premiere or replacing files.*
>
> *For more information, see "Editing a clip in its original application" in Chapter 3 of the* Adobe Premiere 6.0 User Guide.

Creating a simple title

First, you'll create a simple, text-only title. In this exercise, you will add a sample frame to the Title window, add text, change the text attributes, add a shadow, and kern the text.

Adding a sample frame for reference

Before you enter text, you'll add a sample background frame to the Title window. This sample frame will help you determine the best colors to use for the title text. Sample frames are only for reference and do not become part of the title. When you save and close the title, the reference frame is not saved with the file.

Notice that Water.mov is already in the Bin area of the Project window. You'll use this movie as a background reference frame for your title.

1 Drag the Water.mov icon from the Bin area in the Project window to the Title window. Release the mouse. The first frame of Water.mov is now the Title window background.

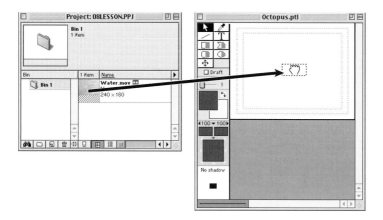

Creating text and changing text attributes

Premiere lets you change the text attributes of words, and of individual characters within a word, using any font available to your operating system.

1 In the Title window, select the text tool (T) and click near the top left corner in the title-safe zone (inner dotted line box).

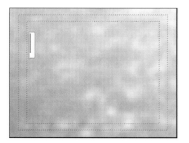

2 Specify the font attributes using the Title menu under the Premiere title bar, as determined by your operating system:

• For Font, select News Gothic Bold.

• For Style, select Bold.

• For Size, specify **30**, and click OK.

Note: As a general rule for video, use a font size of 16 points or larger. Anything smaller may not be visible on a TV monitor.

3 Type **Otto**.

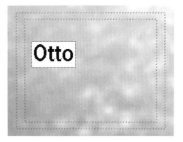

4 Choose File > Save As, open the 08Lesson folder if necessary, and then type **Otto.ptl** for the name, and click Save.

Changing the text color

The default color for text and shadows is black and the default shadow control setting is no shadow. An *Object Color swatch* and *Shadow Color swatch* are displayed under the tools at the left in the Title window, making it easy to see and change the colors of objects and their shadows. Clicking on a swatch opens the Color Picker. You can choose colors in the Color Picker by selecting a color in the color box or by entering values in the Red, Green, and Blue text boxes. The black, white, and gray values are located along the left side of the color box. To switch the object and shadow colors, click the arrow between the swatches.

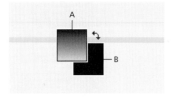

A. *Object Color swatch*
B. *Shadow Color swatch*

Now, you'll change the color of the word "Otto."

1 Use the selection tool ( ) to select "Otto" if not already selected. When selected, a small box or handle appears on each of the four corners of the object's bounding box.

2 Click the Object Color swatch.

The Color Picker appears with the original (default) color of black, displayed in the upper right of the Color Picker dialog box.

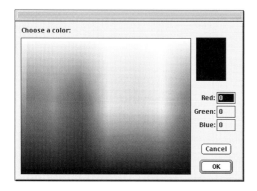

3 Click in the color box to select a deep blue. Now the upper right corner displays the new color you have selected under the original color.

When you have set the Title Window Options to use only NTSC-safe colors, if you select a color that is not NTSC-safe, a gamut warning symbol will appear next to the selected color swatch in the upper right corner of the Color Picker. Such colors may bleed or blur when displayed on an NTSC monitor.

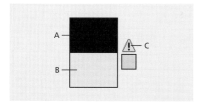

*A. Original color swatch **B.** Selected color swatch **C.** Gamut warning symbol*

♀ *If the gamut warning symbol appears, you can click it to have Premiere choose the nearest color that is within the NTSC color gamut.*

Because the movie you are creating now will only be played on a computer monitor, you don't need to be concerned with the gamut warning if it appears. However, if you were creating a movie that would ultimately be played from an NTSC monitor, you would need to click NTSC-safe colors in the Title Window Options dialog box.

4 To specify the color that was used in the final movie, type **51** for Red, **0** for Green, and **176** for Blue.

5 Click OK to accept the color change and close the Color Picker.

6 Save the title.

Adding a shadow

You can add a shadow to any image or text object in the Title window by selecting the object and then moving the Shadow Offset control near the lower left of the window to the desired amount of shadow. If you have selected text, the Shadow Offset control looks like the text tool (T). If you have selected a graphic object, the Shadow Offset control displays a small preview of it.

First, you'll create a shadow, then you'll change its color. You can change the color of an object or shadow at any time by selecting the object and clicking the color swatch.

1 With "Otto" selected, drag the Shadow Offset control down and to the right until the shadow value indicated in the control area changes from "No shadow" to "4 x 4".

Now, you'll change the shadow for gray (default) to yellow.

2 With the word "Otto" still selected, double-click (Windows) or click (Mac OS) on the Shadow Color swatch to open the Color Picker.

3 Select a light yellow. To use the same color as in the final movie, type **242** for Red, **255** for Green, and **176** for Blue; then, click OK.

By default, Premiere creates soft shadows. You'll change this shadow to a solid shadow, making it more prominent against the aqua-colored background.

4 With the text still selected, choose Title > Shadow > Solid.

Soft shadow and solid shadow

5 Click anywhere in the Title window to deselect the text.

6 Save the title.

Changing opacity

The *opacity* controls in the Title window let you set different amounts of transparency for graphics, text, and shadows. To change the opacity, you first click and hold one of the small black arrows at the top of the opacity controls area, below the Object and Shadow Color swatches, at the left in the Title window. This selects the type of transparency you want. Then, you specify the amount of transparency using the opacity slider.

Overall Transparency sets the effect for an entire image; set it by clicking the center arrow.

Start Transparency lets you vary the opacity from the beginning of the object; set it by clicking the left arrow.

End Transparency lets you vary the opacity from the end of the object; select it by clicking the right arrow.

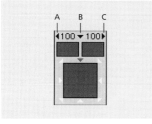

*Opacity controls **A.** Start transparency*
***B.** Overall transparency*
***C.** End transparency*

Shadows have a default opacity value of 50%. Here you'll increase the overall opacity of the shadow, making it less transparent.

1 Use the selection tool (▸) to select the word "Otto."

2 Click once on the Shadow Color swatch to make it active. Now, it overlaps the Object Color swatch.

3 Click the center arrow and drag downward in the Overall Transparency slider to approximately 80%. The shadow becomes stronger and easier to see because less of the aqua-colored background is showing through the shadow.

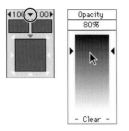

4 Save the title.

For more information on varying the opacity in the Title window, see Chapter 6, "Creating Titles," of the *Adobe Premiere 6.0 User Guide*.

Kerning text

Kerning means changing the distance between two characters in a word. To kern selected text in the Title window, you use the text tool to select the text and then you click one of the kerning buttons. You can either select the text tool and then highlight the two adjacent letters you want to kern or you can select the text tool and then place the text tool icon between the two letters you want to kern. In either case, you click one of the two kerning buttons as often as needed to increase or decrease the space between the letters. Note that the kerning buttons appear under the Draft button only when you select the text tool.

The left Kerning button decreases the distance between two letters; the right Kerning button increases the distance.

Note: *You must use the text tool, not the selection tool, to access the Kerning buttons.*

The text tool and the selection tool affect text in very different ways:

Selection tool Lets you select everything within the bounding box. If you change the font, color, opacity, shadow, or gradient with the bounding box selected, all the text is affected.

Text tool Lets you kern or edit individual characters to change only the font or font attributes of the highlighted characters.

Use the selection tool to edit all text. Use the text tool to edit selected text.

1 Select the text tool (T) and then click between the two Ts in the word "Otto."

2 Click the right Kerning button twice to widen the space between the letters.

3 If kerning caused "Otto" to split over two lines in the Title window, click the selection tool, then drag the lower right corner handle of the bounding box up and to the right. When you release the mouse, the two sections of the word reunite on one line.

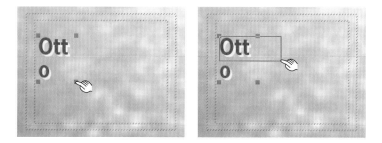

Aligning text

Two types of text alignment are possible in the Title window. You can align the text inside its own bounding box and you can align the text's bounding box inside the window. Here you'll align the word "Otto" using both alignment techniques.

First, you'll align the text within the bounding box. This will be especially noticeable if you resized the box in the last exercise.

1 With the word "Otto" still selected, choose Title > Justify > Center. Notice how the word shifts to the center of the bounding box.

Now, you'll move the bounding box to the top of the window before centering it.

2 Using the selection tool (➤), drag the word "Otto" to the top of the window, so the letters are just inside the title-safe zone. (You can also use the arrow keys to reposition the word in the Title window.)

Now, you can center the bounding box in the Title window.

3 With the word "Otto" still selected, choose Title > Center Horizontally. Notice how the entire bounding box shifts to the center of the window.

4 Save the title.

Adding more text

Now, you'll add more text to the title.

1 Select the text tool (T) and click just below the word "Otto." If you accidently open the text box for the word "Otto," click farther down in the window.

💡 *To select and use a Title window tool one time and then revert to the selection tool, click it once. To use a tool repeatedly, double-click it; otherwise the tool reverts to the selection tool.*

2 Choose Title > Size >18.

3 Type **the octopus**; then, click the selection tool.

Notice that the text has a shadow. This text doesn't require a shadow, so you'll remove it.

4 With "the octopus" still selected, drag the Shadow Offset control out of the Shadow area to return the shadow setting to No Shadow.

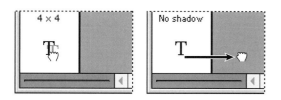

5 With "the octopus" still selected, choose Title > Justify > Center. The text now shifts to the center of its bounding box.

6 Using the selection tool, move the new text so it is positioned in the top one-third in the Title window, directly under the word "Otto." You can also move selected text (or a selected image) by pressing the arrow keys.

7 Choose Title > Center Horizontally.

8 Save the title.

▣ *For more information, see "Creating titles," in Chapter 6 of the* Adobe Premiere 6.0 User Guide. *Also, see "Creating titles > Creating text objects " in the Adobe Premiere 6.0 Technical Guides found in the Support area on the Adobe Web site (www.adobe.com/support/ techdocs/topissuespre.htm).*

Creating a graphic image in the Title window

The Title window lets you create simple graphics. You can use the drawing tools to create rectangles, squares, rounded squares, circles, ovals, lines, and polygons. You can use the drawing tools to create outlined shapes or filled shapes.

Adding a title as a background frame

Before you start drawing the graphic, you'll import the title you just created as the sample frame for this new title. The sample frame will provide a reference of exactly where the Otto title text is located so that you don't draw over the top of it.

1 Choose File > New > Title.

2 Position the new Title window beside the Otto.ptl Title window so that you can see both windows without any overlap.

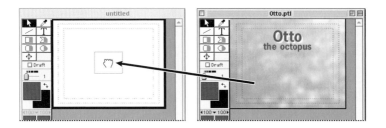

3 Drag the center of the Otto.ptl Title window to the center in the new Title window.

The Otto title appears as a background for your new title. The water background does not transfer to your new title because it is only a sample frame, not a saved component of the Otto.ptl file.

4 Click the new Title window's title bar to make it the active window, and then choose File > Save As. Make sure the 08Lesson folder is open, and then type **Octopus.ptl** for the new title file, and click Save.

5 Close Otto.ptl.

Now, you'll add some graphic images to Octopus.ptl.

Changing the default color before you draw

When nothing is selected in the Title window and you change the color of the Object Color swatch, the new color becomes the default color for everything you draw or type.

Before drawing the first image, you'll change the default color in the Object Color swatch from the deep blue you used for the text to a different blue.

1 Using the selection tool in the Title window, click the Object Color swatch.

2 Select a different blue color in the Color Picker. To specify the color used in the final movie, Type **52** for Red, **0** for Green, and **226** for Blue. Then click OK.

Notice that the Object Color swatch is now dark blue, but no change occurred to the text in the existing text in the Title window. The Shadow Color swatch is also unchanged.

Drawing an image using the polygon tool

The *polygon tool* lets you create random shapes. You first select the polygon tool, click in the title area to set a start point, then move the tool in any direction and click to create end points for each line in your intended shape. To close the polygon, either click the first point you created, or double-click where you want your last line to end. When using the filled tool, as you will in this exercise, double-clicking your last point will automatically connect the last point with the first point.

Now, you'll draw a wave using the polygon tool.

1 Select the filled (right) side of the polygon tool (⬗).

Each drawing shape tool has two options. Clicking the left side of a shape tool produces an outlined shape. Clicking the right side of a shape tool produces a filled or solid shape.

2 Position the cursor in the lower left corner in the Title window, outside the action-safe zone, and click to make the first point.

3 Move the cursor about one-third of the way up the left side of the window and click to make your second point.

4 Continue to click up and down across the entire lower third in the Title window to make a wave effect. You can use the graphic below as a guide.

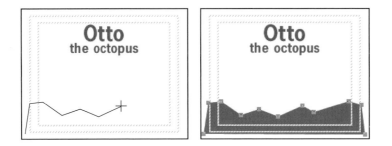

Note: If you make a mistake, there are two easy way to fix the problem. You can double-click to enclose the shape, then press Delete to delete all your points, and then redraw the shape. Alternatively, you can continue adding points, double-click to enclose the shape, then use the selection tool to adjust individual points.

5 When you reach the right side of the window, double-click anywhere in the lower right corner to enclose the polygon. Or, for more precise control, close the shape by clicking your first point. Look for the little indicator circle before clicking your final point to ensure your cursor is directly above the first point.

Premiere automatically adds a line from the last point to the first point, closing the image and filling it with blue because you set the Object Color swatch to blue.

6 With the image selected, drag the Overall Transparency arrow to 50%. (Click and drag down on the center arrow.)

7 Click anywhere outside the image in the Title window to deselect everything.

8 Save the title file.

Repositioning objects

You can reposition text and images in the Title window by bringing them to the front or sending them to the back. Here, you'll draw another wave with a different opacity setting, and then send it to the back.

1 Select the filled polygon tool (⬚).

2 Click the left line of the action-safe zone about halfway up the first wave to create the first point of your new wave.

3 Click to make the second point above the first wave but still in the lower half of the window. You'll make the second wave a little smaller than the first one. Use the graphic below as a guide.

4 Continue clicking points up and down across the window as you did with the first wave. However, for this wave, draw jagged points along the bottom of the wave, instead of a flat bottom.

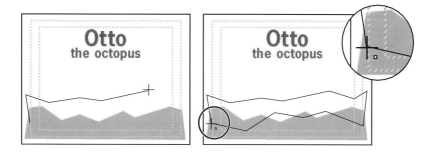

5 When you reach the left side again, enclose the shape by connecting the last point to the first point. You'll know you're clicking on the first point when you see an "o" next to the pointer.

6 With the second wave selected, set Overall Transparency to 25%.

7 Choose Title > Send to Back. The second wave now sits behind the first wave and shows through slightly.

8 Save the title.

Creating a smooth polygon

Now, you'll use the polygon tool to draw an octopus. This time, you'll smooth the lines, because octopuses are round, not pointy.

Before drawing the octopus, you'll change the Object Color swatch. To ensure that you don't change the color of the objects you just drew, first make sure no objects are selected.

1 Using the selection tool ( ), click anywhere inside the Title window (but outside of the waves) to deselect everything.

2 Click the Object Color swatch.

3 Pick a rich orange color from the right side of the color box. To use the exact color we used, type **245** for Red, **42** for Green, and **10** for Blue. Then click OK.

4 Drag the Overall Transparency slider to 100% to make the color completely opaque.

5 Select the filled polygon tool ( ) and click under the words "the octopus" to make your first point for the top left corner of the octopus's head. Then, using the image below as a guide, draw your own octopus in the lower two-thirds of the window, making sure not to draw over the text.

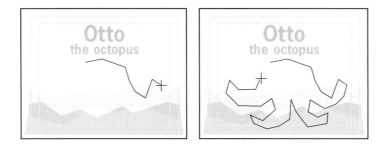

6 Close the shape by clicking your first point. Remember to look for the "o" before clicking your final point to ensure your cursor is directly above the first point.

7 With the octopus selected, choose Title > Smooth Polygon.

8 Save the title.

If you want to adjust any of your images, select the object using the selection tool and drag individual points to reposition them.

Adding an octopus shadow

Now you'll add a light pink shadow to the octopus.

1 Use the selection tool (▶) to select the octopus image if it is not selected.

2 Drag the Shadow Offset control down and to the right so that the shadow dimensions are about 4 x 3.

3 Double-click (Windows) or click (Mac OS) the Shadow Color swatch to open the Color Picker.

4 Click a light pink color between the blues and the reds in the color box. To use the exact color we used, type **255** for Red, **118** for Green, and **174** for Blue. Then click OK.

5 Choose Title > Shadow > Single to remove the shadow's soft edges and create a basic drop shadow that is more apparent against the blue waves.

Repositioning the waves

Now you'll move the first wave you drew to the front so that the octopus appears to be floating between the two waves. Because you added transparency to the wave, you'll be able to see the octopus through it.

1 Using the selection tool (▶), select the first wave you drew. To ensure you selected the first wave, check the Transparency settings in the Title window—they should be 50%. If they're at 25%, select the other wave.

2 Choose Title > Bring to Front.

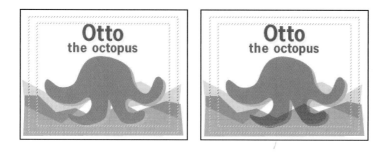

3 To see the shadow effect without the selection points, click an empty area in the Title window to deselect everything.

4 Save the title.

Using the oval tool

Use the oval tool to draw ovals and circles of any size. To make a circle using the oval tool, constrain the tool by pressing the Shift key while drawing. You can also make squares, rounded squares, and 45-degree lines by pressing the Shift key while using the rectangle, rounded rectangle, or line tools.

Before you draw the circles, you'll change the object color to green.

1 To ensure that you don't change the currently selected object's color, click an empty area in the window, and then click the Object Color swatch to open the Color Picker.

2 Pick a bright green color in the color box. To use the same color as the final movie, type **64** for Red, **255** for Green, and **131** for Blue. Then click OK.

3 Drag the Overall Transparency slider to 100%, if it not already set.

4 Now you'll draw one octopus eye, and then copy and paste it to create a second eye.

5 Select the filled oval tool.

6 Hold down the Shift key to constrain the oval to be a circle, and draw a small circle on the octopus's head.

7 Choose Edit > Copy and then Edit > Paste. Premiere pastes a copy of the circle directly on top of the original.

8 Position the selection tool ( ) over the eye, making sure the icon is a pointer, not a finger icon, and then drag the center of the new circle beside the first circle.

 If you accidently stretch the circle instead of moving it, choose Edit > Undo; then deselect and reselect the circle, and use the arrow keys to move it.

9 Click any empty space in the Title window to deselect everything.

10 Save the title file.

Leave Octopus.ptl open. You'll be using it again soon.

Rolling titles and crawling titles

Adobe Premiere 6.0 let's you add motion to titles in rolling titles and crawling titles. *Rolling titles* move across the screen vertically, rolling up or rolling down. *Crawling titles* move across the screen horizontally, crawling left-to-right or right-to-left.

Creating a rolling title

To create a rolling title, you use the *rolling title tool* and enter text in a rolling title scroll box. In this lesson, you'll create a rolling title that rolls up.

First, you'll open a new title window and set the default Object Color to be the same deep blue as the text in Otto.ptl.

1 Choose File > New > Title.

2 Double-click (Windows) or click (Mac OS) the Object Color swatch to access the Color Picker in your new Title window.

3 Type in these values: **51** for Red, **0** for Green, and **176** for Blue, and then click OK.

💡 *Alternatively, you can type in the red value, press the Tab key, type in the green value, press tab, type in the blue value, then press Enter/Return to set the new default.*

4 If a shadow value is selected, drag the Shadow Offset control out of the Shadow area so no shadow is selected.

Now, you're ready to create the rolling title.

5 Select the rolling title tool.

6 With the rolling title tool selected, click and drag inside the title-safe area to define a *rolling title scroll box* from the upper left corner down and to the right about one-third of the way down the window. Be sure the box stays within the title-safe area.

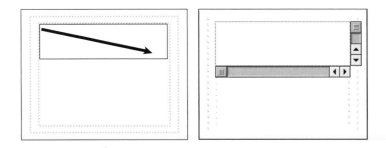

The rolling title scroll box appears with a blinking text cursor at the top. In this box is where you enter the text you want to roll (or crawl) across the screen.

7 From the Title menu, verify that Font is News Gothic and the style is bold.

8 Change the font size by choosing Title > Size > 18.

9 Change the text position to left-justified by choosing Title > Justify > Left.

Now you'll enter the poem text.

10 Type **Octopus.** Then, press Enter (Windows) or Return (Mac OS) twice.

11 Type **Octopus,** again. Then, press Enter/Return twice.

12 Type the following text as shown. Press Enter/Return once at the end of each line or twice where the larger line spaces appear.

how squishy
are thee!

With your
eyes
so bright,

and tentacles
of might,

swimming
the deep

blue

sea.

Note: *You can use the four direction arrows on the keyboard to review the poem. You can click-drag any word to highlight it if it needs to be corrected.*

13 Highlight the word "sea" to select it and choose Title > Justify > Center.

14 Choose Title > Rolling Title Options to access the Rolling Title Options dialog box. Verify or set Direction to Move Up. Then, click OK.

15 Choose File > Save As, open the 08Lesson folder if necessary, and then type **Poem.ptl** for the name and click Save.

Creating a crawling title

To create a crawling title, with the text moving horizontally across the screen, you also use the rolling title tool and enter text in a rolling title scroll box. You can make text crawl left or right. Now, you'll create a crawling title that moves from left-to-right.

1 Choose File > New > Title to open a new Title window.

2 Select the rolling title tool.

3 Drag inside the title-safe area to specify the size of the rolling title scroll box that will contain the crawling title.

4 Verify or set the Object Color swatch, the font, style, size, and justification settings to be the same as for the poem in the rolling title.

5 Type the Octopus poem as follows:

Octopus, Octopus, how squishy are thee! With your eyes so bright, and tentacles of might, swimming the deep blue sea.

This time, don't press Enter/Return after each section; just type the poem continuously until it overfills the box.

Note: To make the text crawl, you must provide enough text to overfill the text box. If you don't have enough text, you can overfill the box using blank spaces. To create blank spaces for crawling text, press the spacebar as often as required to overfill the box.

6 With the rolling title scroll box still selected, choose Title > Rolling Title Options to access the Rolling Titles Options dialog box.

7 In the Direction section of the Rolling Titles Options dialog box, select the direction to Move Right. Then, click OK.

8 Choose File > Save As, open the 08Lesson folder if necessary, and then type **Crawl.ptl** for the name and click Save.

Timing the motion of titles

When you add a moving title to a video program, the speed at which it rolls or crawls is determined by the duration you specify for it in the Timeline. For example, if you specify a duration of 20 seconds for a rolling title, and then change the duration to 10 seconds, the title must roll twice as fast in order to move the same number of lines across the screen in half the time.

To have more control over the rolling or crawling motion in your program, you specify values in the Enable Special Timings section of the Rolling Titles Options dialog box. With a title clip selected ("·ptl" file), you can choose Title > Rolling Title Options and select Enable Special Timings.

Pre Roll specifies how many frames you want to appear motionless starting with the In point of the title clip and ending with the frame in which the title starts moving.

Ramp Up specifies how many frames are used to accelerate the title clip up to normal speed. Type 0 (zero) to start moving the title at normal speed. To accelerate more gradually, specify more frames.

Ramp Down specifies how many frames are used to decelerate the title clip to a halt. For faster deceleration, specify fewer frames. Type 0 (zero) to stop the title immediately. To decelerate more gradually, specify more frames.

Post Roll specifies how many frames you want the title to appear motionless starting with the frame in which the title stops and ending with the Out point of the title clip.

Previewing rolling and crawling titles

You can preview a rolling or crawling titile by dragging the preview slider bar at the bottom of the Title window's toolbox. Premiere plays back the rolling or crawling text object in the Title window.

1   Using the selection tool (➤), click to select the rolling title bounding box for Poem.ptl.

2   Click the Preview Slider button on the *preview slider bar,* located at the bottom left corner in the Title window, and drag to the right.

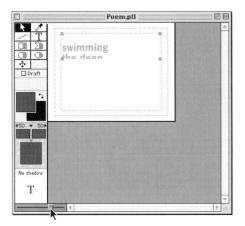

Note: The Title Window Slider previews only the text; not special timings. Special timings depend on the clip's duration in frames; so, you must add the title to the Timeline and preview the title with its special timings in the Timeline.

When you started the preview, you may have noticed that the text was already on the screen at the beginning of the roll; when the roll ended, the last word was still on the screen, at the bottom. To make the text roll onto the screen instead of starting on-screen, you need to insert blank lines before the first word of the text. Similarly, you add blank lines to the end of the text if you want the text to roll all the way off screen at the end.

For this lesson, the Octopus poem rolls onto the screen at the beginning and then stays on-screen at the end.

3 With the Title window of Poem.ptl active, select the text tool and click anywhere in the text area.

4 Scroll to the top of the text and make an insertion point before the first letter of the first word, Octopus.

5 Press Enter (Windows) or Return (Mac OS) three times to add three blank lines at the beginning of the rolling title.

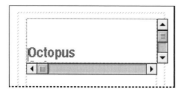

Note: Even though it doesn't appear to move the text off the screen, the carriage returns will create the desired effect when you preview.

6 Click anywhere in the Title window to deselect the text box, and then preview the Octopus title clip again by dragging the preview slider bar.

7 Save the Poem.ptl file.

Using titles in a Premiere project

Now you'll place titles in the Timeline of your project and superimpose them over a video clip. *Superimpose* means positioning a clip, such as a title, still, or video clip, on top of another clip, so that they play at the same time. To superimpose clips in Premiere, you add them to the superimpose tracks (Video 2 track and higher) in the Timeline. Clips in these superimpose tracks play over the clips in the corresponding lower tracks.

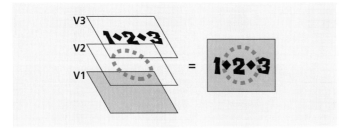

When using titles, Premiere automatically assigns transparency, so clips on the lower tracks display through the title's background. You'll learn more about superimpose tracks and transparency in the next lesson.

How you add a title clip to a Premiere project depends on whether you are creating a new clip or adding an existing clip to a project.

Adding a new clip   A new title clip can be added to a new or existing project.

• Open a new or existing project for which you want to create a new title clip. Use the Title window to create the title. Name and save the new title file. When you save the new title, Premiere automatically adds it to the project and lists it in the Project window. Remember to save the project to keep the title with the Project.

• Open a new (untitled) project and use the Title window to create a new title. When you save the new title clip, Premiere automatically adds it to the new (untitled) project. Close the untitled project without saving it; the new title clip will be available for use in any project because you named and saved the title file.

Adding an existing clip   An existing title clip can be added to a new or existing project.

• Open an existing or new project, then open an existing title file that you want to add to the project. The Title window will open and display the title. Now, drag the title to the Project window. (With the selection tool, click and drag from the center of the Title window to the Project window. Be sure no objects are selected in the Title window, so that the selection tool becomes a hand tool as you click and drag. When the hand tool is properly positioned over the Project window, a black outline appears around the file area of the window. Release the mouse to drop the title into the project.) Save the project.

• Open an existing or new project, then open an existing title file that you want to add to the project. The Title window will open and display the title. With the Title window active, choose Clip > Add This Clip to the Project. (This is useful if your Project window is obscured, making dragging and dropping difficult.) Save the project.

• Open an existing or new project, then choose File > Import > File, specify the title file, and click Open. As with any imported clip, this method adds the title clip to the project without opening the title clip.

Adding titles to the Timeline

So far in this lesson, you have created some title clips and Premiere has added them to the project automatically. You will superimpose two of the titles over the Water.mov video clip; so, you'll need to add a another superimpose track to the Timeline.

Adding tracks to the Timeline

In Single Track Editing mode, a new project opens with two video tracks, a transition track, and three audio tracks. Video 2 and higher tracks are used for superimposing. Adobe Premiere 6.0 supports up to 98 superimpose tracks in the Timeline. You can add or remove superimpose tracks at any time. New video tracks appear above existing video tracks; new audio tracks appear below existing audio tracks.

Note: Video 1, Video 2, Transition, Audio 1, Audio 2, and Audio 3 tracks cannot be deleted.

1 With 08Lesson.ppj open, and either the Project window or the Timeline window active, choose Timeline > Add Video Track.

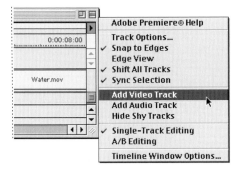

A new track, Video 3, now appears on the Timeline, above the Video 2 track.

You can also add multiple tracks in a single step.

2 Choose Timeline > Track Options or click the Track Options Dialog button at the bottom of the Timeline window.

3 In the Track Options dialog box, click Add.

4 In the Add Tracks dialog box, type a number in the appropriate field to specify the number of Video or Audio tracks to add. In this exercise, add 1 video track and 0 audio tracks. Click OK. Notice that the Track Options dialog box now lists the tracks you just added. Click OK again to exit the Track Options dialog box.

Now, the Timeline shows 4 video tracks and 3 audio tracks.

5 Choose Edit > Undo Add/Delete Tracks so that you have only 3 video tracks and 3 audio tracks.

Adding your titles to the Timeline

Titles are still images with a default duration of five seconds. You can change the duration of a title clip only in the Timeline. You can do this by using the trim tool to drag one edge of the clip to make it longer or shorter, but not shorter than 5 seconds. Alternatively, choose Clip > Duration and specify a new duration.

For information on changing the still image duration preference, see Lesson 12 "Subclips and Virtual Clips" in this Classroom in a Book.

1 Drag Poem.ptl from the Project window to the beginning of the Video 2 track.

2 Choose Window > Show Info to display the Info palette, if it is not visible. You'll need to refer to this palette when editing the duration of the clips in this exercise.

3 In the Timeline, position the selection tool icon on the right edge of the Poem.ptl clip so that it turns into a trim tool ( ).

Note: *You may want to change the Time Zoom Level to 1 Second to see this more clearly.*

4 Drag the edge of the clip to the right and extend the Out point to 10 seconds (00:00:10:00). Use the Info palette as a guide.

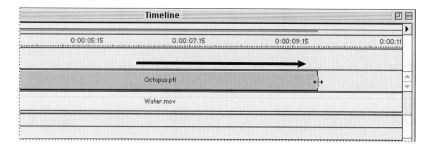

5 Drag Otto.ptl from the Project window to the beginning of the Video 3 track.

6 Select Otto.ptl, and choose Clip > Duration.

7 Type **200** for the new duration and click OK. Otto.ptl is now two seconds long.

8 Drag Poem.ptl from the Project window to the Video 3 track, immediately following Otto.ptl. It should snap to the end of the Otto.ptl clip.

9 Using the selection tool as a trim tool, drag the right edge of Poem.ptl so its Out point is at 10 seconds. It should snap to the end of Octopus.ptl.

Because titles created in Premiere have automatically transparent backgrounds, you don't
need to apply transparency values.

10 Save the project.

11 Do one of the following to set the work area for the preview:

• Drag the work area bar over the section you want to preview.

• Drag the work area markers to specify the beginning and ending of the area to preview.

• Press Alt (Windows) or Option (Mac OS) as you click in the work area band above the
series of clips to preview. This sets the work area to preview a continuous series of clips.

• Double-click the work area band to preview only the section of the Timeline that is
visible in the Timeline window.

12 Do one of the following for the preview:

• Press Enter (Windows) or Return (Mac OS) to build a preview file and preview it in the
Monitor window.

• Hold down Alt (Windows) or Option (Mac OS). When the cursor becomes a
downward pointing arrow, render-scrub within the Timeline window time ruler.

Checking the title-safe zones

Next, you'll check the title-safe zones settings. Safe zones are useful when editing for
broadcast and videotape, because most consumer television sets cut off some portion of
the outer edges of the picture. This process, called *overscan*, permits the center of the
picture to be enlarged. The amount of overscan is not consistent across all televisions, so
it is best to keep titles within the title-safe zone and to keep the important content within
the action-safe zone. The Title window displays the NTSC title-safe and action-safe zones
as dotted-line boxes. The Title Window Options dialog box sets the NTSC title-safe and
color-safe settings.

*Note: The safe zones indicated in Premiere represent NTSC video only; these zones are only
guidelines for other standards, such as PAL and SECAM.*

1 With the Title window open, choose Window > Window Options > Title Window Options, or right-click (Windows) or Control-click (Mac OS) in the Title window and choose Title Window Options from the context menu.

2 In the Title Window Options dialog box, verify (or set) the Show Safe Titles as selected to display NTSC title-safe and action-safe zones. Then, click OK.

For more information about using and adjusting safe zones in the Title window, see "Setting title window options" in Chapter 6 of the Adobe Premiere 6.0 User Guide.

Changing the speed of a rolling title in the Timeline

You can change the speed of a rolling title by changing its duration. The shorter the duration, the faster the title plays; the longer the duration, the slower the title plays.

When you previewed the rolling title, you may have noticed that it played rather quickly. To make it play slower, you'll increase the duration of the Poem clip.

1 Drag the right side Poem.ptl in the Timeline to 14 seconds so that it snaps to the end of Water.mov.

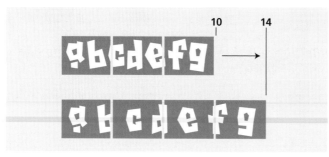

2 Drag the right side of Octopus.ptl to 14 seconds so that it also snaps to the end of Water.mov.

3 Press Enter (Windows) or Return (Mac OS) to preview the project again. Now, the rolling title scrolls much slower and is easier to read.

Updating a title in the Title window

You can open the Title window and update a title by double-clicking the title in either the Timeline or Project window. As soon as you save your changes to the title file, Premiere updates all the references to it in your project.

Now, you will adjust the rolling text of the Poem title so that it doesn't overlap the octopus graphic. To make this adjustment, you'll open Poem.ptl and change the size of the rolling text window using the selection tool.

1 Double-click Poem.ptl in the Timeline.

When the Title window opens, nothing is visible in the window because you entered blank lines at the beginning of the poem. To see the text bounding box, click in the top third of the window.

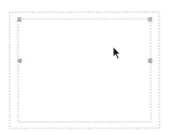

Because you need to make an edit that relies on the position of an object in Octopus.ptl, you'll first import a sample frame to the Title window and use it as a reference.

2 Move the Title window so that it is not obscuring the Project window.

3 Drag Octopus.ptl from the Project window to the Title window. The Octopus title now appears as the background for the Poem title.

Now, you can see exactly how high up in the Title window you need to move the Poem title bounding box.

4 Using the selection tool, select one of the lower handles on the Poem bounding box and move it up just a little so it doesn't touch the head of the octopus.

5 Choose File > Save to save the change to the title file; then, close the Title window.

6 Press Enter (Windows) or Return (Mac OS) to preview the project again.

7 Save the project.

Exporting the movie

Now you'll export the project into a movie for Web viewing. The Save for Web export option provides several different Web output formats.

1 Click the Timeline title bar to activate it.

2 Choose File > Export Timeline > Save for Web. The Save for Web dialog box appears.

3 Click Settings and select a preset to export to the format you have chosen to be the default plug-in for your Web browser. (In this case, choose the download version rather than the streaming version.) Choose one of the following: QuickTime Progressive Download, Real GT Download, or Windows Media Audio.

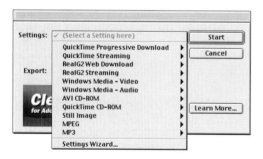

4 Make sure that Entire Project is selected for Export.

5 Click Start.

6 After the export is complete, you can play your Web video in your Web browser. You can also post it to your own Web site to share it with your friends. (Be sure to tell them which plug-in to use for viewing the file).

For more information about preparing video for Web distribution via download or streaming, see any of the following resources:

—"About creating Internet media", in Chapter 10 of the Adobe Premiere 6.0 User Guide.

—"Learn more" in the Save for Web dialog box.

—See "Preparing video for Web distribution via download or streaming" in the Adobe Premiere 6.0 Technical Guides found in the Support area on the Adobe Web site (www.adobe.com/support/techdocs/topissuespre.htm).

—See the Web sites for individual plug-ins: www.apple.com for QuickTime, www.real.com for RealMedia, and www.microsoft.com for Windows Media.

Exploring on your own

Take some time to experiment with the Title window and the 08Lesson.ppj project. Here are some suggestions:

• Apply a gradient fill to the word "Otto" in the Otto.ptl title file. A gradient fill requires a different color in the Start and End Transparency color swatches.

• Create a new title using the poem text but make the text crawl across the screen from left to right. Add empty spaces to make the text start completely off screen, crawl onto the screen, and then crawl completely off the screen.

• Use the Rolling Title Options to apply special timing options to the crawling text so that it slows down as it exits the screen. Save the new title as Crawl.ptl. Replace Poem.ptl in the Timeline with the new Crawl.ptl.

• Change the Octopus graphic to a framed and filled object. Change the color and line weight of the frame.

• Create a graphic in Adobe Illustrator or Photoshop, import it into a Premiere project, then use the Edit Original command to modify the graphic.

Review questions

1 How do you create a new title?

2 How do you change the color of title text?

3 How do you add a shadow?

4 How do you change the opacity of text or a graphic?

5 How do you adjust the speed of a rolling title?

6 What is a reference frame?

7 What is the difference between rolling and crawling text titles?

8 How do you add a title to a video program?

9 How do you add tracks to a project?

Answers

1 Choose File > New > Title.

2 Select the text, click the Object Color swatch and pick a new color from the Color Picker.

3 Select the object, then adjust the Shadow Offset control in the Title window toolbox.

4 Select the text or graphic, then drag one of the Transparency sliders to a new setting.

5 The duration of a title clip can be changed once it has been placed onto the Timeline of a project.

6 A reference frame is a frame from another title, still image, or video clip that you can copy to your title and use as a reference to help determine what colors to use, to precisely position text over an image, or to provide a guideline for drawing an image.

7 Rolling text moves across the screen vertically, either top-to-bottom or bottom-to-top. Crawling text moves horizontally, either left-to-right or right-to-left.

8 Premiere automatically adds a new title to the project that is open when you name and save the new title file. To add an existing title, open the project and title files; then, drag the title from the Title window to the Project window; or choose Clip > Add Clip to Project. Alternatively, with only the project file open, choose File > Import > File and specify the title to import into the project.

9 From the Timeline window menu, choose Add Video Track or Add Audio Track to add a single track. Multiple tracks are added through the Timeline > Track Options box.

Lesson 9

9 | Superimposing

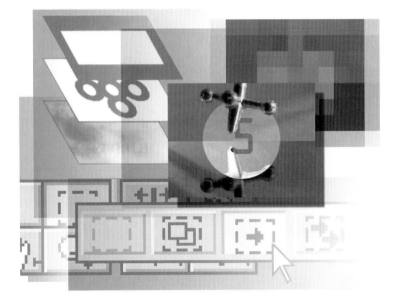

*Using the Timeline in Adobe
Premiere 6.0, you can create up to 98
different video tracks for countless
combinations of layered movies and
stills. With the generous selection of
transparency keys, you can key out
(remove) specific areas of a movie and
create customized effects.*

In this lesson, you'll create a promotional video for CD-ROM distribution. You'll use the superimpose tracks feature in the Timeline to create transparencies, fades, and other special effects. Specifically, you'll learn how to perform these tasks:

- Create a split screen.

- Apply transparency key types and adjust settings.

- Arrange a series of images in a Bin area and specify the display order in the Timeline.

- Use the Shy and Exclude track options.

- Use the fade tools.

Getting started

For this lesson, you'll open an existing project and add clips to the Timeline. Make sure you know the location of the files used in this lesson. Insert the Premiere *Classroom in a Book* CD-ROM disk if necessary. For help, see "Copying the Classroom in a Book files" on page 14 of this *Classroom in a Book*.

Because the files used in this lesson contain font information, you also need to make sure that Adobe Type Manager (ATM) is installed on your system. For information on installing ATM, see "Installing the Classroom in a Book fonts" on page 14 of this *Classroom in a Book*.

To ensure that the Premiere preferences are set to the default values, exit Premiere, and then delete the preferences file as explained in "Restoring default preferences" on page 15.

1 Launch the Premiere 6.0 software and choose Single-Track editing.

2 In the Load Project Settings dialog box, choose Multimedia or Multimedia Quicktime (depending on your operating system), and click OK.

3 Choose Edit > Preferences > General and Still Image and deselect the Open Movies in Clip Window if it is selected.

4 Double-click 09Lesson.ppj in the 09Lesson folder to open the project.

5 If necessary, rearrange windows and palettes so they don't overlap by choosing Window > Workspace > Single-Track Editing.

6 When the project opens, choose File > Save As. If necessary, you may need to open the appropriate folder on your hard disk and type **Promo.ppj**. Press Enter (Windows) or Return (Mac OS).

You'll be superimposing six layers of clips in this lesson, so we've created a project with seven video tracks. Because so many video tracks are open during this lesson, we set the Timeline to display small icons. If you prefer to work with larger icons, choose Window >Window Options > Timeline Window Options and select the medium-sized icons.

Viewing the finished movie

To see what you'll be creating, you can look at the final movie.

1 Choose File > Open and double-click 09Final.mov in the Final folder inside the 09Lesson folder.

2 Click the Play button (▶) to view the movie in the Source view in the Monitor window. The movie remains in the Source view.

Superimposing

Superimposing (often called *matting* or *keying* in television and film production) means playing one clip on top of another. In Premiere, you can add clips to the superimpose tracks (Video 2 track and higher). Then you can add transparency or fades so that the clips placed in lower tracks in the Timeline partially appear as well. If you don't apply transparency to the clip in the highest track, the clips directly below will not appear when you preview or when you play your final movie.

Clips in superimpose tracks with various transparencies applied

Premiere provides 15 *keys* (methods for creating transparency) that allow you to vary the type and intensity of transparency applied to different areas of a clip. When superimposing, you can designate *matte* (specified area) to be totally transparent, or you can apply transparency based on a color or color quality, such as brightness.

It is always best to plan ahead for superimpositions, before you make your video captures. For example, if you videotape a person talking and you want to superimpose a different background behind the person, tape the person in front of a solid-color background, such as a blue screen or seamless background paper. Otherwise, keying out the background will be difficult, if not impossible.

Creating a split screen

A split screen is one of the effects you can create using the transparency settings in Premiere 6.0. A split screen displays a portion of one clip on part of the screen and a portion of another clip on the other part of the screen.

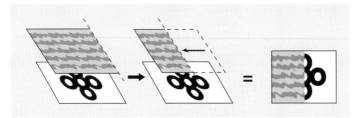

Transparency applied to upper clip; split-screen effect

In this exercise, you'll create a split screen that displays half of one clip on the top and half of another clip on the bottom. But first add the first two clips to the Timeline.

1 Drag Gold.mov from the Bin area in the Project window to the Video 1 track, placing its In point at the very beginning in the Timeline.

2 Scrub through the Timeline ruler to preview the first clip before applying transparency.

3 Drag Amber.mov from the Bin area in the Project window to the Video 2 track, aligning it at the very beginning of the Timeline, as well.

4 Scrub through the Timeline ruler to preview both clips before applying transparency.

Notice that only Amber.mov appears in the Program view in the Monitor window. Without transparency, nothing below this clip displays.

You cannot apply transparency to a clip in the Video 1 track, so you'll apply it to Amber.mov in the Video 2 track. Because Gold.mov is located directly below Amber.mov, after you apply transparency to Amber.mov, Gold.mov will reappear.

5 Select Amber.mov in the Timeline and choose Clip > Video Options > Transparency to see the Transparency Settings dialog box.

Transparency Settings Dialog box: **A.** *Black and white background icon* **B.** *Page peel icon*

6 Leave the Key Type as None.

When you create a split screen, you don't use a transparency key type; instead, you move the corner points on the Sample area.

7 Position the cursor on the bottom left corner of the Sample area (located in the top right corner of the dialog box). When the pointer icon changes to a finger icon, drag it to a point halfway up the left side of the area.

8 Similarly, drag from the bottom right corner of the Sample area halfway up the right side of the area—directly across from the point you placed on the left, to create a straight line halfway up the area.

9 Notice that the lower half of the area has turned white. To see the effect of the split screen, click the page peel icon (⬛) under the Sample area.

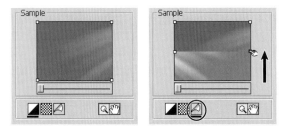

Default Sample area, and Sample area after moving the two bottom corner handles and selecting the page peel icon

Now you can see Gold.mov in the bottom half of the sample area and Amber.mov in the top half.

Note: *You can create vertical, horizontal, or diagonal split screens by moving the sample area corner handles appropriately.*

10 Click OK to close the Transparency Settings dialog box.

11 Use render-scrub to preview the split screen (drag the edit line through the Timeline ruler while pressing the Alt key (Windows) or the Option key (Mac OS.)

If the line that splits the clips is not straight, you can select Amber.mov, re-open the Transparency Settings dialog box, and readjust the points in the Sample area.

12 Save the project.

Applying the Blue Screen transparency key

The two most commonly used transparency keys are Blue Screen and Green Screen. These keys are generally used to substitute the background of one video clip with another. They are favored because they do not interfere with skin tones. For example, TV news programs regularly use blue screens to display footage of the current topic behind the newscaster.

If you use a blue or green background when videotaping footage, and plan to key it out using the Blue or Green Screen key, make sure everything that is to remain opaque is a color other than your key color. For example, if you film a newscaster in front of a blue backdrop and the newscaster is wearing a blue tie, the tie will become transparent along with the background when you apply the Blue Screen key to the footage.

Blue Screen transparency with blue tie and with white tie

Now, you'll add clips to the Video 4 and Video 5 tracks and apply the Blue Screen key and the Chroma key. We're skipping the Video 3 track intentionally for now—you'll add clips to it later in the lesson.

1 Drag Jacklow.mov from the Project window to the Video 4 track, aligning its In point with the very beginning of the Timeline.

Timeline					
⊳0:00		0:00:04:00		0:00:08:00	
Video 7					
Video 6					
Video 5					
Video 4	Jacklow.mov				Jacklow.mov
Video 3					
Video 2	Amber.mov				Amber.mov
Video 1	Gold.mov				Gold.mov

2 Preview this movie by scrubbing through the Timeline ruler. Notice the background is composed of mixed shades of blue. You'll remove this background using the Blue Screen transparency key.

3 Using the selection tool (‹), select Jacklow.mov in the Timeline, and then choose Clip > Video Options > Transparency.

4 Select Blue Screen from the Key Type pop-up menu. If necessary, click the page peel icon (🖾) and look at the Sample area. Notice that the clip's blue background is replaced by the split screen from the Video 1 track and Video 2 track.

The Threshold and Cutoff sliders at the bottom of the dialog box alter the shadows and the extent of color selected and removed.

5 To see how much of the blue background has been keyed out, click the black and white background icon (▨) under the Sample Area. Notice that a blue-gray shadow still appears.

To enhance the appearance of the clip by removing all of this blue background, you'll adjust the Threshold slider.

6 Move the Threshold slider to 60, or until the background becomes completely white.

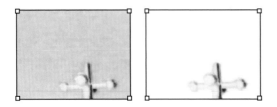

7 Click the page peel icon (▨) again to see the effect. Notice how the background colors become brighter and more true. This is because you're removing more blue value and shadow from the selected clip.

8 Drag the Preview slider in the Sample area to see the effect and then click OK.

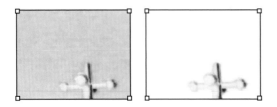

9 Preview the blue screen transparency effect and the split screen by scrubbing through the Timeline ruler while pressing the Alt key (Windows) or the Option key (Mac OS).

10 Save the project.

Applying the Chroma key

The Chroma key lets you select any color as your transparent area. If you can't videotape footage using a blue or green background because of conflicting colors in your clip (such as the color of someone's clothes), you can use any solid color background and then use the Premiere Chroma key to make that color represent your transparent area.

Now, you'll use the Chroma key on a clip with a yellow background.

1 Drag Jackhi.mov from the Project window to the Video 5 track, aligning its In point with the beginning of the Timeline.

2 Scrub through the Timeline ruler to preview the movie before applying transparency.

3 Using the selection tool ( ), select Jackhi.mov in the Timeline, and then choose Clip > Video Options > Transparency.

4 Select Chroma for Key Type.

Notice that the Color box in the Transparency Settings dialog box now displays a frame from Jackhi.mov. You can select a key color from this frame, or you can click the white box above the frame and select a key color from the Color Picker. For this lesson, you'll select a color from the frame.

5 Position the cursor over the frame in the Color box. The pointer turns into an eyedropper tool (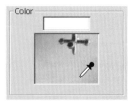).

6 Click the yellow background to select it as your key color.

Because the yellow background in Jackhi.mov is dithered (not a solid color), the background color in the Sample area doesn't change much. You'll need to use the Similarity and Blend sliders to make this clip's yellow background transparent.

The Similarity slider increases the range of colors the key uses for transparency. If you increase the similarity for Jackhi.mov, the range of yellows that are transparent increases.

7 Select the black and white background icon (▧) and move the Similarity slider to 38. Notice how the yellow color gradually decreases as you increase the similarity, until the entire background is white.

The Blend slider blends the edges of the image with the background by gradually changing the opacity where the color pixels meet.

8 Move the Blend slider to 12. Notice how the edges between image and background lose their sharpness.

You don't need to use the Threshold slider or Cutoff slider with this clip.

9 Select the page peel icon (▨)to preview the effect with the split screen and Jacklo.mov in the background.

10 Click OK to close the Transparency Settings dialog box.

11 Preview the clips by pressing Alt (Windows) or Option (Mac OS) while scrubbing through the Timeline ruler. Notice how all the clips now appear on-screen, each with its own unique area of transparency.

12 Save the project.

Adding clips without transparency

Now, you'll add clips to the top two tracks of the Timeline. You won't apply a transparency key to them because you want them to temporarily block the clips below.

1 Drag Ball.mov from the Project window to the Video 6 track, snapping its In point to the beginning of the Timeline.

2 In the Monitor window, drag the Program view shuttle to 0:00:01:00.

3 Drag Excite.ptl from the Project window to the Video 7 track, and snap its In point to the edit line.

Timeline
Video 7
Video 6 Ball.mov
Video 5 Jackhi.mov ... Jackhi.mov
Video 4 Jacklow.mov ... Jacklow.mov
Video 3
Video 2 Amber.mov ... Amber.mov
Video 1 Gold.mov ... Gold.mov

4 Preview the first four seconds of the project by pressing Alt (Windows) or Option (Mac OS) while scrubbing through the Timeline ruler.

Notice how only the bouncing ball and the star graphic appear in the Monitor window. Excite.ptl (the star graphic) is a Premiere title file, so its transparency settings are automatic. Ball.mov has no transparency, so nothing below it in the Timeline is visible.

5 Save the project.

You'll adjust the transition between Ball.mov and the rest of the project a little later.

Applying the Track Matte transparency key type

Premiere's Track Matte key type lets you customize and layer movies. When you apply this key type you can play one movie through the matte of another while yet another movie plays in the background.

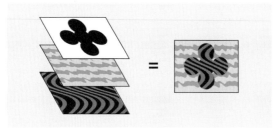

Track Matte key applied to middle clip

When you create a track matte effect, the order of your clips is important. Applying the Track Matte key to different clips and different video tracks results in a wide range of effects. You'll see some of those effects in this lesson. In Lesson 10, you'll apply the Track Matte key to a moving image and create a traveling matte effect. In Lesson 12, you'll also apply several kinds of superimposed transparency effects in combination with virtual and duplicate clips.

Now, you'll create a track matte effect with Ball.mov and Excite.ptl so that the ball bounces inside the Excite.ptl graphic and the clips on the lower tracks display in the background.

First you'll add Ball.mov and Excite.mov to the Timeline again and create an alias for each so you don't confuse them with the clips at the beginning of the Timeline. If necessary, use the Navigator palette to quickly move about the Timeline so that you can see the clips.

1 Drag Ball.mov from the Project window to the end of the Video 6 track, snapping its Out point with the Out point for Jackhi.mov (at 0:00:20:00).

2 Select Ball.mov in the Timeline and choose Clip > Set Clip Name Alias. Type **Ball2.mov** in the text box, and then click OK.

3 Drag Excite.ptl from the Project window to the end of the Video 7 track, snapping its Out point with Ball2.mov's Out point.

4 Select Excite.ptl in the Timeline and choose Clip > Set Clip Name Alias. Type **Excite2.ptl** in the text box, and then click OK.

5 Position the pointer on the left edge of Excite2.ptl and, when the cursor turns into the trim tool, drag to the left until the edge aligns with the beginning of Ball2.mov at 0:00:16:00.

Now you'll apply the Track Matte key.

6 Select Ball2.mov and choose Clip > Video Options > Transparency.

7 Choose Track Matte for the Key Type.

8 Make sure the page peel icon is selected under the Sample area, and then drag the Preview slider to view the effect.

Notice how all the clips in the lower tracks display inside the Excite2.ptl matte (black area). To reverse the effect, so that the background remains constant throughout the video program and only the bouncing ball appears inside the matte, you'll apply the Reverse Key option.

9 In the area below the Sample area, select the Reverse Key option. Drag the Preview slider under the Sample area to view the effect, and then click OK.

10 Save the project.

Adding a series of still images

In this lesson, you'll add a series of title files to the Video 3 track. You'll add six clips at once to the Timeline, but first you'll rearrange them in the order you want them to appear in the Timeline.

You can arrange clips in the Bin area in the Project window in a variety of ways.

To arrange clips alphabetically, click the heading under which you want them to appear. For example, if you want the clips to appear alphabetized by name, click the Name heading in the Bin area in the Project window. If you want the clips to appear alphabetized by media type, click the list view icon (≡) and then click Media Type in the Bin area in the Project window. This puts all the movies together alphabetically, and then all of the still images together alphabetically.

To arrange clips sequentially, select the icon view icon (▯) in the Project window and then drag the clip icons around the window in any order you want. We've grouped all the titles into the Titles bin to make it easy to create a sequential arrangement.

1 Click the Titles bin folder icon in the Project window to open it.

2 With the Project window active, click the Icon view icon (⊡) at the bottom of the window. The titles now appear only as icons, which you can rearrange in the window.

3 Drag the title icons to reposition them in numerical order from left to right. You may need to resize the window.

Note: Alternatively, you can arrange the title clips into a Storyboard and then drag them into the Timeline. Do not choose Automate-to-Timeline, because the clips will be placed on the Video 1 track instead of the Video 3 track. After you've created your storyboard continue with Steps 4–7.

Notice that three of the clips have a white background and three have a black background. The backgrounds vary to create a perceptible transition between clips. Once you apply transparency, the transition from clip to clip will be even more apparent.

Before you drag the clips to the Timeline, you'll set the edit line.

4 Drag the Shuttle slider in the Program view in the Monitor window to the In point of Ball2.mov (at 0:00:16:00).

5 In the Project window, click the Titles bin folder icon to activate the Titles bin, and then choose Edit > Select All.

6 Drag the files to the Video 3 track, aligning the Out point of the last file with the edit line.

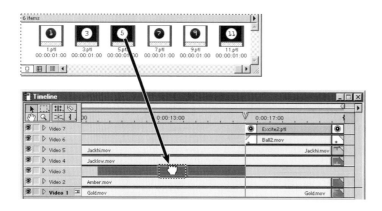

7 If you need to make adjustments to the location of the series of clips in the Timeline, select all the clips using the range select tool (⬚). Then move them as a group. Be careful to only select the clips in the Video 3 track. If you select other clips, click the selection tool to deselect them, then use the range tool again.

Note: You can also use the track select tool (⊞) to select the clips because they are the only clips on the track, but using this tool does not allow you to snap to an edit line or another clip.

8 Close the Titles bin.

9 Preview the titles in the project by pressing Alt (Windows) or Option (Mac OS) while scrubbing through the Timeline ruler.

10 Save the project.

Using transparency to blend clips

When you have a group of clips with identical backgrounds located directly above, below, or beside one another on the Timeline, you can select them as a group and apply transparency.

Several of Premiere's transparency keys let you create special blending and fading effects. For example, to brighten a dark clip you can apply the Luminance key, which replaces the darker colors in the superimposed clip with lighter colors from the clip below it in the Timeline. Here, you'll experiment with different key types and their effects.

1 Select the track select tool and then click the first clip in the Video 3 track to select all the title clips in that track.

2 Choose Clip > Video Options > Transparency.

3 Select Screen for key type. Make sure the page peel icon is selected so you can preview the effect.

When you apply the Screen key to a grayscale image, such as 1.ptl, Premiere substitutes the clip's black areas with the color from the clip below it in the Timeline.

4 Move the Cutoff slider located in the bottom left of the dialog box to see its different effects. This slider lets you gradually change the opacity of the background.

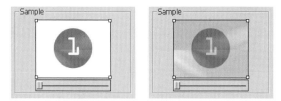

Screen key with Cutoff slider set to 100% and 50%

5 Select Multiply for key type.

The Multiply key creates transparency where the clip is bright. Because you applied it to a black-and-white clip, the white areas are transparent.

6 Move the Cutoff slider and note the different effects. The Cutoff slider adjusts the amount of transparency for the entire clip. As you lower the value, the clip becomes more transparent and the background begins to appear through the black areas. When the Cutoff is at zero, the selected clip becomes completely transparent.

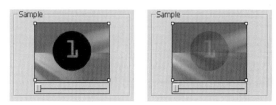

Multiply key type with Cutoff slider set to 100% and 30%

In addition to these transparency key types, you can also use the Track Matte key type to blend images and colors.

7 Select Track Matte for Key Type. Notice how the transparency affects the clips above and below the selected clip, rather than just below, like most keys.

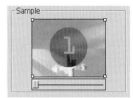

8 Click OK to accept the Track Matte key and close the Transparency Settings dialog box.

Original titles

Titles with Track Matte transparency key applied

9 Preview the transparency effect by scrubbing through the Timeline ruler while pressing the Alt key (Windows) or Option key (Mac OS).

Notice how the alternating black and white backgrounds affect the colors that display in each clip. It is difficult to predict how the Track Matte key type will blend colors; every image generates a different effect. Now you'll make each clip even more distinct by reversing the Track Matte transparency setting on alternating title clips.

10 Using the selection tool, select 3.ptl, and then choose Clip > Video Options > Transparency to open the Transparency Settings dialog box.

11 Select the Reverse Key. Notice once again the shift in colors. Click OK.

12 Select 7.ptl. Choose Clip > Video Options > Transparency, select the Reverse Key, and then click OK.

13 Select 11.ptl. Choose Clip > Video Options > Transparency, select the Reverse Key, and then click OK.

Note: You'll learn how to copy transparency settings from one clip to another in Lesson 11.

14 Preview the transparency effect by scrubbing through the Timeline ruler while pressing the Alt key (Windows) or Option key (Mac OS).

15 Save the project.

Making video tracks shy

Now that you have all the clips added to the Timeline, it's time to start managing the video tracks. You won't be editing Gold.mov or Amber.mov again, so you can mark the Video 1 and Video 2 tracks *shy* and hide them in order to make it easier to see and access clips on the tracks with which you still need to work.

Marking a track as shy does not immediately conceal it in the Timeline, because you must choose the Hide Shy Tracks command to conceal or reveal all shy tracks simultaneously. Although shy tracks, when hidden, don't appear on the Timeline, they are still included when you preview or export the project.

1 Press the Control key (Windows) or Command key (Mac OS) and click the eye icon next to the Video 1 track. Do the same for the Video 2 track.

A solid eye icon represents a visible track; an outlined eye icon represents a shy track.

The eye icon now displays as an outlined eye (👁).

2 From the Timeline window menu, choose Hide Shy Tracks or choose Timeline > Hide Shy Tracks.

The Video 3 track is now the first video track that appears in the Timeline.

Note: You can also hide audio tracks by pressing Control (Windows) or Command (Mac OS) while clicking the speaker icon (◀ْ) next to the track you want to hide.

3 Preview the project by scrubbing through the Timeline ruler while pressing Alt (Windows) or Option (Mac OS).

Notice how even though you can't see the Video 1 and Video 2 tracks in the Timeline, they do appear in the Program view in the Monitor window when you preview.

When you want the tracks to reappear on the Timeline, you choose Show Shy Tracks from the Timeline window menu. If you want to remove the shy designation from a track, press Control (Windows) or Command (Mac OS) and click the outlined eye icon. The outlined eye icon will change to a solid eye icon.

For now, however, you'll leave the Video 1 and Video 2 tracks shy and hidden.

Excluding video tracks

Premiere's exclude feature lets you turn off clips in the Timeline so that they won't appear when you preview or export the project. You won't be using this feature in this lesson. But to learn what it does and how it differs from the shy feature, let's experiment with it on the Video 4 track.

1 Click the eye icon next to Video 4 to hide the track. When you click the eye icon (👁) without pressing Control (Windows) or Command (Mac OS), you enable the exclude feature for the track.

An empty box indicates an excluded track.

2 Scrub through the Timeline while pressing Alt (Windows) or Option (Mac OS) to preview the clips.

The Video 4 track remains visible in the Timeline, but Jacklow.mov does not appear in the Program view window when you preview the project. Also notice that half of the title files display in black and white and half don't appear at all. The Track Matte key type does not create a transparent effect unless there is a clip in the track directly above it.

3 Click the empty eye icon box for the Video 4 track again to include the track, and then save the project.

Note: You can also exclude audio tracks by clicking the speaker icon (🔊).

Fading clips

Premiere's fade controls let you fade in and out of clips on the superimpose tracks, creating shadows, transparencies, and multicamera effects. Now, you'll adjust the opacity rubberband on the top four tracks of the Timeline, starting with the highest track, Video 7.

1 Choose Window > Show Info to open the Info palette so you can use it as a guide, then press the Home key to return the edit line to the beginning of the Timeline.

Note: If a clip is selected in the Timeline, the edit line will return to the beginning of that clip. To deselect the clip, click it again or click the selection tool.

2 Click the triangle to the left of the Video 7 track label to expand the track.

3 Click the red Display Opacity Rubberband icon (◢) to display the opacity rubberband.

Notice the opacity rubberband that appears under the clip name and thumbnail; this specifies the opacity of the entire clip. Every clip has a handle (a small red square) at the beginning and end of the opacity rubberband. You can adjust the fading in and out of clips by moving these handles or by adding handles to the opacity rubberband and moving them up and down. The process is similar to the way you adjusted audio volume in Lesson 5.

4 Using the selection tool, position the pointer on top of the opacity rubberband in the center of the clip, until the pointer turns into a finger icon with plus and minus signs (✥).

5 Move the cursor over the opacity rubberband and when the Info palette's "cursor at" line reads about 0:00:01:15, click to make a new handle. If the new handle is not in the correct location, you can either select it and move it, or drag it off the opacity rubberband to delete it.

6 Select the first handle at the beginning of the Excite.ptl clip and drag it down to the bottom left corner. The Fade Level in the Info palette reads 0%. The clip now starts completely transparent and then becomes fully opaque halfway through.

Note: When selecting a handle on the opacity rubberband, make sure the finger icon is gray before you click to select it, otherwise, you will create a new handle. If you do create a new handle that you don't want, simply drag it off the opacity rubberband to delete it.

7 Drag the last handle in the clip to 0% also.

8 Press Alt (Windows) or Option (Mac OS) and scrub through the Timeline ruler to preview the clips. Now, when the clip begins playing, it is completely transparent; then it gradually becomes completely opaque, and then it gradually dissolves until it's completely transparent again.

9 Click the triangle next to the Video 6 track label to expand the track. Move the cursor over the opacity rubberband and when the Info palette's "cursor at" line reads about 0:00:02:15, click to make a new handle. If the new handle is not in the correct location, you can either select it and move it, or drag it off the opacity rubberband to delete it.

10 Drag the handle at the end of Ball.mov to 0%. Now Ball.mov will play at 100% opacity for 2 seconds and 15 frames, and then it will gradually fade to 0% opacity. As it fades out, all the clips on the lower tracks will fade in.

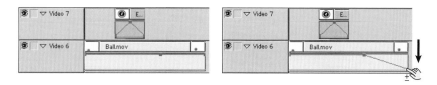

11 Press Alt (Windows) or Option (Mac OS) and scrub through the Timeline ruler to preview the clips.

12 Click the triangles next to the Video 6 and Video 7 track names to collapse them, and then save the project.

Using the fade adjustment tool

Now you'll use the fade adjustment tool to fade in and out of a clip. The fade adjustment tool uniformly moves the fade line between any two handles.

1 Click the triangle next to the Video 5 track name to expand the track.

2 Using the selection tool, click the opacity rubberband for Jackhi.mov at about 6:00 to make a new handle, then click again at about 6:05 to make another handle.

Now you'll use the fade adjustment tool to move the line between the first point on the Timeline and the point at 6:00.

3 Select the fade adjustment tool ( ).

4 Position the tool over the opacity rubberband, between the handle at 0:00 and the handle at 6:00, then drag the line down to 0% opacity. You can view the opacity setting (Fade Level) in the Info palette, as you drag the opacity rubberband.

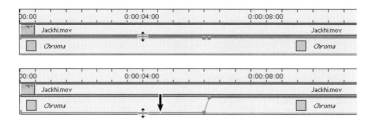

5 Preview the effect by scrubbing through the Timeline ruler while pressing Alt (Windows) or Option (Mac OS).

Jackhi.mov fades in from 0% to 100% over 5 frames. Let's make the fade-in effect last longer, by extending the distance between the second handle (which is at 0% opacity) and the third handle (which is at 100% opacity).

6 Using the selection tool ( ), select the handle at 6:00 on the opacity rubberband, and drag it to the left to about 5:15. Use the Info palette as a guide.

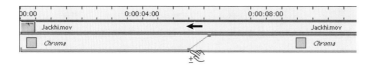

7 Preview the effect by scrubbing through the Timeline ruler while pressing Alt (Windows) or Option (Mac OS).

8 Click the triangle next to the Video 5 track name to collapse the track.

9 Save the project.

Fading the Video 4 track

Now you'll adjust the opacity rubberband for Jacklow.mov so that it fades in and out without reaching 100% until just before the six titles appear. Use the Info palette as a guide when making and moving the fade handles.

1 Click the triangle next to the Video 4 track name to expand the track.

2 Using the selection tool (➤), click the opacity rubberband at about 4:00 to make a new handle, then click again at about 5:00 to make another handle.

3 Select the fade adjustment tool (⬍) and drag the opacity rubberband between the handle at 0:00 and the next handle to 0% opacity.

4 Using the selection tool (➤), click at about 5:15 to make a handle. Then click at about 6:00 to make another handle.

5 Select the fade adjustment tool (⬍).

Position the fade adjustment tool over an opacity rubberband segment and press the Shift key. When you move the opacity rubberband using this technique, the opacity value displays on the opacity rubberband and the entire segment moves as you drag.

6 Press Shift and position the fade adjustment tool (⬍) over the opacity rubberband between the handles at 5:00 and 5:15. Drag the line to 50% opacity.

7 Select the selection tool ( ).

8 Click the opacity rubberband at 7:15 and 9:15 to make two new handles.

9 Using the fade adjustment tool ( ), press Shift and drag the opacity rubberband between the handles at 6:00 and 7:15 to 0% opacity. You may need to drag outside of the Timeline window.

10 Preview the fades by scrubbing through the Timeline ruler while pressing Alt (Windows) or Option (Mac OS).

Notice how all the clips gradually fade in and out, creating a reflection effect.

11 Click the triangle next to the Video 4 track name to collapse the track.

12 Save the project.

Exporting the movie

Now we'll export the project to a QuickTime movie for playback from a CD-ROM. When exporting video for playback from CD-ROM, keep the file size as small as possible, and limit the data rate to 300 or 500K/sec so that it plays back at the highest quality possible from a variety of systems.

1 Make sure the Timeline is active, and then choose File > Export Timeline > Movie.

2 In the Export Movie dialog box, click the Settings button. Make sure QuickTime is selected for the File Type and Entire Project is selected for the Range.

3 Also make sure that Export Video and Open When Finished are selected. Then deselect Export Audio. The default values for other settings, including those for compression, are fine for this project.

4 Click OK to close the Export Movie Settings dialog box.

5 Type **Promo.mov** for the filename; then click Save (Windows) or OK (Mac OS).

A status bar displays the progress and when Premiere is finished creating the movie it opens in its own window.

6 Click the Play button (▶) to view your movie.

Exploring on your own

Feel free to experiment with the project you just created. Here are some suggestions:

• Change the transparency key for the title files to see the different effects.

• Use the Wipe transition to create a split screen between Amber.mov and Gold.mov.

• Create a three-way split screen using the Wipe transition and the Sample area in the Transparency dialog box.

• Change the transparency for Ball2.mov so that the background clips display through the ball.

• Create a title and add it to the project, superimposing it over all the other clips.

• See what other transparency keys will remove the background of the Jackhi.mov and Jacklo.mov clips.

Review questions

1 How do you create a split screen?

2 What is the difference between the Blue Screen key and the Chroma key?

3 Which key lets you customize and layer movies by playing one movie through the mask of another?

4 How do you make a track shy?

5 What is the difference between a hidden shy track and an excluded track?

6 What is the difference between the Similarity slider and the Blend slider?

Answers

1 You move the handles in the Sample Area in the Transparency Settings dialog box.

2 The Blue Screen key only lets you key out the color blue. The Chroma key lets you key out any color you choose.

3 The Track Matte key.

4 Press Control (Windows) or Command (Mac OS) and click the eye icon.

5 A hidden shy track does not display on the Timeline, but does display in the preview. An excluded track does display on the Timeline, but does not preview.

6 The Similarity slider increases the range of colors the transparency key keys out. The Blend slider blends the color pixels around all edges where the transparent pixels meet the opaque pixels.

Lesson 10

10 | Adding Motion

*Motion enhances and enriches the effect
of still image files in a video program.
The Adobe Premiere Motion feature lets
you move, rotate, distort, and magnify
a variety of still image and video files.*

In this lesson, you'll create a 10-second Web advertisement for a flower shop. You'll learn how to animate a still image using the Premiere Motion dialog box and a variety of motion settings. In particular, you'll learn how to do the following:

• Set and change a *motion path*.

• Adjust the Motion timeline.

• Adjust the zoom, rotation, delay, and distortion settings.

• Create a traveling matte from still images.

• Load a saved motion path.

Restoring default preferences

For this lesson, you should restore the default preferences of Premiere to the factory settings before you launch the program or start the lesson. See "Restoring default preferences" on page 15 of this *Classroom in a Book*.

Getting started

For this lesson, you'll open an existing project in which the necessary files are already imported. Then, you'll apply different motion and transparency settings to the clips. Make sure you know the location of the files used in this lesson. Insert the CD-ROM disk if necessary. For help, see "Copying the Classroom in a Book files" on page 14.

1 Launch the Premiere 6.0 software, after you have restored the default preferences, and choose Single-Track Editing.

2 In the Load Project Settings dialog box, choose Multimedia or Multimedia Quicktime (depending on your operating system), and click OK.

3 Choose Edit > Preferences > General and Still Image and deselect Open Movies in Clip Window if it is selected.

4 Click OK.

Open the existing project file

1 Double-click the existing project 10Lesson.ppj in the 10Lesson folder to open it.

2 If necessary, rearrange windows and palettes so they don't overlap by choosing Window > Workspace > Single-Track Editing. Make sure the Effect Controls palette is open for this lesson.

3 Choose File > Save As, select the **10Lesson** folder location on your hard disk, type **Glass1.ppj** for the new project name, and press Enter (Windows) or Return (Mac OS).

Viewing the finished movie

If you'd like to see what you'll be creating, you can open and play the finished movie.

1 Choose File > Open. Select the 10Final.mov in the Final folder inside the 10Lesson folder. The movie opens in the Source view in the Monitor window.

2 Click the Play button (▶) in the Source view in the Monitor window to watch the video program. When the movie ends, the final frame will remain visible in the Source view in the Monitor window.

Creating animation in Premiere

An *animation* is different from a video, in that the motion is generated synthetically, not by shooting live action. You can import animation clips into Premiere from other software programs such as Adobe After Effects. There are also a number of ways to create animations right in Adobe Premiere 6.0.

You can move, rotate, zoom, and distort a still image or video clip in Premiere. But note that you can add motion only to the entire clip; you cannot animate individual elements within the clip.

The motion controls in Premiere 6.0 let you create a motion path along which to animate any still image or video clip. You can specify the path to be completely within the visible area, or to extend beyond the visible area so that the clip appears to enter and exit the frame at the boundaries.

In this lesson, you'll animate a still image by creating a motion path, and learn about using a variety of motion controls in Premiere to enhance the animation.

Applying a motion path to a still image

Here you'll add a simple motion path to Forget.psd, a Photoshop file that contains an alpha channel. As you may recall from Lessons 2 and 8, an alpha channel is a fourth channel in an RGB image that contains a mask (also known as a matte). The mask defines the parts of the image that are transparent or semitransparent

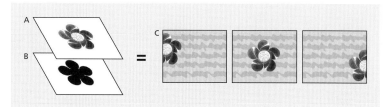

A. Photoshop file B. Alpha channel in Photoshop file
C. Alpha channel key and motion applied

Applying transparency

You'll begin by adding Backdrop.mov to the Source view. Then, you'll preview it and add it to the Timeline.

1 Drag Backdrop.mov from the Bin area in the Project window to the Source view in the Monitor window and click the Play button (▶).

2 After you play it, drag Backdrop.mov from the Source view to the Video 1 track, aligning it with the beginning of the Timeline.

Now you'll add Forget.psd to the Timeline and apply transparency. First, you'll move the edit line to a new position. Then, you'll use it to align the clip in the Timeline.

3 Drag the Shuttle slider in the Program view in the Monitor window to 0:00:00:15.

4 Drag Forget.psd from the Bin area in the Project window to the Video 2 track, aligning its In point to the edit line.

5 Move the Shuttle slider in the Program view to about 0:00:03:00.

6 Drag the right edge of Forget.psd to the edit line. Resizing a clip like this is an easy way to change the duration of a still image.

7 Select Forget.psd in the Timeline and choose Clip > Video Options > Transparency.

8 In the Transparency Settings dialog box, choose Alpha Channel for the Key Type. Make sure the page peel icon (▨) is selected so that you can preview the effect.

When Forget.psd was saved in Adobe Photoshop, the white background was saved as an alpha channel, which is easy to key out using either the Alpha Channel key or the White Alpha Matte key.

9 Click OK to accept the transparency settings and close the dialog box.

Applying motion

Now you'll add motion.

1 With Forget.psd still selected in the Timeline, do one of the following to open the Motion Settings dialog box:

• Choose Clip > Video Options > Motion.

• If the Effect Controls palette is not open, choose Window > Show Effect Controls. Then click the box to the left of the word Motion in the Effect Controls palette.

In the top left corner of the Motion Settings dialog box, a sample of the selected clip moves along the default motion path. To the right of the sample is the motion path. The default path locates the Start and Finish keyframes outside the visible area of the video program so that the clip enters the visible area from the left, moves across, and exits on the right.

Note: In Windows, the last keyframe on the motion path is labeled End, rather than Finish.

2 Click the Pause button by the preview thumbnail in the Motions Settings dialog box to stop the motion. Click the Play button to view the motion.

Notice that the default motion is straight, as represented by the horizontal line in the upper right panel. This line is called the *motion path*. If you were to click OK without making any changes, the selected clip would move in a horizontal line.

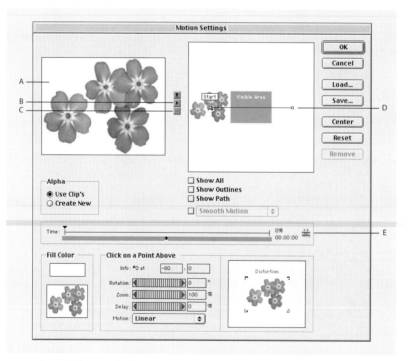

A. Preview window B. Play button C. Pause button D. Motion path E. Motion timeline

3 Make sure the Alpha option under the motion thumbnail is set to Use Clip's, and then select Show All to see a preview of the motion superimposed over Backdrop.mov.

When you select Use Clip's, Premiere uses the clip's alpha channel for transparency. When you select Create New, Premiere uses the clip's frame as the transparent border, so a white box surrounds the image.

Notice that each end of the motion path has a small box, called a *keyframe*. You use keyframes to change the direction and shape of the path.

4 Position the pointer on the Start point of the motion path. The pointer icon becomes a pointing finger icon.

Note: If you are working in Windows, the pointing finger icon turns gray if you position it directly over a keyframe. If you position it over the path, it turns white. In Windows, clicking while the finger icon is gray selects a keyframe; clicking while the finger icon is white creates a new keyframe. In Mac OS the pointing finger icon remains white.

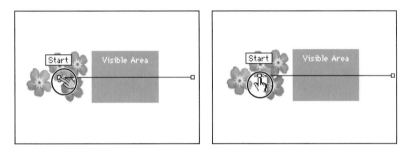

Motion path with pointing finger icon in Windows and in Mac OS

Note: The finger icon may flicker when you position it over a keyframe along the motion path, because of the constant screen redraw in the preview window or because of memory-related issues. Pausing the preview may help control the flicker.

5 Click the Pause button by the motion thumbnail to stop the preview from playing and to preserve memory.

The motion thumbnail requires memory in order to display the motion settings. Leaving it active all the time may slow your system's performance. Pausing the preview increases the memory available for other functions in Premiere.

6 Drag the start motion keyframe to the lower left corner, so that the image is just outside of the Visible Area.

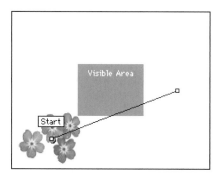

The Visible Area represents what you can see on-screen. Any keyframes or paths outside this area will not be fully visible when you view the video program. When you want clips to gradually enter or exit the screen, place keyframes outside the Visible Area.

7 Drag the last keyframe up to the top right corner so that the entire image is outside the Visible Area.

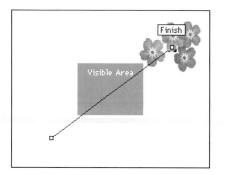

8 Click the Play button by the motion thumbnail to view the motion. When you're finished viewing, click the Pause button.

Adding keyframes and distorting an image

You can add keyframes to the motion path in two ways. To move keyframes in space, move them on the motion path; to move keyframes in time, move them on the Motion timeline.

• Click anywhere directly on the motion path. The pointer turns into a pointing finger. Click again to add a keyframe to the motion path, and drag to adjust its position, creating a new segment of the path. You can drag the Start and Finish keyframes to any location within or outside of the visible area.

• Click anywhere along the motion path timeline (located directly below the motion path). The pointer turns into a downward-pointing triangle. Then drag the keyframe on the motion path to adjust its position.

For now, you'll use the first method of adding keyframes. You'll be introduced to the second method, which uses the motion path timeline, later in this lesson.

1 Click the motion path about one-third of the way from the start keyframe to make a new keyframe, and drag it to the top left corner of the Visible Area.

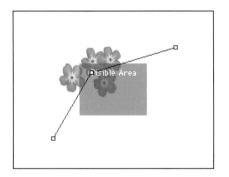

While the keyframe is still selected, you'll distort the image.

2 In the bottom right corner of the Motion Settings dialog box is the Distortion area. Place the pointer over the top left corner keyframe in the Distortion area until it becomes a pointing finger, and then drag it up and to the left.

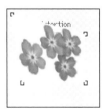

3 Click the bottom right corner keyframe, and then drag down and to the right.

4 Click the top right corner keyframe, and then drag it toward the center of the Distortion area. Click the bottom left corner keyframe, and then drag it toward the center of the Distortion area. The image should look something like this:

When previewed, the clip will slowly distort as it approaches this keyframe, and then it will gradually return to its original shape.

5 Click the Play button (▶) to view the motion, and then click the Pause button.

You'll end the distortion effect sooner by adding another keyframe and returning the clip to its original shape (although smaller) in the Distortion area.

6 Click about two-thirds of the way across the motion path to make another keyframe, then drag it down to the lower right corner of the Visible Area.

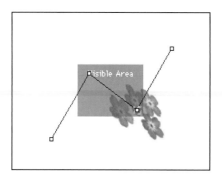

7 While this keyframe is still selected, move the corner keyframes of the clip in the Distortion area back to their original square positions, but make the clip about one-third of its original size. Use the picture below as a guide.

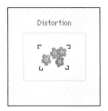

8 Click the Play button in the motion thumbnail to preview the changes.

9 Click OK to close the Motion Settings dialog box.

10 Save the project.

For more information, see "To fine-tune the position of a keyframe on the motion path" in Chapter 8 of the *Adobe Premiere 6.0 User Guide*.

Applying transparency settings

Now you'll animate Lotus.psd using the motion path, zoom, and rotation options. First, you need to add Lotus.psd to the Timeline and apply transparency.

1 Move the edit line to 0:00:02:15, using the timecode in the Monitor window's Program view as a guide.

2 Choose Timeline > Add Video Track to display the Video 3 track if it is not already open.

3 Drag Lotus.psd from the Project window to the Video 3 track, aligning its In point to the edit line.

4 Move the edit line to about 0:00:06:15.

5 Drag the right edge of Lotus.psd to the edit line.

	Timeline		
	00:15	0:00:02:15	0:00:04:15	0:00:06:
▷ Video 3		LOTUS.PSD	
▷ Video 2	FORGET.PSD	⟶	
▷ **Video 1**	Backdrop.mov		Back
▷ **Audio 1**			

6 Select Lotus.psd in the Timeline and choose Clip > Video Options > Transparency.

Lotus.psd was created in Adobe Photoshop with a blue-green background (Red = 0, Green = 255, and Blue = 255). As you recall from Lesson 9, with this color, you could make the background transparent using the Blue Screen, Green Screen, Chroma, or RGB Difference key.

Because the RGB Difference key includes the option to add a drop shadow to the remaining opaque image, we'll use it on Lotus.psd.

7 Choose RGB Difference for Key Type.

8 In the Color area, click the blue-green background of the thumbnail to select it as the transparent value.

Make sure the black and white icon (◩) is selected under the Sample area so that you can clearly view the transparency effect.

9 Move the Similarity slider to 60 to increase the range of colors affected by the key type. Click the page peel icon (◪) to view the transparency in relation to the other clips in the Timeline.

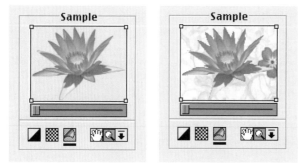

Sample area before and after moving Similarity slider

💡 *It's a good idea to plan ahead. Notice that Lotus.psd was created so that the background color is not used anywhere in the image, allowing for a high Similarity value to generate a good mask.*

10 In the lower right corner of the Transparency Settings dialog box, select Drop Shadow. Notice the new shadow that appears on the remaining opaque image (the flower).

11 Click OK to close the Transparency Settings dialog box.

Applying motion to a clip with a colored background

Now you'll apply motion to Lotus.psd. Because this clip has a colored background, you'll need to adjust the Fill Color in the Motion Setting dialog box.

1 Select Lotus.psd in the Timeline, if it's not already selected.

2 Choose Clip > Video Options > Motion.

3 To view the motion, click the Play button. Make sure Show All is selected so that you can see the clip on the lower track as you preview the motion.

Notice that as the clip moves across the screen, a white background follows and precedes it. By default, Premiere uses white to fill the area around the clip's frame when the frame does not fill the screen. Because you applied transparency to a color other than white, the white fill area is not transparent. The Fill Color option lets you select the color Premiere uses for the fill area, so that it appears transparent.

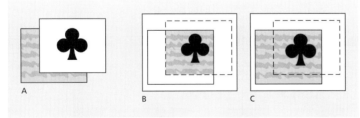

*A. Clip with a transparency value other than white **B.** Before choosing the motion Fill Color **C.** After choosing the motion Fill Color*

4 Position the pointer on the clip thumbnail in the Fill Color area in the lower left corner of the Motion Settings dialog box. The pointer turns into an eyedropper tool (🖋).

5 Click the blue-green background to select it. Notice how the white box disappears from the preview, which now displays with a completely transparent background.

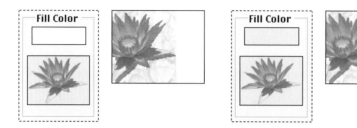

Applying zoom and rotation

Now you'll add keyframes to the Motion timeline and apply zoom and rotation. When you add keyframes directly to the Motion timeline rather than to the motion path, you can select the exact time at which you want the effect to occur.

1 If you prefer to work without the motion, click the Pause button to stop the preview.

2 Position the pointer over the middle of the Motion timeline. When the pointer turns to a solid triangle icon, click and drag until the Motion timeline percent is at 55%. Then release the mouse to make a keyframe.

3 Click the Center button to position the new keyframe directly in the center of the Visible Area. This button centers the keyframe visually, but not chronologically.

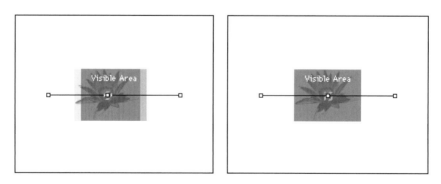

4 With the keyframe still selected, type **300** in the Rotation text box below the Motion timeline. One complete rotation is 360 degrees. By entering 300, you're rotating the image almost one full rotation.

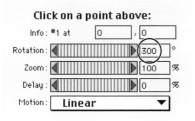

5 Press the Tab key to move to the Zoom text box and type **180**, and then press Tab again. A zoom value of 100% represents the original size of the clip. Entering a zoom value of 180 increases the image size by 80%.

6 Click the Play button (▶) to preview your edits in the motion thumbnail, and then click the Pause button to stop the motion.

Notice how the flower begins rotating clockwise as it moves from the first keyframe to the second keyframe, and then turns counterclockwise as it moves from the second keyframe to the last keyframe. Because the first and last keyframes on the motion path have rotation values of 0 (zero), the flower must rotate to 300 degrees by the time it reaches the second keyframe, and then return to 0 degrees by the time it reaches the last keyframe, thus creating a backwards rotation effect between the second and last keyframe.

Now, you'll edit the first keyframe of the motion path.

7 Select the Start keyframe on the motion path and click the Center button.

8 Type **0** in the Zoom text box, and then press the Tab key.

9 Click the Play button by the motion thumbnail and notice how the clip now zooms in from 0 to 180% in the center of the Visible Area. Click the Pause button to stop the preview.

Now, you'll move the last keyframe of the motion path out of the Visible Area, making the clip move off the screen.

10 Drag the last keyframe of the motion path to the top right corner so the image is just outside of the Visible Area.

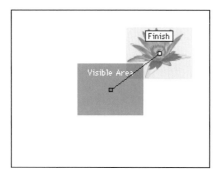

11 With the last keyframe still selected, type **150** in the Rotation text box; then press the Tab key.

12 Preview the effect by clicking the Play button by the motion thumbnail.

This effect may not be too obvious, but the 150 degree rotation on the last keyframe slows down the spinning flower as it leaves the Visible Area. Now, the image only needs to return to 150 degrees instead of 0 while traveling from the second keyframe to the last keyframe.

Adjusting the speed of the motion

You can adjust the speed of motion effects by changing the Motion or Delay option, or by moving the keyframes on the Motion timeline.

Here, you'll make the zoom effect on the second keyframe appear more realistic by accelerating it with the Motion option.

1 Select the second keyframe on the Motion timeline.

Note: *When selecting a keyframe on the Motion timeline, make sure the pointer appears as a finger icon before clicking. If the pointer appears as a triangle, each click will create a new keyframe rather than select an existing keyframe.*

2 Choose Accelerate from the Motion pop-up menu at the bottom of the dialog box. Click the Play button (▶) to preview the results.

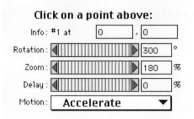

The motion now speeds up as the flower approaches its full magnification of 180%.

💡 *When you zoom out of a keyframe, use the Decelerate Motion option to make it appear more realistic. The Linear option keeps the motion at a constant rate between two keyframes.*

Now, you'll adjust the keyframes on the Motion timeline, to increase the speed at which the clip moves off the screen.

3 Click the Pause button to stop the preview.

4 Drag the second keyframe on the Motion timeline to the left until it is at 46%.

The time it takes the flower to get from the first keyframe to the second keyframe is less than what it takes to get from the second keyframe to the last keyframe.

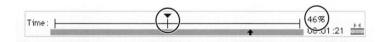

5 Click OK to close the Motion Settings dialog box, and then save the project.

6 Drag the work area bar over Forget.psd and Lotus.psd, and then press Enter (Windows) or Return (Mac OS) to preview the new motion settings.

Creating a traveling matte

Traveling mattes are moving track mattes. You can create a traveling matte by using a still image with applied motion or by using a black-and-white or grayscale video clip. The motion applied to a still image can be as simple as a zoom or it can be complex, involving rotations, distortions, and delays.

First let's add two more clips to the Timeline.

1 Drag Logo.ai from the Bin area in the Project window to the Video 3 track, aligning its In point with the end of Lotus.psd.

2 Drag the right edge of Logo.ai until its Out point snaps to the end of Backdrop.mov.

3 Drag Green.psd from the Project window to the Video 2 track, aligning its In point with the In point of Logo.ai.

4 Drag the right edge of Green.psd until its Out point also snaps to the end of Backdrop.mov.

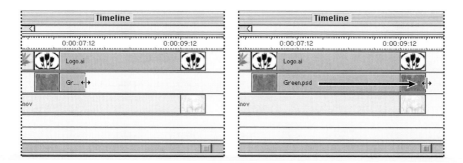

Applying transparency to traveling matte clips

When creating a track or traveling matte transparency effect, always apply the Track Matte key to the clip located below the matte in the Timeline. Here you'll apply the Track Matte key to Green.psd, so that it will play through the black area (matte) in Logo.ai, which is located above it.

1 Select Green.psd in the Timeline and choose Clip > Video Options > Transparency.

2 Choose Track Matte for Key Type. Make sure the page peel icon is selected.

Notice how Green.psd becomes the background and Backdrop.mov (the video program's background) displays through Logo.ai's matte. We want to reverse this effect, so that the background remains constant throughout the video program and Green.psd plays through Logo.ai's matte.

3 Select the Reverse Key.

Before and after selecting Reverse Key

4 Click OK, and then save the project.

Applying preset motion settings

You can save motion settings and use them repeatedly on different clips and in different projects. Here you'll load a previously saved motion file and apply it to Logo.ai.

1 Select Logo.ai in the Timeline and choose Clip > Video Options > Motion.

2 Click Load and double-click Logomoti.pmt in the 10Lesson folder. A motion path appears in the Visible Area.

3 Preview the motion by clicking the Play button.

4 Click the Start keyframe on the motion path. Notice the different settings for Rotation, Zoom, and Delay.

5 Press Tab to move to each keyframe along the path.

Note: *If a text entry box is active in the Motion Settings dialog box, pressing Tab highlights successive boxes rather than selecting successive motion keyframes.*

The motion path begins with a zoom value of 450%, shrinks to 37% by the second-to-last keyframe, and ends at 75%. The block at the end of the Motion timeline represents a delay on the last keyframe.

6 Click the last keyframe on the Motion timeline to see the details of the delay setting. Notice that the delay is set to 7%.

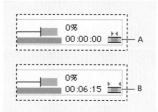

7 Click OK to close the Motion Settings dialog box.

8 Save the project.

Delaying a keyframe on the motion path

Preview the motion in the Monitor window, and then you'll make some changes to the delay.

1 Drag the work area bar over all the clips in the Timeline; then press Enter (Windows) or Return (Mac OS) to preview the project.

Currently, the logo reaches its final position right before Background.mov stops playing. We want the logo to appear at its last keyframe sooner, and remain there longer, so a longer portion of Background.mov plays after the logo stops moving. To achieve this effect, we'll increase the length of the delay on the last keyframe to one-half second, or 15 frames.

2 Select Logo.ai in the Timeline and choose Clip > Video Options > Motion.

You'll use the Motion timeline's time display ( ), located to the right of the Motion timeline, to set the delay in the Motion Settings dialog box to exactly 15 frames.

A. Time display showing timecode for the clip B. Time display showing timecode for the entire project

The time display shows you whether the Motion timeline timecode represents the timecode for your entire project or for the selected clip. Using this information, you can determine the exact time at which a motion effect occurs in the video program or in the video clip.

Set the time display to show the timecode for the entire project, which is 10 seconds long. Once it's set, you can accurately set the delay to 9 seconds 15 frames, which is one-half second in from the end of the project.

The time display (▸▸) is currently set to show the timecode for the selected clip.

3 Click the time display's red arrows to display the location of the selected keyframe in relation to the timecode for the entire project (▸▸).

4 Select the last keyframe on the Motion timeline, and notice that the time display reads about 00:09:22. The delay setting stops all motion at this keyframe, and the image remains constant for the last 8 frames of the project.

5 Click the arrows on either end of the Delay text box until the time display reads 00:09:15. The Delay text box should be at approximately 14%.

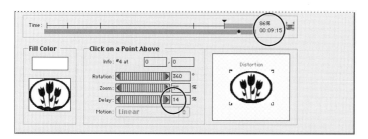

6 Click OK to close the Motion Setting dialog box, and then save the project.

7 Press Enter (Windows) or Return (Mac OS) to preview the project.

Exporting the movie

If you were really creating an advertisement to be broadcast on television, your clips would all be 640 x 480 resolution so that they would display optimally on a NTSC monitor. Your project Timebase would be 29.97 or 30, and you'd export your project using a hardware codec and print the final movie to videotape.

However, because 640 x 480 resolution files require an exceptional amount of hard disk space to store and memory to edit, we kept the tutorial files to 240 x 180 resolution. You'll export this project using this smaller file size, a 15 fps Timebase, and a software codec.

1 If necessary, click the Timeline title bar to activate it, and then choose File > Export Timeline> Movie.

2 Click the Settings button. Choose QuickTime for the File Type, and Entire Project for the Range.

3 Deselect Export Audio, and then click Next.

4 Select Cinepak for the Compressor and choose 15 for the Frame Rate.

5 Click OK to close the Export Movie Settings dialog box.

6 Type **FlowerAd.mov** for the filename, and then click Save to export the movie. Premiere displays a status bar providing the estimated time it will take to process the movie.

When the movie is complete, it opens in a separate window.

7 Click the Play button to play the movie.

Printing to video

When you want to print your finished movie to videotape, you use the Print to Video option. This option lets you display the movie at full screen on your computer monitor. If your movie is not in full screen resolution (640 x 480), which requires an exceptional amount of hard disk space to store and memory to edit, you can zoom the movie to fill the screen, or you can display it at its smaller resolution (240 x 180) with a black border.

1 With the Clip window still active, choose File > Export Timeline > Print to Video.

2 Enter 1 second for Color Bars, 1 second for Play Black, and then select Full Screen (Windows) or Zoom Screen (Mac OS). Click OK.

The movie plays at full screen on your computer or peripheral monitor. Because your movie is not full resolution (640 x 480), it appears pixelated or jaggy.

3 Choose File > Export Timeline > Print to Video again and don't select Full Screen. Now the movie plays in high resolution at its smaller size.

Exploring on your own

Take a few minutes to experiment with the project and try out some of your new skills. Here are some suggestions:

• Change the motion path for Forget.psd so that it continually rotates along the path. Save the path as a file.

• Create a one- or two-word title for the flower advertisement. Place the title at the beginning of the project in the Video 3 track and change the duration so it ends when Lotus.psd begins. Add motion to the title, making it zoom in from 10% to 100%.

• At different keyframes along Logo.ai's motion path, set the Motion to Accelerate and Decelerate and notice the effects.

• Apply a zoom effect to Backdrop.mov using only the Center button and the distortion area.

Review questions

1 Under what circumstances would you need to use the Fill Color setting in the Motion dialog box?

2 When should you accelerate a motion path?

3 If you want to set a keyframe on the Motion timeline that matches a specific time in the clip, should the time display's red arrows be close together or far apart?

4 What are two different ways to add keyframes to a motion path?

5 How do you convert a track matte to a traveling matte?

6 How do you adjust the time between two keyframes on the motion path?

Answers

1 When your clip has a colored background, such as blue.

2 When your image zooms in to a larger size.

3 Close together.

4 Clicking on the motion path and clicking on the motion path timeline.

5 Add motion to the clip that has the track matte applied.

6 Move the keyframe on the Motion timeline. The farther the keyframes are from each other, the longer the time between them.

Lesson 11

11 Applying Video and Audio Effects

Adobe Premiere provides a broad range of video and audio effects you can use to solve problems and to enhance your video projects.

To learn about using effects in Adobe Premiere 6.0, you'll create a short promotional spot for a coffee bar. Specifically, you'll learn how to do the following:

- Apply video and audio effects.

- Change effects and settings.

- Use multiple effects and change their order.

- Change effects over time using keyframes and transitions.

- Copy effects and settings from one clip to another.

- Apply an effect to part of an image.

- Use the Image Pan and ZigZag effects.

Restoring default preferences

For this lesson, you should restore the default preferences of Premiere to the factory settings before you launch the program or start the lesson. See "Restoring default preferences" on page 15 of this *Classroom in a Book*.

Getting started

For this lesson, you'll open an existing project with most of the files already imported. Be sure you know the location of the files used in this lesson. Insert the CD-ROM disk if necessary. For help, see "Copying the Classroom in a Book files" on page 14 of this *Classroom in a Book*.

1 After you have restored the default preferences, launch the Premiere 6.0 software, and choose Single-Track Editing.

2 In the Load Project Settings dialog box, choose Multimedia or Multimedia Quicktime (depending on your operating system), and click OK.

3 Choose Window > Workspace > Single-Track Editing mode. Then choose Window > Workspace > Effects. This lesson is practiced in the Effects Workspace.

Opening the existing project file

1 Double-click the existing project 11Lesson.ppj in the 11Lesson folder to open it.

2 Choose File > Save As, select the **11 Lesson** folder location on your hard disk, type **Coffee.ppj** for the new project name, and press Enter (Windows) or Return (Mac OS).

Viewing the finished movie

To see what you'll be creating, you'll first take a look at the finished movie.

1 Choose File > Open and select the 11Final.mov file in the Final folder, inside the 11Lesson folder.

Because you are working in the Effects workspace, the video program opens in the Source view in the Monitor window.

2 Click the Play button (▶) in the Source view in the Monitor window to watch the video program. When the movie ends, the final frame will remain visible in the Source view in the Monitor window.

Why use effects?

Video and audio *effects* (known as "filters" in previous releases of Premiere) serve many useful purposes. You can use them to fix defects in video or audio material, such as correcting the color balance of a video clip or removing background noise from dialogue. Effects are also used to create qualities not present in the raw video or audio, such as softening focus or giving a scene a sunset tint, or adding reverb or echo to a sound track.

You can add an effect to a clip at any time, and even apply the same effect multiple times to a single clip with different settings. By default, when you apply an effect to a clip, the effect is active for the duration of the clip. However, by using keyframes, you can make the effect start and stop at specific times, or make the effect more or less intense over time.

⧉ *For more information, see "Applying Effects > Video effects" or "Applying Effects > Audio effects" in the Adobe Premiere 6.0 Technical Guides found in the Support area on the Adobe Web site (www.adobe.com/support/techdocs/topissuespre.htm).*

Many of the video and audio effects in Adobe Premiere 6.0 are different from those included in earlier releases of the software. In fact, to enhance compatibility, many of the older versions' effects (filters) have been replaced with effects developed for Adobe After Effects software. You can identify such effects by the After Effects icon (⬚) next to the effect name.

If you want to work on a project created in Premiere 5.x (or earlier) that uses an effect which has been replaced in Premiere 6.0, you can continue to use it in Premiere 6.0. The settings will remain intact and replaced effects can be found in the Obsolete folder in the Video Effects palette.

For more information about working with obsolete effects, see "Obsolete Effects" in Chapter 9 of the *Adobe Premiere 6.0 User Guide*.

Getting to know the Effects workspace

The Effects mode is designed for easy access to both audio and video effects. You'll begin by opening the Effects workspace and getting familiar with its components.

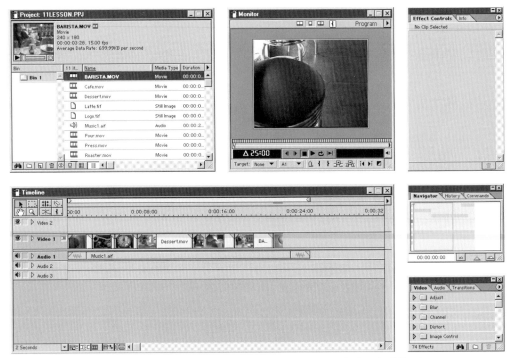

Default Effects workspace for Lesson 11 in Single-Track Editing mode described in the following text

When you choose Window > Workspace > Effects, Premiere sets up the
following conditions:

- In the Monitor window, Single View is displayed. Clips open in a separate Clip window.

- The Info palette and the Effect Controls palette are grouped into one palette window.

- The Navigator, History, and Commands palettes are grouped into another palette window.

- The Video Effects, Audio Effects, and Transitions palettes are grouped into a third palette window.

How effects are organized

All effects are stored in the Audio Effects palette and the Video Effects palette, grouped by
type. For example, all video effects that create a blur are grouped within a Blurs folder in
the Video Effects palette. You can customize the palettes by creating new folders. For
instance, you can group effects that you use frequently or group effects that you rarely use.
You can also change settings to show or hide a folder or an effect.

Note: You use the same tools to organize or manipulate folders in either palette.

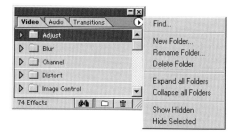

Showing and hiding effects

Premiere provides two menu items in the Video Effects palette and the Audio Effects
palette for showing and hiding effects and folders of effects from view. Hide/Show
Selected is used to dim or "shy" an effect (Hide Selected) in the palette or make it active
again (Show Selected). Hide/Show Hidden is used to make dimmed effects disappear or
reappear in the menu.

Applying effects

An effect can be added to a clip that is already in the Timeline window, or the effect can be dragged to the Effect Controls palette if the clip is selected in the Timeline. Effects can be added to clips or removed at any time. You apply video effects and audio effects in the same way: you select the clip and you apply a selected effect. Video effects are listed in the Video Effects dialog box; Audio effects are listed in the Audio Effects dialog box. A clip that has an effect applied to it appears with a blue-green bar at the top of it in the Timeline window. An effects can be modified after it has been applied. For instance, it is easy to make adjustments after you preview an effect.

After you've applied effects to a clip, you can temporarily turn off one or all of those effects to concentrate on another aspect of your project. Effects that are turned off do not appear in the Program window and are not included when the clip is previewed or rendered. Turning off an effect does not delete the keyframes created for any of the effect's settings; all keyframes remain until the effect is deleted from the clip.

In this exercise, you'll apply effects to create a monochrome appearance, using a yellow tint that will be applied to a number of clips. Three video effects are used to achieve this result: Black & White, Color Replace, and Tint. You'll start by applying the Tint effect to the Stool.mov clip.

Before you begin working on effects for this project, mute the audio tracks to avoid the distraction of audio while previewing the video effects.

1 Click the speaker icon (🔊) on the left side of the Audio 1 track so that the speaker icon disappears. The blank box indicated that the audio is muted for that Audio track.

Audio 1 track is muted;
Audio 2 track is not.

2 Double-click Stool.mov in the Timeline to open it in the Clip window, and then click Play to preview it.

For this project, you want this clip to resemble an old photograph, using a brown tint to simulate the sepia tone of early photographic prints. As you apply effects to the clip, it will be helpful to keep the original clip displayed in the Clip window so that you can compare it to the preview image in the Clip window.

3 Drag the Clip view Shuttle slider all the way to the left to display the first frame of Stool.mov in the Source view of the Clip window.

4 In the Video Effects palette, click the binocular icon () to search for an effect in the Find Video Effect dialog box.

5 Type in **Tint** and click Find. The Tint effect is located and highlighted. Click Done to exit the Find Video Effect dialog box.

6 Drag the Tint effect to the Stool.mov clip in the Timeline window. Or, if the Stool.mov clip is selected in the Timeline window, drag the Tint effect to the Effect Controls palette.

7 In the Effect Controls palette, click the Map Black Color box to open the Color Picker dialog box.

8 Select a medium-dark brown color for your tint or type in the following values to match the final movie: (Red: **85,** Green: **42,** and Blue: **0**). Click OK to close the Color Picker dialog box.

9 Do one of the following to set the Tint level to 35%:

• Drag the Level slider to 35%.

• In the Effect Controls palette, click the underlined percentage amount to open the Edit Amount to Tint dialog box. Type in 35% and click OK to close the Edit Amount to Tint dialog box.

10 Render-scrub to preview this effect by dragging in the Timeline ruler while holding down the Alt key (Windows) or the Option key (Mac OS).

When compared to the original image in the Source view of the Clip window, you should see a brown tint applied over a color image in the Program view of the Clip window, especially in white areas. Notice the blue-green bar along the top of the clip indicator in the Timeline. This indicates that an effect has been applied to the clip.

Applying effects in the correct order

When you apply multiple effects to one or more clips, the order in which you apply them can affect the final result. If a clip has multiple effects applied, the Effect Controls palette identifies them in an ordered list. They are rendered from this list, in order, from the top to the bottom. You can reorder the list to change the sequence in which the effects are rendered. In this exercise, you'll change the render order.

Now, you'll add an additional effect to the Stool.mov clip. You apply the Black & White effect to strip out the original color from the clip, making it look more like an early black-and-white photograph.

1 In the Video Effects palette, click the binocular icon (🔍) to search for an effect in the Find Video Effect dialog box.

2 In the Find Video Effect dialog box, type in **Black & White.** Now, click Find. The Black & White effect is located and highlighted. Click Done to close the Find Video Effect dialog box.

3 Drag the Black & White effect to the Stool.mov clip in the Timeline window, or if the Stool.mov clip is selected in the Timeline window, drag the Black & White effect to the Effect Controls palette.

4 Render-scrub to preview the result of both effects by dragging the edit line in the Timeline ruler while holding down the Alt key (Windows) or the Option key (Mac OS).

Now, instead of seeing the brown tint over a black-and-white image, you see only the black-and-white image. This is because the Black & White effect removed all color from the image. Ordering the effect sequence is important. It's easy to put these effects in the right order.

5 With Stool.mov still selected, click the triangle next to each effect to collapse the settings in the Effect Controls palette.

6 In the Effect Controls palette, click the Tint effect and drag it to its new location on the list, below the Black & White effect.

7 Render-scrub to preview the effect of both effects again by dragging the edit line in the Timeline ruler while holding down the Alt key (Windows) or the Option key (Mac OS).

This time when you preview the clip, you see a brown tint over a black-and-white image. This is just what you want. Now, you'll add the last effect to this clip. You'll change highlights of a color by applying the Color Replace effect.

Customizing an effect

Some Premiere effects can be customized. If an effect can be customized, the Setup option appears next to the effect. You can click Setup for that effect to open its specific Settings dialog box. The settings you choose here apply to the first keyframe of a clip (if you change settings for other keyframes in the same clip) or apply to the entire clip (if you make no changes to a keyframe).

Note: If you use effects in a Premiere project that are created in After Effects, that effect must be customized in the Effect Controls palette, not in the Audio Effects or Video Effects palette.

1 In the Video Effects palette, click the binocular icon (🔍) to search for an effect in the Find Video Effect dialog box.

2 Type in **Color Replace** and click Find. The Color Replace effect is located and highlighted. Click Done to exit the Find Video Effect dialog box.

3 Drag the Color Replace effect to the Stool.mov clip in the Timeline window. Or, if the Stool.mov clip is selected in the Timeline window, drag the Color Replace effect to the Effect Controls palette.

4 The Setup option appears next to this effect, indicating that the Color Replace effect can be customized. Click Setup to open the Color Replace Settings dialog box.

The settings you choose in the Color Replace Settings dialog box apply to the entire clip if you make no changes to any keyframe later in the clip. Alternatively, the settings you choose here apply to the first keyframe if you change the effect settings for other keyframes in the clip.

To establish which color you'll replace, you'll use the eyedropper tool ( ) in the Color Replace Settings dialog box.

5 Position the pointer in the Clip Sample image so that it turns into the eyedropper icon ( ). Move the eyedropper over the bright area in the upper left corner. Click to capture the color.

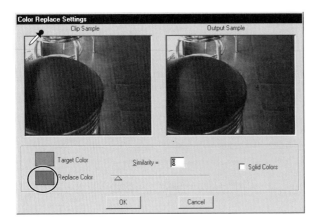

6 Now, click the Replace Color swatch to access the Color Picker. Then, click a light orange color. Or, to match the color in the final movie, type in these values: Red: **255,** Green: **210,** Blue: **115** to replace your first color selection. Click OK.

Now, you'll set the Similarity slider to indicate the range of colors to be replaced, based on their similarity to the color you selected. This setting determines the smoothness of the transition from original colors to the replaced color.

7 Using the Similarity slider in the Color Replace Settings, set Similarity to about 70. Click OK to close the Color Replace Settings dialog box and to apply the settings.

8 Preview the cumulative color effects of the effects you just applied by scrubbing in the Timeline ruler while holding down the Alt key (Windows) or the Option key (Mac OS).

9 Save the project.

Copying effects, keyframes, and settings

Once you have set up and applied one or more effects to a clip, you may want to use the same effects and settings on other clips. Doing this manually would be a lot of work, but there is a much easier way. Using the Paste Attributes command, you can apply identical effects and settings to any number of clips. You'll use this technique now to copy the effects and its keyframes from the Stool.mov clip and apply them to the Roaster.mov, Press.mov, and Dessert.mov clips.

1 Make sure Stool.mov is still selected in the Timeline. Choose Edit > Copy.

2 In the Timeline window, select Roaster.mov and choose Edit > Paste Attributes.

3 In the Paste Attributes dialog box, select Settings.

4 Click Paste.

5 Preview Roaster.mov by scrubbing in the Timeline ruler while holding down the Alt key (Windows) or the Option key (Mac OS).

The effects you originally applied to Stool.mov are now also applied to Roaster.mov, along with the settings you selected. You also need to apply the same effects to the Press.mov and Dessert.mov clips, so this time you'll select those clips using the range select tool, which lets you select more than one clip at a time.

6 In the Timeline window, select the range select tool.

7 Drag over Press.mov and Dessert.mov in the Timeline to select them.

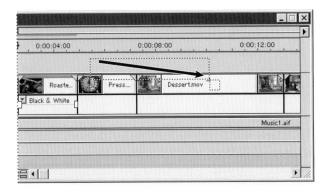

Because you have not used the Copy command since you copied Stool.mov, the Paste Attributes command still contains the effects and settings from that clip. You can simply use the Paste Attributes Again command to reuse these settings.

8 Choose Edit > Paste Attributes Again.

The effects and settings from Stool.mov have been applied to the clips you selected, so that the first four clips in the project now have identical effects and settings.

9 Deselect the range select tool by selecting the selection tool (↖).

10 Preview the project by scrubbing in the Timeline ruler while holding down the Alt key (Windows) or the Option key (Mac OS).

11 Save the project.

Changing effects over time

Some Premiere effects change dynamically; some change over time. Effects that change dynamically use *keyframes* to tell them when to make changes. Effects that don't have settings associated with them, such as the Black & White effect, don't need or use keyframes, so they can't be changed in this way.

For effects that don't use keyframes, you can often create change over time using transitions, although this technique is not as flexible as using keyframes.

Changing effects using keyframes

A keyframe is a marker in time that contains a video effect's settings for a specific point in a clip. By default, Premiere creates a beginning and ending keyframe when you apply an effect to a clip. But, you can change the keyframes to have the effect change gradually over time.

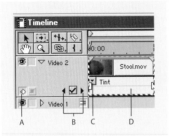

A. Effect keyframe button B. Keyframe navigator C. Effect pop-up menu D. Keyframe line

Each effect has a default keyframe at the beginning and end of the clip, indicated by half-diamonds on the keyframe line in the Timeline window. If an effect has adjustable controls, you can change the start or end time of the effect or add additional keyframes to create an animated effect. If you don't make any changes to the default keyframes, the settings for the associated effect apply to the entire clip.

After you add an effect to a clip, the effect appears under the clip in the keyframe line in the Timeline window. This menu displays each of the applied effects. If the effect has adjustable controls, you can set keyframes for it in the keyframe line. In order to view the Opacity Handles (✐) button, the clip must be on the Video 2 track or higher. The keyframe line for an audio file can display effect, volume, or pan (✐) keyframes. To display effect keyframes for either type of clip, click the Effect Keyframe button (◈), on Video 2 track or above.

1 In the Timeline window, click the triangle to the left of the Video 1 track name which will display the keyframe line once a clip is selected.

Note: When you add more than one effect to a clip, a menu of effects that have been applied to it appears at the left edge of the clip.

2 Make sure Stool.mov is selected in the Timeline window to view the clip's effects in the Effect Controls palette.

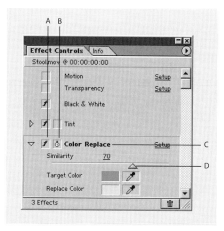

A. *Effect Enabled button with the stopwatch icon visible* **B.** *Keyframing Enabled button* **C.** *Effect name* **D.** *Effect controls*

Applying the Replicate effect

Now you'll use the Replicate effect to add an effect to Press.mov, and use keyframes to indicate when the effect starts and what its settings are at that point. Then, you'll use another keyframe to change the effect again at a different point in time.

1 Select Press.mov in the Timeline window and make sure the Effect Controls palette is showing.

2 In the Video Effects palette, click the binocular icon (🔍) to search for an effect in the Find Video Effect dialog box.

3 Type in Replicate and click Find. The Replicate effect is located and highlighted. Click Done to exit the Find Video Effect dialog box.

4 Drag the Replicate effect to the Press.mov clip in the Timeline window, or if the Press.mov clip is selected in the Timeline window, drag the Replicate effect to the Effect Controls palette.

5 The Setup option appears next to the Replicate effect on the Effect Controls palette. Click Setup to open the Replicate Settings dialog box.

The settings you choose in the Replicate Settings dialog box apply to the first keyframe (if you change settings for other keyframes) or to the entire clip (if you make no changes to any keyframe).

6 In the Replicate Settings dialog box, drag the slider to see the different effects created by varying the settings for this effect. Set the slider back to the 2-by-2 format as shown below, and then click OK to close the dialog box.

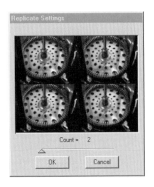

To create and position keyframes and edit their settings, you use the keyframe line in the Timeline window. The appearance of a keyframe icon depends on where it is on the track. The default (first and last) keyframes are white rectangles (□) that rest at the edges of the clip. By default, the first and last keyframes are active when you select an effect. Once you add additional keyframes (◇), the initial keyframes become white half-diamonds. Once you move the keyframes from the edges, they become full diamonds. The first keyframe is gray on the left half (◈), and the last keyframe is gray on the right half (◈).

Because you want the effect to start near the middle of the clip, you'll move the first keyframe on the keyframe timeline to that point. Then you'll add a new keyframe and change its effect settings. Finally, you'll change the settings for the last keyframe.

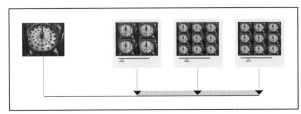

The Replicate effect will change at keyframes along the keyframe timeline, from one image to four to nine.

7 In the Timeline window, click the triangle to the left of the Video 1 track label to expand the track and display the keyframe line.

8 Position the edit line just before the point where the shiny lid of the coffee maker enters the frame to create a keyframe (at about 05:18).

9 Select the Press.mov clip. Position the pointer on the first keyframe until it becomes the pointing finger icon, and drag it to 05:18.

This indicates where the effect starts in the clip.

Note: The pointer becomes a shaded finger when it is on a keyframe.

Next, you'll create a new keyframe and set the Replicate effect value for that keyframe.

10 Position the edit line just midway between the first and last keyframes. Click the keyframe navigator box to create a new keyframe and adjust its settings.

11 Click Setup to open the Replicate Settings dialog box. The Replicate Settings dialog box opens with the same settings as the previous keyframe.

12 Drag the slider so that the preview shows the 3-by-3 format, and then click OK.

Once you insert a keyframe for an effect other than the beginning or the end keyframes, the Effect Enabled icon (☉) appears next to the effect name in the Effect Controls palette, and the beginning and end keyframe symbols change into triangles. A grey triangle points in the direction where there is no effect established.

Now you'll select the effect settings you want at the end of the clip. The last keyframe is currently set to the 2-by-2 format. Because the last keyframe affects only the last frame of the clip, a change at that keyframe would cause a distracting one-frame flash of the new setting. To avoid this, you'll make it the same as the previous keyframe, the 3-by-3 format.

13 Position the edit line on the last keyframes to adjust its settings.

14 Click Setup to open the Replicate Settings dialog box. The Replicate Settings dialog box opens with the same settings as the previous keyframe.

15 Drag the slider so that the preview shows the 3-by-3 format, and then click OK.

16 Preview this effect by scrubbing in the Timeline ruler while holding down the Alt key (Windows) or the Option key (Mac OS).

The Replicate effect applied to Press.mov maintains a single image throughout the first half of the clip. At that point it changes to four images and then to nine images.

17 Save the project.

Changing effects using transitions

Some effects do not include keyframes, so to change the effect over time, you can use a transition to accomplish the same thing. Simply position the transition (usually a cross dissolve) between two versions of the same clip that are identical except for the effect settings.

This method of changing an effect over time works best with certain effects, such as those that control image quality, such as hue, saturation, and contrast.

Here, you'll use a cross-dissolve transition to fade changes in the Dessert.mov clip over time, returning the clip to its original color. In this case, you need to use a transition to make the change, because the Black & White effect applied to Dessert.mov cannot be changed dynamically.

1 Click the Track Mode button on the right side of the Video 1 track to expand it.

2 Position the edit line in the Timeline at 10:04, which is the mid-point of the Dessert.mov clip.

3 Position the pointer over the Out point of Dessert.mov and drag it to the left until it snaps to the edit line. The Dessert.mov has just been trimmed to half of its original length.

Now, you'll make a smooth lingering cross dissolve between the first half of Dessert.mov, with its three effects, and the second half in its original form.

4 In the Bin area in the Project window, select Dessert.mov and choose Edit > Copy.

5 With the Timeline active, select the empty space you created between Dessert.mov and the clip on its right, Cafe.mov.

6 Choose Edit > Paste Attributes.

7 In the Paste Attributes dialog box, choose Content. Choose Move Source In Point and click Paste.

Note: The Paste Attributes command has several functions. In this exercise, it will not be used to copy effects, but to trim the In point of a clip.

The Paste Attributes command automatically trimmed the full-color source clip of Dessert.mov, and fit it into the empty space. The two Dessert.mov clips are now exactly contiguous. Each clip has been trimmed to one half of its original duration. The first half has multiple effects, and the second half is original footage.

8 In the Transitions palette, click the Dissolve folder and locate the Cross Dissolve transition.

9 Click the Transitions palette menu, located in the top right corner of the palette, and choose Set Selected As Default. The Default Effect dialog box appears.

10 Change the Effect Duration to 170 frames, which is the entire duration of the Dessert.mov clip. The cross dissolve will transpire gradually over this run length.

11 Click OK.

12 Drag the Cross Dissolve transition from the Transitions palette to the Video 1 Transition track, placing it between the two Dessert.mov clips.

13 To preview Dessert.mov, resize the work area bar so that it covers the clip, and then press Enter (Windows) or Return (Mac OS).

The Dessert.mov clip changes gradually over the duration of the clip from yellow highlights on brown shadows into full color.

14 Save the project.

Using the Image Pan and ZigZag effects

Next, you'll animate a still image of a cup of espresso (Latte.tif) by applying the Image Pan effect and the Motion effect to create a zoom, and applying the ZigZag effect to add a swirling motion. These effects can be set to change gradually over time, in contrast to the Replicate effect you used earlier in this lesson, which can be changed only in discrete steps.

The instance of Latte.tif in the Timeline has a duration of 30 frames. For this project, this clip should be 3:23 long, and you'll want to set the clip to this duration before you apply the Image Pan effect. You'll make this change using the Duration command.

1 In the Project window, select Latte.tif, choose Edit > Locate Clip, and then click Done.

2 Choose Clip > Duration.

3 Type **323** in the duration box, and then click OK to close the dialog box. You've just changed the duration of Latte.tif from 00:30 to 3:22.

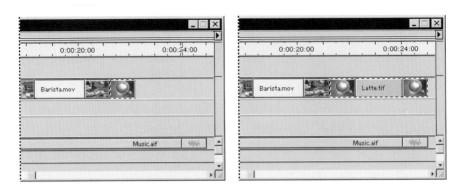

You'll now apply the Image Pan effect to the clip to simulate a zoom.

When you shoot film or video, panning refers to the movement of the camera from side-to-side or up-and-down, either to follow a subject or so that the subject moves across the frame. Zooming refers to the movement of the camera (or camera lens) so that the subject progressively appears larger in the frame (closer to the camera), or smaller in the frame (further away). You can use effects in post production to simulate panning and zooming with the camera. In Premiere, you use the Image Pan effect to simulate panning or to crop a clip.

4 In the Video Effects palette, click the binocular icon (🔍) to search for an effect.

5 Type in **Image Pan** and click Find. The Image Pan effect is located and highlighted. Click Done to exit the Find Video Effect dialog box.

6 Drag the Image Pan effect to the Latte.tif clip in the Timeline window, or if the Latte.tif clip is selected in the Timeline window, drag the Image Pan effect to the Effect Controls palette.

7 In the Timeline window, click the first keyframe in the Latte.tif clip.

8 In the Effect Controls palette, the Setup option appears next to the Image Pan effect. Click Setup to open the Image Pan Settings dialog box.

You can change the size of the image in the Source view of the Image Pan dialog box in two ways: by entering values for width and height, and by dragging the handles at the corners of each box. First, you'll crop the image slightly by entering a new frame size, in pixels.

9 In the Image Pan Settings dialog box, type **392** in the Width box and type **287** in the Height box.

10 With the cursor inside the selected rectangle, adjust the image to center the cup in the revised frame. Click OK.

Notice that the image in the Source view is cropped (as indicated by the white selection box) and there is no motion.

Add an image pan by dragging the handles of the selection box to size it.

Now you'll specify the area of the image for the image pan to end.

11 In the Timeline window, select the end keyframe of the Image Pan effect in the Latte.tif clip.

12 In the Effect Controls palette click the Enable Keyframing box, the one directly left of the words "Image Pan."

13 Click Setup. The Image Pan Settings dialog box appears.

14 In the Source view, locate the lower right handle on the selection box. While holding down the Alt key (Windows) or the Option key (Mac OS), drag this handle near the right edge of the cream in the cup. Dragging while holding down the modifier key maintains the *aspect ratio* (ratio of height to width) of the original image, and is important because we don't want to distort the image. Use this technique to drag the other handles so that they make a selection box about the size of the cream. Then drag inside the selection box to center it over the cream. Use the image below as a guide. You may need to adjust the handles of the selection box, or slide the whole frame around with the hand cursor to position the frame over the cream only.

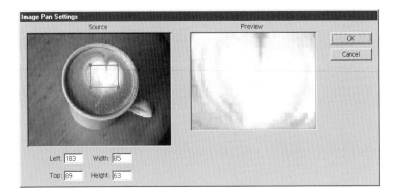

15 When you are satisfied with the image pan you have set up, click OK to close the Image Pan Settings dialog box.

16 Save the project and preview the Image Pan effect.

Next you'll add the ZigZag effect to animate Latte.tif, making the cream appear to swirl. You'll set the effect to start with very little distortion and to change over time to the desired intensity at the end of the clip.

17 In the Video Effects palette, click the binocular icon ( ) to search for an effect.

18 Type in ZigZag and click Find. The ZigZag effect is located and highlighted. Click Done to exit the Find Video Effect dialog box.

19 Drag the ZigZag effect to the Latte.tif clip in the Timeline window, or if the Latte.tif clip is selected in the Timeline window, drag the ZigZag effect to the Effect Controls palette.

20 The ZigZag Settings dialog box opens automatically.

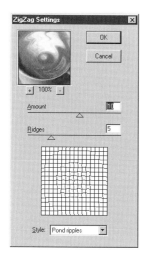

By default, the first keyframe is selected, although keyframes are not yet displayed in the dialog box at this point.

Now, you'll select the settings for this keyframe.

21 In the ZigZag Settings dialog box, type **0** for Amount (represents the magnitude of distortion), type **1** for Ridges (represents the number of direction reversals of the zigzag from the center of the clip to its edge), and set Style to **Around Center** (which rotates pixels around the center of the clip). With these settings, the effect will have little or no effect on the clip. Click OK to close the ZigZag Settings dialog box.

Now, you'll select the settings for the last keyframe in this effect.

22 Click the last keyframe on theLatte.tif clip to select it. In the Effect Controls palette, click the Enable Keyframing box to the left of the ZigZag effect and the Enable Keyframe icon appears ( ). Then click Setup to open the ZigZag Settings dialog box.

23 Type **41** for Amount, type **5** for Ridges, and then click OK to close the ZigZag dialog box.

24 Preview the effect you just applied: Resize the work area bar so that it covers the clip you just worked on, and then press Enter (Windows) or Return (Mac OS).

The image in Latte.tif zooms in while the ZigZag effect gradually intensifies.

25 Save the project.

Adding a logo

You'll add a logo to the last scene in this project. To do this, you'll simply make the logo clip visible. Logo.tif is already in the Video 3 track, but that track has been made shy and the shy tracks have been hidden to keep them out of your way. To eliminate it from your previews, the track has also been excluded. Note that the eye icon is missing from the left of the track. Its absence indicates that the track is excluded.

For a full explanation of shy and excluded tracks, see "Hiding tracks" in *Premiere Online Help* or "Hiding and excluding tracks" in Chapter 3 of the *Adobe Premiere 6.0 User Guide.*

1 From the Timeline window menu, choose Show Shy Tracks to display the Video 3 track and Logo.tif. You may need to resize the Timeline window or scroll the video tracks vertically to view this track.

2 Preview Barista.mov and Logo.tif by scrubbing in the Timeline ruler while holding down the Alt key (Windows) or the Option key (Mac OS).

The logo doesn't appear in the preview because the Video 3 track is still excluded, as indicated by the blank box (▢) on the far left edge of the Video 3 track.

3 Click the blank box on the far left side of the Video 3 track so that the outlined eye icon (👁) appears, indicating that the track is still shy but is no longer excluded. This means the track will now be included in previews and exported video.

4 Preview Barista.mov and Logo.tif again by scrubbing in the Timeline ruler while holding down the Alt key (Windows) or the Option key (Mac OS).

The logo is superimposed over Barista.mov and Latte.tif, but it is difficult to see over the clips because the backgrounds are too dark for a black logo. Adding a matte would enable you to use an effect to lighten just the area of Barista.mov under the logo.

Applying an effect to specific areas of an image

In Lesson 10,"Adding Motion," you used a travelling matte to create a motion effect. Here, you'll use an image matte to apply an effect to just one area of an image. To do this, another instance of the clip must be placed in the superimpose (Video 2) track, and an effect must be applied to make one of the clips different from the base clip.

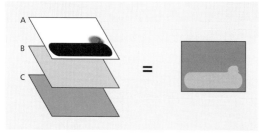

*A. Matte B. Lightened instance of clip with matte applied
C. Original clip*

Because an effect is applied to the superimposed clip, the parts of that clip showing through the image matte will be different from the areas you see of the base clip—the areas not masked by the matte.

You'll start by adding an instance of Barista.mov to the superimpose track.

1 Drag Barista.mov from the Project window into the Video 2 track, snapping it to the first instance of Barista.mov in the Video 1 track so that the two clips are aligned.

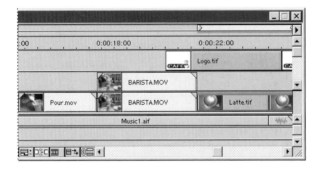

Now, you'll apply an effect to lighten the instance of Barista.mov you just added to the Video 2 track.

2 In the Video Effects palette, click the binocular icon (🔍) to search for an effect.

3 Type in **Brightness & Contrast** and click Find. The Brightness & Contrast effect is located and highlighted. Click Done to exit the Find Video Effect dialog box.

4 Drag the Brightness & Contrast effect to the second instance of Barista.mov clip in the Timeline window (on the Video 2 track). Or, if Barista.mov is selected in the Timeline window, drag the Brightness & Contrast effect to the Effect Controls palette.

5 In the Effect Controls palette, set Brightness to +**100** and set Contrast to -**35**.

Now you'll set the transparency options and apply the matte for the instance of Barista.mov that you added to the Video 2 track.

6 With Barista.mov still selected in the Video 2 track, choose Clip > Video Options > Transparency to open the Transparency Settings dialog box.

7 For Key type, choose Image Matte.

8 For Matte, click Choose, and then double-click Matte.tif in the 11Lesson folder.

9 Click the page peel icon (🖼), and select the Reverse Key.

Transparency Settings

Matte   Color   Sample

Choose...

Key type: Image Matte

☑ Reverse Key
☐ Drop Shadow
☐ Mask Only

Smoothing: None

OK   Cancel

10 Drag the slider in the Sample box to preview the effect of your settings, and then click OK to close the Transparency Settings dialog box.

11 Preview Barista.mov and Logo.tif by scrubbing in the Timeline ruler while holding down the Alt key (Windows) or the Option key (Mac OS).

The area of the image from the original Barista.mov clip, above the logo, displays normal brightness and contrast values, while the area of the copy below the logo is lighter, to go under our logo.

Right now, the matte starts before the logo, which is unnecessary. To fix this, you'll trim the beginning of the top instance of Barista.mov.

12 Move the pointer to the beginning of Barista.mov in the Video 2 track and drag right until it snaps to the beginning of Logo.tif.

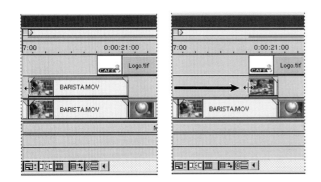

Next, you'll set up Latte.tif the same way you set up Barista.mov, so the logo is visible in both clips. To start, you'll add a copy of Latte.tif to the Video 2 track and add an effect to it. Then you'll copy the transparency settings from Barista.mov and paste them into the copy of Latte.tif in the Video 2 track to set up the matte.

13 Select Latte.tif in the Timeline window and choose Edit > Copy.

14 Select the Video 2 track by clicking the space to the right of Barista.mov, and then choose Edit > Paste.

The copy of Latte.tif has the same duration, Image Pan effect, and ZigZag effect you applied earlier to the original Latte.tif.

15 Now you'll apply the Brightness & Contrast effect to the copy of Latte.tif. Drag the Brightness & Contrast effect to the Latte.tif clip in the Video 2 track of the Timeline window. Or, if Latte.tif is selected in the Timeline window, drag the Brightness & Contrast effect to the Effect Controls palette.

16 With the copy of Latte.tif still selected, make sure the Effect Controls palette is open.

17 In the Effect Controls palette, set Brightness to **+100** and set Contrast to **-35**.

Now you'll copy the transparency settings, which include the matte, from Barista.mov to Latte.tif.

18 Select Barista.mov in the Video 2 track, and choose Edit > Copy.

19 Select the copy of Latte.tif in the Video 2 track, and choose Edit > Paste Attributes.

20 In the Paste Attributes dialog box, select Settings; then deselect all options except Transparency Settings, and then click Paste.

Note: You didn't choose Filters in the Paste Attributes dialog box because that would have affected the effects already applied to the copy of Latte.tif.

21 To see the completed effect, including the logo, preview Barista.mov and Latte.tif by scrubbing in the Timeline ruler while holding down the Alt key (Windows) or the Option key (Mac OS).

22 Save the project.

Applying audio effects

Audio effects and video effects are applied in about the same way. Here, you'll first remove noise from an audio clip, and then add some reverberation to the same clip.

1 Set the Time Zoom Level pop-up menu in the Timeline to 2 Seconds.

2 Using the scroll bar on the right side of the Timeline, scroll the audio tracks, if necessary, so that the Audio 1 and Audio 2 tracks are visible.

3 Drag Voice1.aif from the Project window into the Audio 2 track so that its Out point snaps to the end of the last clips in the project.

You'll need to unmute the Audio tracks before you work with Voice1.aif and the other audio clips.

4 Click the box on the far left of the Audio 1 and Audio 2 tracks so that the speaker icon (🔊) appears.

5 Preview Voice1.aif by moving the edit line to the beginning of the clip and pressing the Play button under the Program view. Notice the constant noise in the clip.

The Notch/Hum Filter effect in Premiere can be used to remove or reduce hum (low-frequency noise) or other single-frequency noise in an audio clip. You'll use the Notch/Hum Filter effect to remove noise from the Voice1.aif clip.

6 In the Audio Effects palette, click the binocular icon (🔍) to search for an effect.

7 Type in **Notch/Hum** and click Find. The Notch/Hum Filter effect is located and highlighted. Click Done to exit the Find Audio Effect dialog box.

8 Drag the Notch/Hum Filter effect to the Voice1.aif clip in the Timeline window. Or, if the Voice1.aif is selected in the Timeline window, drag the Notch/Hum Filter effect to the Effect Controls palette.

9 The Setup option appears next to the Notch/Hum Filter effect. Click Setup to open the Notch/Hum Filter Settings dialog box.

10 Click the Preview sound box. Premiere plays a short loop of audio from the audio track.

The frequency of the noise in Voice1.aif is 800 Hz.

11 Drag the slider in the Notch/Hum Effect dialog box to 0, then type random settings less than 800 Hz in the effect setting text box and listen to the audio preview.

Notice that as the effect setting (to the right of the slider) approaches 800 Hz, the noise is reduced. To set the effect precisely at 800 Hz, enter that value.

12 Type **800** in the Hz box, and then click OK to close the Notch/Hum Effect dialog box.

13 Preview Voice1.aif again. The noise is now nearly inaudible. Also notice that the audio sounds flat. Add some life to it adding reverberation to the same audio clip. The Reverb effect simulates sound bouncing off hard surfaces in either a medium-sized room or a large room.

14 In the Timeline window, select Voice1.aif.

15 In the Audio Effects palette, click the binocular icon (🔍) to search for an effect.

16 Type **Reverb** and click Find. The Reverb & Delay folder effect is located and highlighted. Click Done to exit the Find Audio Effect dialog box. You then have to expand the Reverb & Delay folder and highlight Reverb.

17 Drag the Reverb effect to the Voice1.aif clip in the Timeline window. Or, if the Voice1.aif is selected in the Timeline window, drag the Reverb effect to the Effect Controls palette.

18 The Setup option appears next to the Reverb effect. Click Setup to open the Reverb Settings dialog box.

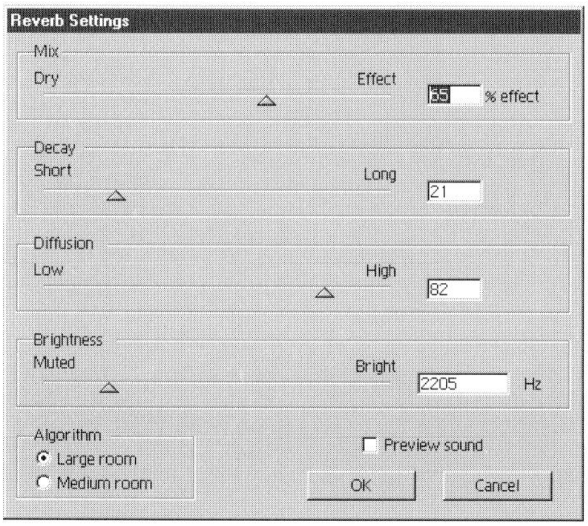

19 Select Preview Sound, select Medium room, and set Mix to about **20%**. Set Decay to a value that makes the audio sound like it is coming from a medium-sized room (the final movie uses **20%**).

20 Click OK to close the Reverb dialog box.

21 Preview Voice1.aif and Music1.aif together by moving the edit line to a point several seconds before the beginning of Voice1.aif and pressing the Play button under the Program view. You have just improved the quality of the sound in your project significantly!

22 Save the project.

Exporting the movie

Now that you've finished your editing, it's time to generate a movie file.

1 Make sure the Timeline is active, and then choose File > Export Timeline > Movie.

2 In the Export Movie dialog box, click the Settings button and choose your settings. Make sure QuickTime is selected for the File Type and Entire Project is selected for the Range. Also make sure that Export Video, Export Audio, and Open When Finished are selected. The default values for other settings, including those for compression, are fine for this project. Click OK to close the Export Movie Settings dialog box.

3 In the Export Movie dialog box, specify the 11Lesson folder for the location and type **Coffee.mov** for the name of the movie. Click Save (Windows) or OK (Mac OS).

Premiere starts making the movie, displaying a status bar that provides an estimate for the amount of time it will take.

4 When the movie is complete, it is opened in its own window.

5 Click the Play button to play the movie.

Exploring on your own

Feel free to experiment with the project you have just created and to explore various ways of working with the Audio Effects and Video Effects palettes. Here are some suggestions:

• Create and name a new folder in the Video Effects palette, using the palette menu or the New Folder button in the palette. Drag some of your favorite effects into the folder.

• Select a folder in the Audio Effects palette that you don't expect to use frequently, and use Hide Selected in the palette menu to dim the folder. Now, use the Hide Hidden command in the palette menu to hide the folder.

• Find effects to reverse an image (left-to-right), invert an image (top-to-bottom), and reverse a clip (front-to-back).

• Try this method of making an effect start changing at an exact point in a clip. Select a keyframe either by clicking it, using the keyframe navigator to move the edit line to it, or manually positioning the edit line on it. Specify where you want the change to start by making your changes using the available settings controls.

• Split a clip into a number of equal-sized segments using the razor tool, and then apply an effect to every other segment using Paste Attributes and Paste Attributes Again.

Review questions

1 How can you tell if an effect has been applied to a clip?

2 What does a keyframe contain?

3 Why would you need to use a transition to change an effect over time?

4 What is the quickest method of applying identical effects and settings to multiple clips?

5 What does the speaker icon do in the Timeline window?

Answers

1 A blue-green bar is displayed at the top of the clip in the Timeline.

2 A keyframe contains the values for all the controls in the effect and applies those values to the clip at the specified time.

3 Effects that do not use keyframes can be changed over time only by using a transition.

4 Using the Paste Attributes command is the quickest way to apply identical effects and settings to multiple clips.

5 The speaker icon can be used to mute the audio track or unmute it.

Lesson 12

12 | Duplicate Clips and Virtual Clips

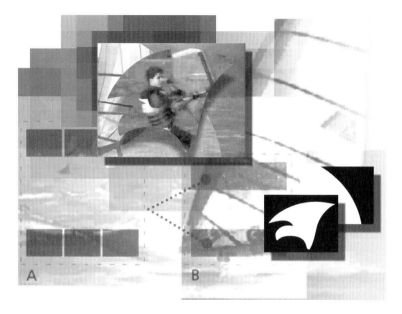

Duplicate clips and virtual clips are two powerful tools for assembling a video program in Premiere. Duplicate clips can be useful for splitting clips into a number of shorter clips that appear in the Project window. By contrast, a virtual clip can combine one or more clips, effects, and transitions into a single clip to simplify the Timeline and allow you to use effects and transitions repeatedly on the same source material.

You can create two other types of clips from video clips you import into a Premiere project: duplicate clips and virtual clips. You'll learn about using duplicate clips and virtual clips in Premiere by creating one component of a television spot for a resort.

In this lesson, you'll learn the following skills:

- Creating and naming duplicate clips.

- Using duplicate clips in a project.

- Creating virtual clips.

- Nesting virtual clips.

- Editing virtual clips.

- Compiling a virtual clip into an actual clip.

Restoring default preferences

For this lesson, you should restore the default preferences of Premiere to the factory settings before you launch the program or start the lesson. See "Restoring default preferences" on page 15 of this *Classroom in a Book*.

Getting started

For this lesson, you'll open an existing project in which the necessary files are already imported.Then, you'll create and use duplicate clips and virtual clips. Make sure you know the location of the files used in this lesson. Insert the CD-ROM disk if necessary. For help, see "Copying the Classroom in a Book files" on page 14 of this *Classroom in a Book*.

1 Launch the Premiere 6.0 software after you have restored the default preferences, and choose Single-Track Editing.

2 In the Load Project Settings dialog box, choose Multimedia or Multimedia Quicktime (depending on your operating system), and click OK.

3 Choose Edit > Preferences > General and Still Image and deselect Open Movies in Clip Window if it is selected.

4 Click OK.

Opening the existing project file

1 Double-click the existing project 12Lesson.ppj in the 12Lesson folder to open it.

2 If necessary, rearrange windows and palettes so they don't overlap by choosing Window > Workspace > Single-Track Editing. Make sure the Effect Controls, Navigator, and Transitions palettes are open for this lesson.

3 Choose File > Save As, select the **12Lesson** folder location on your hard disk, type **Windsurf.ppj** for the new project name, and press Enter (Windows) or Return (Mac OS).

Viewing the finished movie

If you'd like to see what you'll be creating, you can open and play the finished movie.

1 Choose File > Open. Select the 12Final.mov in the Final folder inside the 12Lesson folder. The movie opens in the Source view in the Monitor window.

2 Click the Play button (▶) in the Source view in the Monitor window to watch the video program. When the movie ends, the final frame will remain visible in the Source view in the Monitor window.

Understanding duplicate clips

Each component of a video program has a name that describes its function in the program and its location in the Premiere Workspace.

Master clip A *master clip* is a file containing video that has been digitized. All of the files currently in the Project window of this project are master clips.

Instance You can drag copies of a master clip from the Project window into the Timeline as many times as you want. Each copy you use in this manner is called an *instance*.

Duplicate clip You can also create a *duplicate clip* from a master clip in the Project window. Although a duplicate clip can include all of a master clip, it is most useful to create duplicate clips that are shorter than the master. Like a master clip, a duplicate clip appears in the Project window, and is identified by the name you specify when you create it. You can use any number of instances of a duplicate clip in a project.

Note: *Don't confuse a duplicate clip with an* alias. *Applying an alias to a clip simply changes the name of the clip but doesn't create a new clip.*

To create a duplicate clip that is a subset of a master clip, you must first open an *instance* of the master clip in the Source view to set new In and Out points for the duplicate clip.

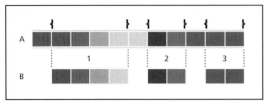

*From one master clip (**A**), you can create many different duplicate clips (**B**).*

Note: *It's important to understand that if the master clip is deleted from the Project window, the instances and duplicate clips created from that master clip will also be deleted, both from the Project window and from the Timeline.*

Creating duplicate clips

You'll start this lesson by creating three duplicate clips from the Surf.mov master clip. These duplicate clips are automatically added to the Project window when you create them. You'll use them in the next exercise to create your program.

You can create a duplicate clip by copying a clip in a Bin area in the Project window and then pasting the copy to a specified bin. Using this method, you name the duplicate clip when you paste it in a bin. Alternatively, you can drag a clip from the Source view to a specified Bin area in the Project window. This method allows you to set new In points and new Out points for duplicates that are shorter subsets of the original master clip.

Note: *Copying from or pasting to the Timeline creates the same effect as dragging to or from the Timeline. Specifically, Premiere creates another instance of the clip, not a duplicate clip.*

1 In the Project window, double-click Surf.mov to open it in the Source view in the Monitor window.

2 Preview it by pressing the Play button (►) in the Source view.

Notice that Surf.mov contains a number of separate scenes. You'll make duplicate clips of three of these scenes.

3 In the Source view, set the In point (⊣) for the first duplicate clip where the scene changes, at 1:22.

4 Set the Out point (▸) at 9:26.

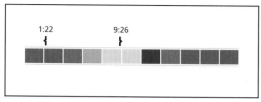

In and Out points define the source of a duplicate clip.

5 Click the Loop button (↺) to preview only the portion of Surf.mov defined by the In and Out points you just set. Press the Stop button (■) when you are finished previewing.

6 Choose Edit > Duplicate Clip.

7 In the Name box in the Duplicate Clip dialog box, type **Surf1.mov** for the duplicate clip name. Make sure the Location box specifies **Project: Windsurf.ppj**, and then click OK. Surf1.mov now appears in the Project window.

One way to rename a duplicate clip is to use the Project window. First select the List view in the Project window, by clicking the list view icon (▤). Then, double-click the duplicate clip name in the Project window, type the correct name, and then press Enter (Windows) or Return (Mac OS).

Now you'll make the second duplicate clip.

8 Make sure the Source view in the Monitor window is active, and choose Clip > Clear Clip Marker > All Markers to clear the In and Out point markers.

9 For the second duplicate clip you're going to create, set the new In point at 13:20.

10 Set the new Out point at 21:24.

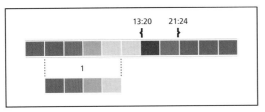

In and Out points for the first duplicate clip are cleared
and new ones are set for the second duplicate clip.

11 Click the Loop button (↻) to preview the material you just defined. Press the Stop button to end previewing.

12 Choose Edit > Duplicate Clip.

13 In the Name box in the Duplicate Clip dialog box, type **Surf2.mov** for the duplicate clip name, and then click OK.

Now, you'll make one more duplicate clip.

14 Choose Clip > Clear Clip Marker > All Markers to clear the In and Out point markers.

15 For the third duplicate clip you're going to create, set the In point at 23:10.

16 Set the Out point at 29:04.

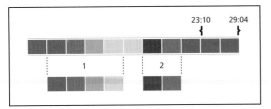

In and Out points are set for the third duplicate clip.

17 Click the Loop button (↻) to preview the material you just defined. Press the Stop button to end previewing.

18 Choose Edit > Duplicate Clip.

19 In the Name box in the Duplicate Clip dialog box, type **Surf3.mov** for the duplicate clip name, and then click OK.

The Surf1.mov, Surf2.mov, and Surf3.mov duplicate clips are now included in the Project window, ready for you to use in the project.

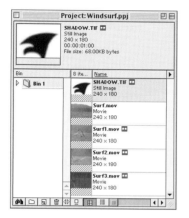

20 Save the project.

Editing duplicate clips

Duplicate clips can be edited in several ways. Just like any other clip, you can trim either end, change various settings, or apply effects.

Understanding virtual clips

In creating duplicate clips, you make a number of clips from a single master clip. In creating Virtual clips, you do just the opposite: You create a single clip from a specified area of the Timeline, which can include any number of clips. A virtual clip is much like a program exported as a movie that includes multiple clips, tracks, effects, and transitions. A virtual clip can be reused in a program any number of times. Premiere treats a virtual clip as a single clip. So, you can edit and apply settings to it just as you would to a simple source clip. By using virtual clips to organized and group sequences, you can save time editing complex video programs.

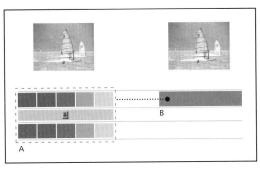

*Multiple clips (**A**) can be combined into a virtual clip (**B**).*

For example, if you create a short sequence involving four superimposed video tracks and three mixed audio tracks, and you want to use the sequence ten times in a project, just build the sequence once, create one virtual clip from it, and add ten *instances* of the virtual clip to the Timeline.

You can apply effects, transitions, or other settings to the source clips that define a virtual clip to simultaneously make global changes to all instances of the virtual clip in the Timeline. You can also apply settings more than once to the same clip. For example, certain effects can be achieved only by combining transitions. You cannot apply more than one transition to the same point in time. To accomplish multiple overlapping transitions you must use virtual clips.

You can also apply different settings to copies of a sequence. For example, if you want a sequence to play back repeatedly but with a different effect each time, you can create a virtual clip and just copy that for each instance where you want it to appear with a different effect. As with duplicate clips, each clip in the source area for a virtual clip refers back to a master clip in the Project window.

Note: *Deleting the master clip or the clip in the source area for the virtual clip will also delete the corresponding portion of each instance of the virtual clip.*

For more information on using virtual clips, see "Nesting edits using virtual clips" in Chapter 3 of the *Adobe Premiere 6.0 User Guide*.

Creating virtual clips

In this exercise, you'll create a virtual clip that will be combined with other clips to make the final project.

Before you can create a virtual clip, you must assemble the source clips that will make up the virtual clip. To create a virtual clip, you use the block select tool ( ). This tool selects material in all tracks in the area defined by the *block select marquee*. Although you can use any part of the video program in the Timeline to create a virtual clip, the ideal location for the source material is at the beginning of the Timeline, ahead of the main video program. This is because you don't want changes you make in the main video program to shift or otherwise affect the clips in the source area for the virtual clip.

Assembling source clips

You'll now assemble the source clips from which you will create a virtual clip. The result you want is a virtual clip that combines two clips of windsurfers. You'll set one clip to be partially transparent; the other clip will show through the transparent clip.

1 Drag Surf1.mov from the Project window into the Video 1 track, at the beginning of the Timeline window.

2 Drag Surf2.mov from the Project window into the Video 2 track, also at the beginning of the Timeline window.

With your clips in place, you'll select the transparency key type for one of them.

3 Select Surf2.mov in the Timeline, and then choose Clip > Video Options > Transparency to open the Transparency Settings dialog box.

4 Click the page peel icon ( ) under the Sample window to view a thumbnail of the actual clip.

5 Select Luminance for the Key Type, and leave Threshold set to 100 and Cutoff set to 0, and then click OK.

Now you'll set up a fade to make Surf2.mov partially transparent.

6 Click the triangle to the left of the Video 2 track label to expand the track.

7 Select the fade adjustment tool.

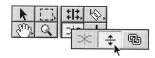

8 Press and hold the Shift key, and then drag the red fade control line down to 50%. You will need to drag outside the clip to reach this value.

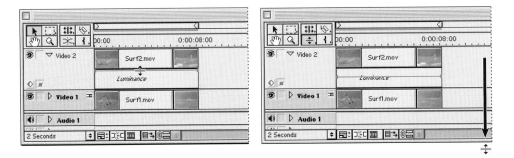

9 Select the selection tool (▶) to deselect the fade adjustment tool.

10 Clean up the Timeline by clicking the arrow in the Video 2 track to collapse the track. You have assembled the source clips for the first virtual clip.

Now, preview your work so far.

11 Render-scrub to preview the assembled clips by dragging the edit line through the Timeline ruler while pressing the Alt key (Windows) or Option key (Mac OS).

12 Save the project.

Making and positioning the virtual clip

Now that you have assembled the source clips, you are ready to make a virtual clip from them.

1 Set the edit line to 08.21 to establish that frame as the In point for the virtual clip to be made in step 5, below.

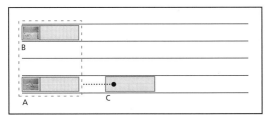

Select Surf1 (A) and Surf2 (B) to create a virtual clip (C).

2 In the Timeline, select the block select tool ().

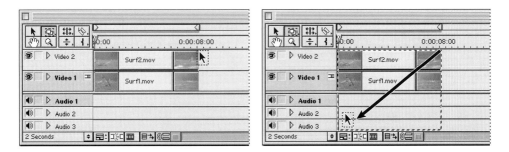

💡 *When using the block select tool to select clips at the beginning of the Timeline, the easiest method is to drag from right to left.*

3 Drag to select Surf1.mov and Surf2.mov, from which the virtual clip will be created. Be sure all of both clips are inside the selection marquee. Any part of a clip outside the marquee will not be included in the virtual clip.

4 Position the pointer in the selected area so that it changes to the virtual clip tool (♣).

5 Drag the selected block to the Video 1 track in the Timeline—until the beginning of the newly created virtual clip snaps to the edit line at 08:21.

After you release the block select tool cursor from this location, the virtual clip looks like any other clip in the Timeline, except for three items: The color is different from source clips, the clip is identified as Virtual Clip, and there are numbers below the name. The numbers indicate the beginning and end points of the block you selected in the Timeline. So, the numbers on your virtual clips may vary somewhat from those in the illustrations.

By default, Premiere creates a companion virtual audio clip when you create a virtual video clip. In this case, the virtual audio clip is empty. Because you won't be adding audio in this project, you'll delete the audio clip.

6 Deselect the block select tool by selecting the selection tool (⬉).

7 Make sure Sync Selection is not selected in the Timeline window.

8 Select the virtual audio virtual clip and press the Delete key.

9 Render-scrub to preview the virtual clip you just created by dragging through the Timeline ruler while pressing the Alt key (Windows) or Option key (Mac OS).

Note: *If you included any blank space (without clips) when you selected the source area in the Timeline for the virtual clip, you'll see black frames in that part of the virtual clip.*

All virtual clips are named Virtual Clip when they are created. To make this virtual clip easier to distinguish from other virtual clips, you'll give it an *alias*.

10 Select the virtual clip and choose Clip > Set Clip Name Alias.

11 When prompted, type **Background**, and click OK.

The name of the virtual clip changes to Background.

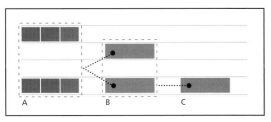

12 Save the project.

You've just created a virtual clip, a second generation clip growing out of modified trimmed source clips. As you'll see in the next exercise, you can use this virtual clip in ways you couldn't use the two individual source clips that it comprises.

Nesting virtual clips

In this exercise, you'll make another virtual clip using the one you just created. When assembling clips to create a virtual clip, you can include other virtual clips in the source material. This process of putting one virtual clip inside another is called *nesting*.

*Source areas (**A**) are selected to make several virtual clips (**B**), which are nested in a new virtual clip (**C**).*

Now, you'll assemble two instances of the virtual clip you just made and apply an effect to each of them. Then, you'll add the Image Mask transition between the virtual clips to show both at the same time. Finally, you'll make a nested virtual clip from these clips, creating a third-generation clip.

Assembling source clips

First, you'll make a copy of Background and position it in the Timeline.

1 Select Background and choose Edit > Duplicate Clip.

2 When prompted, type **Background 2**, and click OK.

3 Background 2 now appears in the Bin area in the Project window. Drag the Background 2 clip from the Project window to the Video 1 track in the Timeline, so that its In point snaps to the end of Background.

4 Select the audio portion of Background 2 and press the Delete key.

Next, you'll apply an effect to Background and Background 2. When you apply an effect to a virtual clip, it applies to all the images that make up the virtual clip but does not affect the source clip. This is an efficient way to apply an effect to more than one clip at a time. Here, you'll make the effect settings different for each virtual clip so that when you add the transition, you'll be able to see the difference between the two.

5 In the Video Effects palette, click the binocular icon (🔍) to search for an effect.

6 Type in **Brightness & Contrast** and click Find. The Brightness & Contrast effect is located and highlighted. Click Done to exit the Find Video Effect dialog box.

7 Drag the Brightness & Contrast effect to the Background 2 clip in the Timeline window. Or, if the Background 2 clip is selected in the Timeline window, drag the Brightness & Contrast effect to the Effect Controls palette.

8 In the Effect Controls palette, set Brightness to +**19** and set Contrast to -**20**.

9 In the Video Effects palette, find the Brightness & Contrast again. Click Done to exit the Find Video Effect dialog box.

10 Drag the Brightness & Contrast effect to the Background clip in the Timeline window. Or, if the Background clip is selected in the Timeline window, drag the Brightness & Contrast effect to the Effect Controls palette.

11 In the Effect Controls palette, set Brightness to +**50** and set Contrast to -**20**.

In Lesson 11, "Applying Video and Audio Effects," you used the Transparency Settings dialog box to apply an effect to an area of an image. Here, you'll use the Image Mask transition to do the same thing to the Background and Background 2 virtual clips.

Trimming the source clips

Background and Background 2 currently have a duration of 08:05 or 245 frames each. In order for the transition to cover the full duration of Background, you'll need to trim both virtual clips.

1 To trim Background to use only the first half, set the edit line to 12:23.

2 With the selection tool, drag/trim the end of Background to its midpoint until it snaps to the edit line. Check the Info palette or the duration dialog box to be sure that the new duration for Background is 4:02.

3 Locate the halfway point of Background 2 by moving the edit line to 21:00.

4 This time, trim from the beginning of Background 2 to the right until it snaps to the edit line.

5 Drag Background 2 to the left until it snaps to the end of Background.

6 Locate the Cross Dissolve transition in the Transitions palette. Click it to select it. From the Transitions palette menu, select Set Selected as Default.

7 Set or change the Effect Duration to 243 frames, Center at Cut. Click OK.

8 Next, locate the Image Mask transition and select it.

9 Drag the Image Mask transition from the Transition palette to the Transition track, positioning it between the two virtual clips.

10 In the Image Mask Setting dialog box, click Select Image, locate the 12Lesson folder, and double-click Mask1.tif. Then click OK to close the Image Mask Setting dialog box.

Timeline

11 Double-click the transition in the Timeline. As you can see in the dialog box previews, the Background 2 clip shows through the black part of the mask, while the Background clip shows through the white part. Click Show Actual Sources to see the results on the virtual clips. Click OK to close the Image Mask Settings dialog box.

12 Render-scrub to preview the effect you just created by dragging through the Timeline ruler while pressing the Alt key (Windows) or Option key (Mac OS).

Next, you'll create a third generation virtual clip from the clips you just assembled.

Making and positioning the third generation virtual clip

1 Set the Time Zoom Level to 2 Seconds. This will allow you to better view this exercise.

2 Set the edit line to 17:12.

3 In the Timeline window, select the block select tool (⊞).

4 Drag to select Background, Background 2, and the Image Mask transition footage.

This time, you'll use a keystroke combination to create a virtual clip without audio.

5 Press and hold the Shift key and the Alt key (Windows) or the Shift key and the Option key (Mac OS) and then drag the selected block to the Video 1 track, leaving a small gap in the Timeline between the selected block and the new virtual clip, by snapping the beginning of the new virtual clip to the edit line.

6 Deselect the block select tool by selecting the selection tool (▸).

You now have a new virtual clip with the previous virtual clips nested inside. Because the Timeline contains only one Transition track, you can normally use only one transition at a time. By nesting virtual clips that contain transitions, you can apply multiple transitions to one set of clips for more complex results. However, nesting virtual clips does slow down the previewing and exporting of movies—especially if you are using transitions, effects, and superimposition.

Now, you'll give the virtual clip an alias that will be a more descriptive clip name.

7 To select this new virtual clip, choose Clip > Set Clip Name Alias, type **Masked Background**, and click OK.

8 Preview the virtual clip you just created by render-scrubbing through the Timeline ruler while pressing the Alt key (Windows) or Option key (Mac OS). The results of the effects and the transition look just like they did when you previewed the source clips.

9 Save the project.

Assembling the final video program

You'll now nest the virtual clip you just made inside a new virtual clip. In this new virtual clip, you'll combine the Masked Background virtual clip with another video clip and some still images, adding another Image Mask transition. This time, you'll use this transition to make a clip and a collection of still images play on top of the background effects through the image mask. First, you'll add a new scene to the project.

Note: The pictures of the Timeline shown in this exercise reflect several different Time Zoom Levels, for clarity and ease of viewing. As you have seen in the lessons in this book, it is normal to frequently adjust the navigation and zoom levels to settings that are most comfortable for the video artist as you work on projects in Premiere.

1 Set the Time Zoom Level to 1 Second so that you can see more detail.

2 Scroll the Timeline or drag in the Navigator palette so that just Masked Background is displayed.

The Masked Background will be moved three times in this exercise.

3 To begin, move Masked Background directly above its current position into the Video 2 track. Do this by setting the edit line to 17:12 and then snapping the clip to the edit line in the Video 2 track.

4 Drag Surf3.mov from the Project window into the Video 1 track so that it snaps to the beginning of Masked Background.

The still images you'll be adding to this project will be inserted into the middle of Surf3.mov. To make this insertion possible, you'll use the razor tool to split the clip into two pieces.

5 Set the edit line to 20:10. Then, in the Timeline window, select the razor tool (✎), and click in the middle of Surf3.mov, at the edit line.

Now, Surf3.mov is split into two pieces.

6 Select the selection tool (▸) to deselect the razor tool.

Before you add the still images to the project, you'll make a change to the preferences that will set the duration of the stills automatically as they are imported.

Note: You must make the preference changes before you import the still images to have the duration set automatically.

7 Choose Edit > Preferences > General and Still Image. Under Still Image, type **5** for the Default Duration for Frames, then click OK.

8 Choose File > Import > Folder, select the Images folder in the 12Lesson folder, and click OK (Windows) or Choose (Mac OS).

You'll add all 10 still images at once between the two portions of Surf3.mov that you created with the razor tool.

9 In the Project window, double-click the Images bin to open it and choose Edit > Select All to select all 10 files in the bin. Drag all these files at once into the Video 1 track, between the two segments of Surf3.mov. Close the Images bin.

The Masked Background virtual clip is slightly longer than the clips you've assembled in the Video 1 track. Because you want the material in the Video 1 and the Video 2 tracks to be the same length, you'll trim the virtual clip, just as you would trim any other clip.

10 With the selection tool ( ) selected, position the pointer on the right end of Masked Background and drag left until it snaps to the end of the last Surf3.mov segment below it.

11 The second timeline shift for Masked Background is to drag it until its In point snaps to the Out point of the last Surf3.mov, at 24:28, keeping it on the Video 2 track for the next few steps.

In order for the next transition to work properly, you'll make all of the Surf3.mov footage on the Video 1 track into a new virtual clip.

12 Select the block select tool (⊞) and select all of the Surf3.mov footage, including both parts of the razor cut and the 10 images.

13 Press and hold Shift and Alt (Windows) or Shift and Option (Mac OS) and drag the block select tool on the Video 1 track next to the Surf3.mov footage so that it snaps at the end of the second part of the Surf3.mov razor cut.

You have made a virtual clip of the 12 pieces selected.

14 Now, select the selection tool (⬐).

15 Rename the virtual clip to be Surf3 Virtual Clip.

16 Now, for the final positioning move of Masked Background, drag it down to the right into the Video 1 track until it snaps to the end of Surf3 Virtual Clip.

17 Preview the last two virtual clips, Surf3 Virtual Clip and Masked Background, by render-scrubbing in the Timeline.

18 Save the project.

Next, you'll add the Image Mask transition with a new mask shape.

Adding the Image Mask transition with a new mask shape

First, you'll trim the virtual clips to prepare them for the transition.

1 Set the edit line to the mid point of the Surf3 Virtual Clip at 28:21.

2 Trim Surf3 Virtual Clip by dragging the end point to the left until it snaps to the edit line.

3 Set the edit line to the midpoint of Masked Background at 36:06.

4 Trim Masked Background by dragging the beginning to the right until it snaps to the edit line at 36:06.

5 Drag Masked Background until it snaps to the end of Surf3 Virtual Clip.

6 In the Transitions palette, select Cross Dissolve.

7 In the Transitions palette menu, select Set Selected as Default.

8 Change the Effect Duration in the Effect Settings dialog box to 225 frames. Click OK.

9 From the Transitions palette, drag the Image Mask transition into the Video 1 track between Surf3 Virtual Clip and Masked Background.

10 In the Image Mask Settings dialog box, click Select Image, make sure the transition direction is from A to B, and double-click Mask2.tif in the 12Lesson folder. Then click OK to close the Image Mask Settings dialog box.

11 Save the project.

As you preview this transition, notice that two unaffected frames remain at the end of Masked Background. This is the result of using 225 frames for the transition, so it works properly. You'll perform a precision razor cut on these 2 frames to achieve the same result as the final movie.

12 Preview the two clips and the transition you just assembled by render-scrubbing through the Timeline ruler.

13 Set the edit line to the end of the program at 32:12.

14 Zoom/Navigate to the 1 Frame view of the Timeline.

15 Select the razor tool and cut the Masked Background clip at the edit line.

16 With the selection tool (➤), select the 2 frame clip you just made and delete it.

17 Preview the last transition again. Notice the clean end to the sequence.

18 Save the project.

Adding unnumbered keyframe markers

With the transition in place, you'll apply the Invert effect to Masked Background and set the keyframe markers so that the Invert effect applies to this clip only when the still images are playing. You'll add two unnumbered markers to aid in setting where the effect starts and ends.

1 Click the Track Mode button (▱) in the Video 1 track to reveal Masked Background in the lower Video 1 track.

2 In the Program view, drag the Shuttle slider to position the edit line at 27:26. This is the beginning of Still01.tif, in Surf3 Virtual Clip.

3 Choose Clip > Set Clip Marker > Unnumbered.

4 In the Program view, drag the Shuttle slider to position the edit line at 29:15, in the last segment of Surf3.mov in the Timeline. Click the Previous Edit button (◄) to move the edit line to the first frame of the last segment of Surf3.mov. Now, click the Previous Frame button (◄|) under the Program view to move the edit line to the last frame of Still10.tif and choose Clip > Set Clip Marker > Unnumbered. Move the edit line away from the marker so it won't interfere when you align the keyframe to the marker.

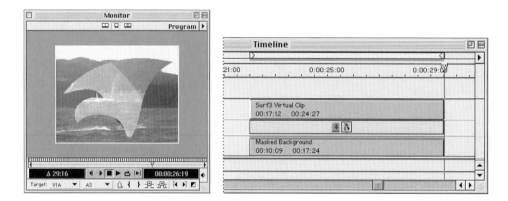

Now, you'll apply the Invert effect to Masked Background. This effect inverts each color to its complementary color.

5 In the Video Effects palette, click the binocular icon (🔍) to search for an effect in the Find Video Effect dialog box.

6 Type **Invert** and click Find. The Invert effect is located and highlighted. Click Done to exit the Find Video Effect dialog box.

7 Select Masked Background in the Timeline window and drag the Invert effect to the Effect Controls palette.

8 In the Timeline window, click the triangle to the left of the track label to display the keyframe line.

9 Drag the first marker on the keyframe line to the right until it is aligned with the unnumbered marker at the beginning of Still01.tif.

In the same way, drag the end marker on the keyframe line to the left until it is aligned with the marker at the end of Still10.tif.

10 Preview the clips you have assembled by render-scrubbing through the Timeline ruler while pressing the Alt key (Windows) or Option key (Mac OS).

11 Save the project.

Editing virtual clips

Virtual clips can be edited in several ways. Like any other clip, you can trim either end of a virtual clip, change various settings, or apply effects, as you did earlier in this lesson. In addition, you can edit the clips in the source area from which the virtual clip was made, and the changes are automatically reflected in all instances of the virtual clip. You have already modified virtual clips directly by applying effects. Now, you'll use the second method, editing the clips in the source area, to modify the last virtual clip you just created and all previous virtual clips.

Here, you'll add a shadow under the shape you created with the Image Mask transition. To do this, you'll add a clip to the source area of Masked Background.

💡 *To quickly find the source area for a virtual clip, simply double-click the virtual clip.*

1 Double-click Masked Background. The source area is selected by the marquee and the block select tool is active. Select the selection tool (▸).

2 Drag Shadow.tif from the Project window into the Video 2 track, directly above the beginning of Background and Background 2.

To match the final movie, you want Shadow.tif to be the same length as Background and Background 2, so you'll change the duration of the Shadow.tif clip.

3 Position the pointer over the end of Shadow.tif and drag to extend it until it snaps to the end of the virtual clips.

4 Select Shadow.tif, and then choose Clip > Video Options > Transparency to open the Transparency Settings dialog box.

5 Select Luminance for the Key type, set Threshold to **0** and set Cutoff to **100**.

6 Click the page peel icon (▨) under the Sample window to view a thumbnail of the actual clip, and then click OK.

Now, you'll set up a fade to make Shadow.tif partially transparent.

7 Click the triangle to the left of the Video 2 track label to expand the track.

8 Select the fade adjustment tool (↕).

9 Press and hold the Shift key and then drag the red fade control line down to 50%. You will need to drag outside the clip to reach this value.

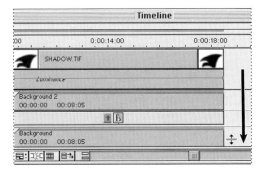

10 Select the selection tool ( ) to deselect the fade adjustment tool.

11 Preview the effect you just created by render-scrubbing through Background and Background 2 in the Timeline ruler.

Adding Shadow.tif to the source area has added a shadow effect to the Background and Background2 virtual clips.
Preview Masked Background and the clips above it in the same way.

Adding Shadow.tif to the source area changed Masked Background. Notice that the effect you applied to Masked Background inverts the shadow.

12 Clean up the Timeline by clicking the arrow in the Video 2 track to collapse the track.

13 Save the project.

Compiling virtual clips

When a virtual clip is in its final form and needs no more changes, you can compile the source components into an actual clip. This step saves time when previewing and eliminates the need to keep the source material in the Timeline.

Note: Deleting any of the clips in the source area in the Timeline or deleting associated master clips in the Project window has no effect on the compiled clip.

Now that your second virtual clip is finished, you can compile it. In addition to greatly reducing the time it takes to preview and export movies, compiling a virtual clip prevents further changes at the source clip level. You can still edit the compiled clip as you can any other clip. If you want to make changes at the source clip level, you can edit the clips and compile again.

1 Select Background in the Timeline.

2 Choose Clip > Replace with Source to display the Export Movie dialog box.

3 In the filename box, type **Background.mov** to name the clip you are about to compile.

4 Make sure the Export Movie dialog box is set to save in the 12Lesson project folder, and then click Save (Windows) or OK (Mac OS).

When Premiere has finished compiling, the virtual clip changes to the new named clip in the Timeline and also appears in the Project window.

5 In the Source view, preview the clip you just compiled.

6 Save the project.

Exporting the movie

Now that you've finished your editing, it's time to generate a movie file. You'll export just the last virtual clip you created, Masked Background, and the clips above it.

1 Scroll across the Timeline so that Masked Background is visible.

2 To quickly resize the work area bar to cover Masked Background and the clips above it in the Timeline, hold down the Alt key (Windows) or Option key (Mac OS) and click between the title bar and the ruler, above Masked Background.

3 Choose File > Export Timeline > Movie.

4 In the Export Movie dialog box, click Settings and choose your settings as necessary.

5 Make sure that QuickTime is selected for the File Type and Work Area is selected for the Range.

6 Also make sure that Export Video and Open When Finished are selected. Then deselect Export Audio. The default values for other settings, including those for compression, are fine for this project.

7 Click OK to close the Export Movie Settings dialog box.

8 In the Export Movie dialog box, specify the 12Lesson folder for the location, and type **Windsurf.mov** for the name of the movie. Click Save (Windows) or OK (Mac OS).

Premiere starts making the movie, displaying a status bar that provides an estimate for the amount of time it will take.

9 When the movie is complete, it is opened in a separate window.

10 Click the Play button to play the movie.

Congratulations! You just completed a complicated lesson and gained more experience with some of the powerful features of Premiere. Refer to any of the lessons in this book at any time, especially if there is a process with which you want more practice.

Exploring on your own

Feel free to experiment with the project you have just created. Here are some suggestions:

• Use the Paste Attributes command to copy just the fade control settings from Surf1.mov to Background 2.

• Use the razor tool to cut one of the virtual clips into several segments and apply different effect settings to each segment.

• Add the Strobe effect (in addition to the Invert effect) to the last virtual clip you created. Set Visible Frames to 4, Hidden Frames to 1, and pick a bright color. Set keyframes identical to those used in the Invert effect.

Review questions

1 What are two ways to rename a clip?

2 What is the advantage of nesting virtual clips while creating effects and transitions?

3 To create a new clip that appears in the Project window, would you use a duplicate clip, an alias, or a virtual clip?

4 What are the advantages and disadvantages of compiling a virtual clip?

5 Can a duplicate clip contain more than one source clip?

6 Can a virtual clip contain more than one source clip?

7 What are three ways to change the duration of a still image?

Answers

1 Assign an alias to it or change the name in the Project window with the list view selected.

2 You can use transitions and effects more than once on the same material.

3 A duplicate clip.

4 Compiling a virtual clip protects it against being accidentally modified, eliminates the need to keep its source material in the project, and shortens the preview time. Once a virtual clip is compiled, however, you can't change it by modifying the source material. Also, if the source area is deleted, you can't identify the source clips by name, or see the effects, transitions, or settings used to create it.

5 A duplicate clip cannot include more than one source clip.

6 A virtual clip can consist of more than one source clip. It can also consist of more than one virtual clip.

7 You can change the duration of a still image in the following ways:

• Before importing the clip into the project, set Default Duration for Still Image in the General and Still Image Preferences dialog box.

• Choose Clip > Duration and then enter a new duration after the clip is imported into the project.

• Position the selection tool pointer on the edge of the clip and drag to a new location in the Timeline.

Index